MEDIA AND TRIBAL DEVELOPMENT

About the Author

Jagannath Pati is Deputy Director, Central Adoption Resource Agency, Ministry of Social Justice and Empowerment, Government of India. He did his M.A. in social work from the Institute of Social Sciences, Agra University, Agra (now Dr. Ambedkar University) and his Ph.D. from Ranchi University. He also has degrees in Law and Journalism.

Dr. Pati has published over 50 research papers in national and international journals of repute and presented over 25 papers at different seminars and workshops in India and abroad. He has edited a seminar volume entitled *Women in Agriculture*. Also, Dr. Pati has produced several programmes for All India Radio, in addition to completing a project on 'Stories of Tribal Women Involved in Local Brewing', sponsored by Ministry of Social Justice and Empowerment, Government of India.

MEDIA AND TRIBAL DEVELOPMENT

JAGANNATH PATI

CONCEPT PUBLISHING COMPANY, NEW DELHI-110059

ISBN-81-8069-068-7

First Published 2004

Published and Printed by
Ashok Kumar Mittal
Concept Publishing Company
A/15-16, Commercial Block, Mohan Garden,
NEW DELHI-110059 (India)

Phones : 25351460, 25351794
Fax : 0091-11-25357103
E-mail : publishing@conceptpub.com

PREFACE

Eulogised by many, ridiculed by some and believed by millions, the All India Radio (AIR) continues to rule the air-waves in country side despite the onslaught from the visual media. AIR continues to be the medium of the masses. Unlike western nations, the state controlled media have done more service to the Indian public. Thopugh broadcasting in India started as early as 1923, AIR came into being in 1936. In the six decades after that, as things changed in the country and outside, the number of AIR stations installations also multiplied. At present, AIR covers nearly 98 per cent of the population through its 185 stations or more as a three tier system comprising the national, regional and local channels. Whether it is news, weather forecast, cricket commentary or agricultural programme, AIR has no comparison and its music programmes have contributed in a great way to keep our traditions alive. Agriculture scientists say that green revolution was possible because of AIR for the extensive kisan programmes form time to time. Many innovations were done to satisfy the listeners. FM and digital broadcasting service are the latest one.

Despite its achievements in the last six decades, media critics say the AIR losing its listenership and it has failed to adopt itself to the changing environs. Though AIR played crucial role in certain development activities, it failed to make breakthrough in certain other areas.

The study has been taken up at a time when AIR is moving steadily to take the shape of a fullfledged corporation. Here it is worth-mentioning to state that all those Committees set up recently by the Government of India including that of Paswan Committee and Sengupta Committee have strongly advocated in favour of Public Service Broadcasting whose expenditure should be separately borne by Parliament if Corporation fails to arrange fund on this head. This is essential because millions of people are still leading difficult life without access to appropriate information and minimum needs. They are illiterate, ignorant and prejudiced. The fate of tribal people who silently lead their uneventful life need some more attention because of their helplessness and vulnerability. Thus, I have chosen the topic keeping in mind the fact that the electronic media have enormous potential to cater to the development goals of the tribal people in remote places. A high priority area is communication support to antip-overty programme and active participation in the process of information dissemination.

The present volume bearing the title, "Media and Tribal Development" brings together eight chapters which speak that man has another fundamental need beyond the physical requirements of Food and Shelter : the need to receive information. This book brings out the role of broadcasting media and how it can be effectively used for influencing tribal and rural mass in the southern plateau region of Jharkhand state where about fifty per cent of inhabitants are tribals.

I must also put on record that ideas, views and insights presented here have evolved and crystalised through the process of ten long years of experience in broadcasting media and interaction with different media personalities. My engagement with OB (Outside Broadcast) duties and regular interviews with tribal and folk artists was certainly a stirring experience. All those gave me an inside view of the complex problems including that of media deprivation experienced by majority of tribals in the region.

New Delhi JAGANNATH PATI

ACKNOWLEDGEMENTS

At the outset, I wish to express my sense of gratitude to all those who have helped me in my research work. First and foremost among such luminaries, is my esteemed supervisor Dr. A. K. Singh, Professor in UGC Centre for Advanced Study, Department of Anthropology, Ranchi University, Ranchi who has been a constant source of inspiration from the inception to the final stage of the submission of the thesis.

I had the benefit of discussing the theme and contents of the research work with important radio personalities, folk artists, tribal leaders and welfare activists and anthropologists who inspired me to take up the work. I have got sincere regards for them all. I am grateful to all tribal people who were part of the interview schedule.

I thank All India Radio : Ranchi, my work place for over eleven years and a centre of media and cultural activities which has sustained my interest in programmes and academics. I am also thankful to the librarian and staff of Jawaharlal Nehru University (JNU), New Delhi, Indian Institute of Mass Communication (IIMC), New Delhi; Xavier Institute of Social Services (XISS), Ranchi; and Tribal Research Institute (TRI), Ranchi.

My debt to my parents, family members and wife, Varsha is beyond words. She coped cheerfully with the heavy burden of typing out drafts of each chapter included in the book. I am equally thankful to my son Golu and daughter Anu who beared long periods of my absence from home.

My close friend Vicky deserves a mention here who has rendered a good deal of support during the period.

New Delhi JAGANNATH PATI

CONTENTS

LIST OF PLATES

Frontispiece Map

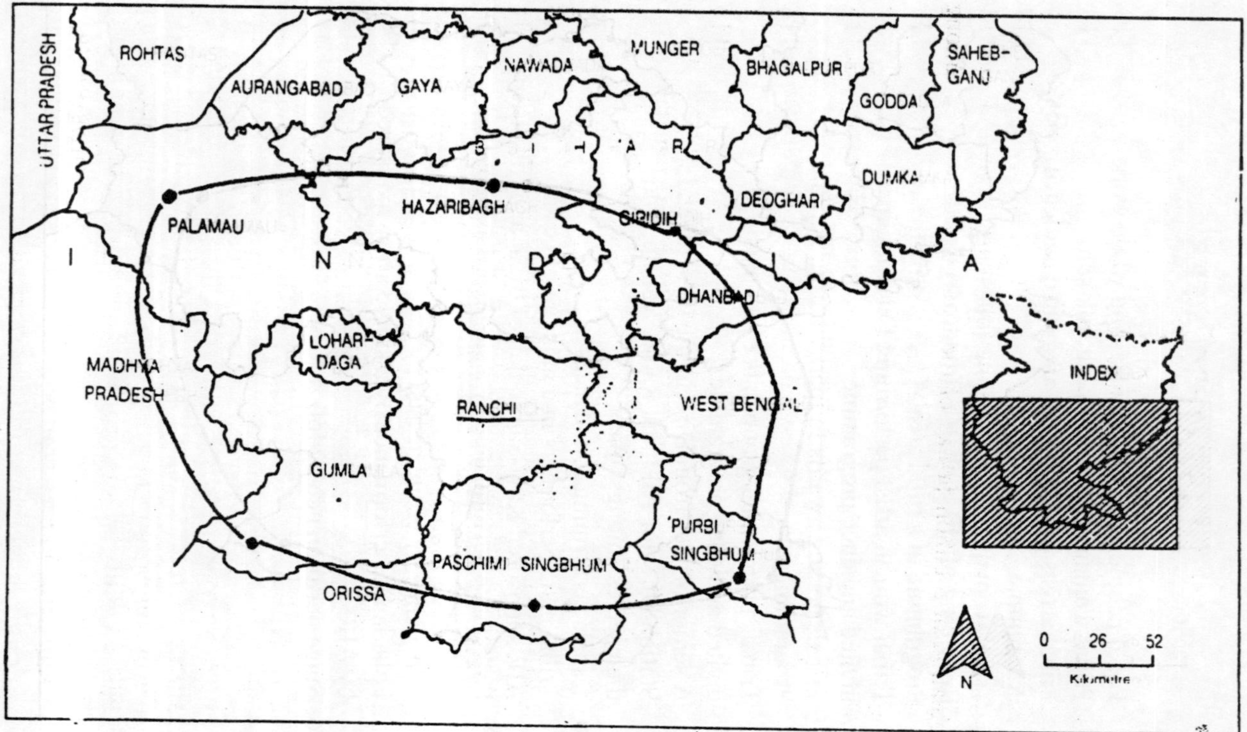

Primary Broadcast area of Ranchi AIR station

1

INTRODUCTION

Since the dawn of history, every power, whether religious, political or private, knew that control over communication is control over society. Today, all over the civilised world, there is a debate on how to give the people access to the media of communication including that of broadcasting. The inequality of progress possesses perhaps the most important single challenge and threat to human kind. The notions of equality and liberty don't have the same connotation everywhere. The predicament is that most of us in this subcontinent are struggling between life and death and their voice hardly reach limelight.

According to an observation of US Supreme Court, "It is right of the viewers and listeners, not the right of the broadcaster, which is paramount. It is the right of the public to receive suitable access to social, political, aesthetic, moral and other ideas and experience which is crucial here. That right may not be constitutionally abridged either by Congress or by the Federal Communication Commission". It is not easy to devise a communication policy for a country so large and so varied as ours, broke up into many linguistic regions. Communication policies are not ends in themselves but set principles, which emanate from the political, social, economic and other conditions of society. Addressing the "One Asia" Assembly in February. 1973, the then Minister of Information and Broadcasting declared that a realistic Communication Policy in a developing society involves striking a balance among three factors :

(i) What is socially desirable,
(ii) What is economically meaningful, and
(iii) What is technologically feasible.

Before the advent of modern electronic media, mass communication in INDIA took place through traditional media only. The peoples freedom struggle in the nineteenth and twentieth centuries against the alien domination was largely inspired by the creative use of art forms such as singing and story-telling, dance and folk theater including the puppet. These arts have continued to play a meaningful role in rural areas, in educating the rural and the tribal people about the consequences of social evils like alcoholism, illiteracy, untouchability, superstitions, communalism, population explosion, malnutrition and sanitation, dowry, sati and so on. Even today, in the midst of hi-tech media scenario, the traditional performing arts continue to be popular. A national committee which deliberated on the media of communication in India, reported, "from the point of view of it's great appeal to the masses and it's quality of touching the deepest emotions of the illiterate millions, the medium of song and drama is matchless" (UNESCO Report, the Mac Bride Commission; 1980).

Thus the broadcasting medium which is having greater potential to influence people through entertainment (song, music, play etc.) and make them aware of social, political, economic, cultural and moral issues has got to be emphasized.

The poverty induced life cycle affects most of the people here in tribal Jharkhand. South-Chotanagpur having tribal concentration of about fifty percent of the total inhabitants are a impoverished lot. Nutritional deficiencies, ill-health, growth retardation, slow learning, small body size, low productivity, excess of ill paid and unorganised work, low earning capacity, unemployment, least facility of communication and transportation etc. are some of the common features of tribal life here.

Community participation is the key to the success of rural development programmes. Village panchayats, cooperatives, block development committees etc. attempt to involve the people in decision-making, implementation and monitoring of development programmes, *i.e.* the IRDP, ICDS, Community

Health Care and Total Literacy Movement are all seen as peoples movement. Since awareness is one of the factors contributing to effective participation, local people should have free and easy access to

(i) Information relating to all aspects of community life including health, education and family planning,
(ii) Policies and procedures with regard to agriculture, health and housing, employment, welfare etc., and
(iii) Available state funds and other resources.

For people in tribal areas, there lies a challenge, that is technical innovation. Let information make our people think that there are better ways to milk cows; there are profitable ways to market our goods, there are improved methods to protect our vegetables from rotting and life can become more productive than what it is now. No government in India can eradicate poverty and improve the standard of living of the millions unless the people themselves feel a strong desire to change their centuries old life style which is less productive in today's economic environment. Development communications which include information on improved methods on growing of rice, wheat, vegetables, pulses, bee-keeping, poultry, pisciculture and setting up of small scale industries through this powerful medium will be much more relevant for people at the grass-roots level. To create the necessary impact on the tribal population who are bound by age old beliefs and customs, the medium has to be effective. Improved dissemination of information is not possible in any country or any regime without the primacy of listening to others the superiority of dialogue over monologue, the dedication to intelligence rather than to indoctrination.

The present study is based on two major tribes, *i.e.* Munda and Oraon spread over in different tribal pockets of Ranchi district. The Chotanagpur plateau is not only distinguished geographically from the surrounding areas, in many respect, it is a distinct cultural area as well. A heterogeneous, multi-ethnic population, linguistic diversity, and a tribal cultural base have all contributed to its distinct character and cultural configuration. At the same time, centuries of interaction between diverse cultural groups has shaped a regional culture in which all groups participate, though in different ways and to different extents.

According to 1991 census, every twelveth Indian is a Scheduled Tribe. They are specified as per provisions in Article 342 of the Constitution. The two hundred fifty and odd tribes and tribal communities tend to confirm the norm sought to be applied consisting of

(i) Geographical isolation,
(ii) Primitive traits,
(iii) Distinctive culture,
(iv) Shyness of contact with community at large, and
(v) General backwardness.

Communication through various media including radio can be effective for tribal development only if the communicators identify themselves with the tribal poor and the unprivileged. The objective should be to create a new awakening among those for whom development plans are intended. They should be fully involved to ensure their active participation in development. The present study is based on some of the dominant tribes of Chotanagpur but there are about two lakhs of primitive tribes in the state who are, we can say, the most deprived mass. At a time, when we claim to have third largest technical manpower in the world and welcome almost all global changes into our subcontinent, there are few millions of primitive tribes in the country who are deprived of basic necessities of life. Naturally, the percentage of people possessing receiver sets may be very low among the primitive tribes.

We need entirely a new media order for this sensitive electronic media which should be based on quality, equity and relevance especially after the advent of satellite communication (Television). Bread is not the whole of life and economic life is not the whole of nation building. In our country, there are two main social hurdles to nation building; their ignorance and the reconciliation of the linguistic and regional animosities. In the country, social change and development have picked up speed and it requires momentum to carry forward the task of national reconstruction through media.

Traditional communication agencies, which have been supporting traditional agriculture and industry, can't meet any longer the information requirements of a technological progressive economy. A dynamic economy calls for a far more sophisticated and efficient communication system which can reduce the time required for transfer of reliable and relevant message and information from one point to another and which can also overcome the formidable constraints created by vast distances in transmitting information inputs. There is ample evidence that during last forty five years of India's planned development, radio has played an important role as a development agent, specially as aid to the Green Revolution. Reference can be made to the Farm and Home units of Akashvani which were started in 1966 to support different developmental activities. It is noteworthy that one of the high yielding varieties of Rice –ADT27 popularised by Radio came to be known to the farmers of Tanjore District as 'Radio Rice' (Joshi, 1989).

In this emerging era of shift from centralism to decentralisation, homogenisation to diversification and manipulative to participatory communication, radio broadcasting has an inherent superiority over television. This arises partly from its easy accessibility to vast masses and partly from its easy adaptability to local needs and massage making and above all, from its amenability to becoming a medium of participatory two-way communication (as stressed long back so forcefully by Burtold Brecht, the German playwright).

The Mac Bride Commission says, "In developing countries, radio is the only medium that can really be labelled 'mass' where as large proportion of the population can be reached by radio broadcasts and possesses the means to receive them". No other medium now has the potential to reach so many people so efficiently for information, education, culture and entertainment. Radio can be used easily and economically to reach distant regions. There is another reason why radio will remain a very important mass medium in the developing world for a very long time. The production of radio programmes is much cheaper as compared to television and, therefore, radio is today the least transnationalised mass medium in terms of ownership and programme flows because almost all countries have a certain capacity to radio programmes in line with their political needs, cultural patterns and basic values (Srivastava, 1989).

What Lord Irwin said in 1927 about radio, holds true even today. 'India offers special opportunities for the development of broadcasting. Its distances and wide spaces alone make it a promising field. In India's remote villages, there are many, who, after the day's work is done, find time hangs heavily enough upon their hands. Both for entertainment and for education, its possibilities are great and as yet we perhaps scarcely realise, how great they are'.

Among the mass media, radio is an established medium of communication in India because of its inherent ability to obtain reactions from a large number of people at the same time, its merit of immediacy, its ability to break the literary barrier and also its high effectiveness at low cost. In recent years, many useful programmes of intensive broadcasting in agriculture have been introduced in order to help a large number of farmers and also extension workers to get quick, correct and succinct information. The important role of extension largely lies in narrowing down the gap between the researchers and the farmers in bringing about social change by way of introducing innovations among farmers. The reach of radio today is geographically, linguistically and numerically much greater than that of all other media in the country. That is where it's great potential lies. Introduction of FM and digital broadcasting are important innovations.

The basic fact about radio art is that it is entirely an aural art with a complete absence of visual components. This is at once the weakness as well as strength of radio as an art form. As far as broadcasting is concerned, according to N. Menon, former Director General of All India Radio, 'We have to create a language which is as near the language of speech as possible. The sound of words should be the operative factor in this language, not the shape. The voice can persuade, condemn, doubt, hesitate, approve, question and assert. It can bring rhythm and life to speech'.

Development of Tribals

Development is the development of man, as an individual and as a social being, aiming at his liberation and at his fulfilment.

Development of tribals should be geared to the satisfaction of needs beginning with the eradication of poverty in harmony with the environment. The elimination of poverty, social inequality and unemployment has been considered as the essential theme of development for each developing country. Development is essentially intended to bring about the desired change in various sectors of social life, at the same time, taking roots in the national soil so as to make the whole process of change indigeneous and legitimate.

Tribal development poses a challenge to the policy makers, administrators and social workers. Even after five decades of planned development, due to the inaccessibility of the tribal areas, hilly and tough topography as well as extreme variations in the climate conditions, the tribals have not been able to share the gains of development equally with the non-tribals and as a result, they have remained backward and poor.

When we talk 'tribals', we are of the opinion that they share a very low standard of living, they live in ethnic groups in interior areas where civic amenities are very acute. They are illiterate, they are vulnerable and poor for so many reasons. Broadcasting being the cheapest medium of information has got to play quite a significant job for the people having little access to resources.

Radio disseminates facts, transmits knowledge of many things and provides the speediest and the most effective means where the national leaders can approach the people at the time of national crisis and strains. Besides news, it provides information on different aspects of life and its problems, cultural fair and entertainment. It can provide the motivation for social change, create the climate for development and influence attitudes and traditional practices. It can also help in imparting various types of education and training to the farmers in the field, to the small entrepreneurs in village industries, to teachers in training institutions, to the extension personnel on various subjects to the social education personnel etc.

How radio can be more communicative and benefit to the poorest of the poor is the main theme of our study. Unlike the entertainment part, radio has failed to attract substantially its listeners to its various educational, welfare and informative programmes. Radio can be the most important link between the knowledgeable and the ignorant.

Importance of the Study

(i) In recognition of the role of broadcasting in society, it's importance for the dissemination of information and spread of education, influence on public opinion, all Govts. seek to regulate this powerful media. Right to information is a fundamental right and radio being cheapest medium of information, communication and education, the poor and tribal people in remote part of the countryside can derive benefit out of it.

(ii) As a friend – philosopher and guide, this vital electronic media can amount to conscientization of the mass through a systematic step-by-step identification, description, dis-cussion, analysis and solution of the issues concerning them.

(iii) Right now, the participation and involvement of tribals in different special audience programmes fall short of the estimation. It is important to explore as to how they can have effective participation in programmes for their own development.

(iv) Radio can't survive with its limited roles, which are basically traditional. It has to adapt itself with the changing social scenario. By the modes of information prevailing right now, radio can't bring about to public the real issues and challenges of it's listeners most of whom belong to lower socio-economic strata. On the other hand, it has to be more communicative and popular. The methodology adopted by programme planners while communicating with it's targeted listeners is subject to criticism.

(v) Poverty, population explosion, illiteracy, malnutrition and environmental degradation have become chronic problems in the countryside adversely affecting the schemes and strategies for tribal uplift. Development programmes fail mostly due to non-involvement, non-participation of the local people minimizing the chances of the success.

Objectives of the Study

(i) To study the social relevance of broadcasting service as viewed by the tribal listeners.

(ii) To study the opinion of tribal people towards radio programming as an educational information entertainment sub-system.

(iii) To study and analyse the media behaviour of different target groups like tribal women adults, children and youth.

(iv) To explore the areas for greater listenability, participation and feedback what is called democratic decentralisation of media.

(v) To study measures that can be initiated to bring about further mass-credibility for AIR.

(vi) To study the undiscovered potential areas of broadcasting media that can ensure maximum involvement of the people at the grass-roots level and suggest new fields of enquiry.

Hypothesis of the Study

(i) By its reach and impact, radio provides the most powerful mass-communication. It is specially important as a medium of information and education in tribal pockets where the coverage of the press is not extensive. It is worth mentioning that with the high percentage of illiteracy and low information level higher among tribals, radio is the medium with a vast potential, which can influence the mass.

(ii) There is an increasing demand of a new media order inviting more participation, more decentralisation and more credibility particularly for tribal pockets.

(iii) It is now generally recognised that there is a marked imbalance in development among the tribals. Traditional means of communication are most effective means of communication among tribal people in rural areas. Very few among tribals in countryside have exposure to modern mass-media.

(iv) Radio is having much significance as a powerful mass-medium in tribal areas where population is scattered over vast distance and methods of access are difficult.

(v) Only few among tribals are having access to this modern medium of mass-communication in remote part of Jharkhand while many migrate to nearby urban places to improve their standard of living, with access to other modern mass media.

(vi) The medium can leave substantial impact on rural tribals promoting their language, providing them healthy entertainment, education and timely information in the local dialect.

(vii) Both software and hardware connected with radio requires substantial improvement.

Area of Study

Mother nature has blessed Chotanagpur with a wide array of natural beauty. Rugged and richly wooded mountains, serene and secluded valleys, serpentine rivers and gorgeous water falls about in this region providing ideal habitat for people with thirst for beauty of nature, peace and tranquility. Chotanagrpur is also blessed with the munificence of verdant forest wealth as well as sumptuous mineral reserves like coal, mica, bauxite etc. It is also home for numerous ethnic tribals like santhals, Hos, Mundas, Oraons, Cols, Cheros, Kharias, Pahadias etc. who have their own rich tradition of at, craft and culture.

In keeping with the Government's policy to bring the backward areas on the path of progress, All India Radio was set up in Ranchi on 27.7.1957. Now it is having a high powered transmitter which almost covers eleven districts of Jharkhand.

Chotanagpur

The Chotanagpur plateau which is a distinct geographical area, set off from flat, fertile plains to its north, northwest, and east by its undulating plateau with rocky outcroppings and ranges of rugged hills with steep passes, ravines, rivers, streams and often spectacular waterfalls. In elevation, the plateau areas range from an average of 1000 to 2000 feet, the highest hills rise to over 3000 feet above sea level. The steeper hill areas are unsuitable for cultivation, and thus many of these areas are still covered by forests, predominantly of sal, sakhua and sarjom trees (Carol, 1991).

The southern forest region of Bihar state, Jharkhand, is world famous for holding mineral wealth in abundance in its womb. Its resources include mica, iron-ore, coal, copper, bauxite, limestone, asbestos and clay. The Britishers established mining and steel industries in the area in the early 1900's, and the area has grown as a center of industry since then.

The climate here is healthful and the weather is generally cool. Small rivulets and cascades can be seen in large number here. Despite the fact that people of other castes also live in Chotanagpur, it is this region which is the chief habitat of tribals. The tribals of this region have got a rich culture. They have always remained economically deprived. They have always faced the hardship of life despite their glorious culture which has secured a place of honour for them in the human civilization. When a woman of this region, clad in clothes just enough to hide her body, with her child tied with a piece of cloth at the back, supporting a pitcher on the waist by one hand and a basket on the head, walks in a rhythmic style, it becomes a graceful scene and the feeling of respect swells up in one's heart. Within the limits of honour and dignity, like free flowing waves, the life of the tribal women is quite noticeable in the sense that they provide meaning and life to their special traditions without fail and strive eagerly at the same time to break the chains of their economic dependence on men. They are the people who are satisfied with the minimum of possessions. Dressed only in the minimum of clothes, they work in their fields in the scorching heat and torrential rains. In their leisure, they look like monuments of patience and satisfaction – be it with their children or with their pitchers of wine.

The tradition of pleasing Gods by singing, dancing and by playing musical instruments continue till today. Nature is reflected in all their art forms. Talking of beauty, it can be said that all creatures possess a consciousness for beauty. Some embellish themselves with the objects of nature while others decorate themselves with manmade ornaments. There are various means of embellishment among the tribals in the region, for wearing ornaments, getting the ears pierced, applying kohl to the eyes, putting flowers on their head, tattooing etc.

The awareness level of tribals in country-side is very insignificant in comparison to their brothern living in urban areas. There is a big gap of standard of living between these two places. Exposure to mass media is perhaps the most important key to development

The whole Jharkhand can be divided into Santal Pragana and Chotanagpur. The region of Chotanagpur is divided into two parts : South Chotanagpur and North Chotanagpur. There are eleven districts in all. In North Chotanagpur, there are six districts i.e. Hazaribag, Giridih, Dhanbad, Daltanganj, Bokaro and Godwa while South Chotanagpur comprises of five districts, *i.e.* Ranchi, Gumla, Lohardaga, East Singbhum and West Singhbhum.

K.B. Sexena holds the view that the traditional society characterised by a greater degree of homogeneity, group action, community feeling has received severest jerk in their process of development which has disintegrated their solidarity and diluted their cultural values. His view raised eyebrows of many because of the fact that the tribals of Chotanagpur in particular have remained backward only for two reasons–their long isolation from the general society and their exploitation by the non-tribals specially the zamindars, the money lenders, contractors on the one hand and their own brothers on the other (Saxena. 1983).

A Description on the Selected Field Areas

Ranchi is not only capital of Jharkhand but is an industrial city. According to 1991 census, total population of the district is 22,14,048, out of which 9,64,422 (43.56%) are scheduled tribes. Chotanagpur region as a whole and Ranchi in particular, has several big and small industrial set-up. Since 1951-52, serious efforts were started through multipurpose development projects.

All the programmes aim at tribal development but much remains to be done since the awareness level of the tribal people is very low.

Various schemes were launched after getting the recommendations of Varrier Elwin Committee of 1956. The traditional home for STs confined to four divisions of Bihar in eighteen districts. Ranchi, being one of them, is the headquarter of South Chotanagpur Division consisting of Ranchi, Lohardaga, Gumla, East Singhbhum and West Singhbhum districts.

The Commission under the chairmanship of U.N. Debar recommended for the need of comprehensive legislation to cover entire tribal population and evolve a feasible system suited to the local situation for the upliftment of the whole region. Bihar Tribal Sub Plan was formed in the year 1974-75 to improve quality of life of tribals to accelerate socio-economic pace of the whole region and bring significant change in organisational capacities of the area. Integrated Tribal Development Project and Modified Area Development Approach have not been able to bring about perceptible change in their quality of living. More stress on income generating programmes and more involvement of the masses are important.

The district of Ranchi with the geographical area of 7,593 square kilometers sits in the middle of the Chotanagpur plateau. The population of Ranchi city is more diverse in terms of ethnicity, social status and language than other field areas *i.e.* Mandar and Rania, the former being a very small town and the latter a remote tribal area. Most of the villages in Rania are accessible only on foot, or in dry weather, by bicycle. All the villages coming under Rania block are without electricity. Villages vary in size ranging from a dozen households to around one hundred and fifty. A large village encompasses a number of smaller hamlets, each a cluster of houses surrounded by fields. Plough are usually pulled by bullocks. The population of Hatma (Ranchi city) is more diverse in terms of ethnicity, social status, and language than other field areas, *i.e.* Mandar and Rania.

Since the area surrounding Ranchi gets only one monsoon a year, from mid-June to August followed by a cold winter and then a very dry hot season, only one rice crop is possible every year. That crop is the mainstay of subsistence from most villagers. In certain parts of the plateau cultivation of wheat and cash crops are also possible. Vegetables are grown in plenty in plain area of Chotanagpur. Water is carried to houses from large open wells, although deep tube wells are becoming more common in these days. Weekly and, biweekly markets are a continuing process in rural Chotanagpur. The markets are centers of social, economic, political and cultural activities. In Rania and Mandar, weekly and biweekly markets are the important communication channels for the tribal people; so also radio has been accepted as a fairly common electronic device for entertainment, education and information.

Rania

Rania about eighty kms away from Ranchi town is one of the most underdeveloped blocks in the whole state of Jharkhand. The tribal people inhabitating in the region are mostly Mundas and they are subject to evil forces *i.e.* ignorance, malnutrition and poverty. The people have no access to modern and civilized means of living. They any how survive hand to mouth and they are too poor to afford the basic necessities of life. Agriculture, animal husbandry and nature are their important sources of livelihood. There was no electricity in the whole of the block due to theft of electricity wires and transformers as observed during field work in the year 1998.

As per 1991 sensus, total population of the block comes about 31,822 while the strength of the tribals is 22,114.Total literacy comes about 25.22 percent of the total population.

The only pacca road connecting Rania with the outside is in a hopeless state. The block of Rania consists of ten panchayats. Out of Lohagara and Khatanga panchayats, two villages from each panchayat were selected. Lohagara and Digri from Lohagara panchayat and Tangerkela and Kulhei from Khatanga panchayat were chosen for survey of household enumeration schedule as well as for village profile.

Each village consists of few Tolas and each Tola consist of 10-30 houses. Only one can find narrow access through agricultural land and hilly tracks in between each Tola. Each area is difficult to locate. Weekly market plays a significant role in the life of the tribals. There is still barter system in the market and the selling and purchasing of goods depend much on traditional practices. The postman delivers letters and telegrams to people in the weekly market only. Life is very slow indeed.

Only private transport thrice a day during morning hours is available for travelling to Rania. Although there exist few NFE centers run by the Government and voluntary agencies, also anganwaris under ICDS (Integrated Child Development Scheme) Project, the progress is very slow. As the economic condition of tribals is deplorable despite their hardwork and labour throuh out the day, few of them hardly manage twice a meal. In such a situation, they can't think of educating their children. Long distance from school teachers absenteeism and apathetic attitude of teachers are a few causes of low literacy among tribal people.

Large scale deforestation and migration are some of the unhealthy features of tribal life. The place is generally characterised by hot summer and extreme cold in winters. Weekly markets and interpersonal relations play quite meaningful role in the life of the tribals. People have got very limited exposure to modern mass media.

Mandar

Mandar block is situated at about 30 kms away from Ranchi city on the way to Lohardaga and Daltanganj. The place is well connected with out side and the satellite villages are connected with motorable roads on either side of the state highway running from Ranchi to Lohardaga. Near the block area, the inhabitants are observed to have better social status and most of them are non-tribals. As the researcher enters into the nearby villages, he finds that majority of the population belongs to Oraon tribe. As far as quality of living is concerned, except agricultural labourers, tribals engaged in service and business who are quite less in strength are well off. Village Ambatoli was contacted for eliciting information from the respondents.

Hatma

The tribals of Hatma which is centrally located in Ranchi city are much better in terms of quality of living in comparison to tribals of Mandar and Rania. There is a mixed population of tribals here. Almost all of the tribals are migrants from the villages. Conversion to Christianity is more among Oraon than Munda tribe. Out of the two major tribes residing in the area, most of the families are properly settled either in business or having suitable employment. There are some families who belong to working class and are engaged in the task of rickshaw pulling and daily labour. In some cases, both husband and wife are found to have employment. TV, Radio, and news papers are important communication channels here. Some of the tribals here lead a better socio-economic status. Besides Munda and Oraon population in the two villages (Sarna Toli and Hatma Toli), there are also quite good number of people belonging to Scheduled Castes and Backward Castes. Hindi, Sadri and Mundari are the important languages here.

Details about selected areas have been mentioned in chapter 5.

RESEARCH METHODOLOGY

The criteria for the selection of the field areas were that they should encompass a range of geographic, economic and cultural conditions. It was thought feasible to choose areas that would be representative, in any true sense, of Chotanagpur with it's great variety of people and socio cultural conditions.

The field work was planned in four phases.

(i) The first phase was an initial period of participant observation in the three selected areas. The idea was that the insights gained at this preliminary stage could be fed into the design of subsequent stages. In the event, this initial period was extended to about one month to have impression about the dynamics of village life. In all the three places where field work was conducted (urban, rural and remote-rural), levels of development as seen in the infrastructural facilities such as media exposure of the people, standard of living, etc. were taken into consideration. Some of the major aspects of social, economic and cultural life in the selected areas were also observed. Through informal interviews and discussions, information on the history of the inhabitants and different aspects of their social life were collected.

(ii) Once the first phase had been completed, the sample survey that constituted the second phase was prepared. The Study was intended to produce results regarding the effectiveness of broadcasting media and it's different expected roles. The sample consisted of 100 respondents each from each selected area. Children youth, women, men and aged people were covered. Radio listening was the only pre-requisite on the basis of which the respondents were selected. The actual data collection work started in this phase through simple random sampling.

Quantitative as well as qualitative data were collected by administering tools and undertaking indepth observations.

(iii) In the third phase, village profile (door to door) survey was undertaken to find out tribe, occupation, family income, radio-TV ownership, exposure to print media etc. As the tribals don't have adequate access to modern mass media in rural areas, it was felt to take up a house hold enumeration survey particularly in Rania and Mandar.

(iv) In the fourth and final phase, the respondents numbering thirty and coming in the category of media personalities, radio talkers, anthropologists, tribal leaders and social workers were contacted, through interview schedules comprising various issues on tribal development and the broadcasting media. In this category, the schedule was structured to contain both open-ended and closed questions.

Since it is not possible to distinctively devise the communication potential of a particular media, attempts have been made here to extract opinion from the tribal respondents about their listening behaviour, awareness and reactions on different function areas. On the other hand, in the expert category, some important suggestions have come up on broadcasting media.

First Phase : Observation
Second Phase : Interview schedule for common tribal listeners
Third Phase : Household enumeration survey in selected rural areas only
Fourth Phase : Interview schedule for the category of experts.

Data Analysis

Data collected with the help of various tools were manually analysed. While drawing inferences various statistical techniques were used. The response given by the respondents to the interview schedules in different phases were analysed systematically in terms of frequencies and percentage.

A Plan of Chapters

The whole book has been divided into eight chapters.

1. In the introductory chapter, the following information have been included
   - An outline of the subject including a brief discussion on 'development'
   - Importance of the Study
   - Objectives of the Study
   - Hypothesis of the Study
   - Research methodology
   - Area of the Study

2. In chapter 2, attempts have been made to collect some of the important extracts of literature available on Communication, Broadcasting Media and Tribal Development.

3. "Communication and Development" is the theoretical chapter which deals with the following :
   - Meaning of Communication
   - Elements of Communication
   - Access to Communication

- Problems in Communication
- Theories of Communication
- Feedback in Communication
- More exposure – More Development
- Roles of Communication
- Functions of Communication
- The Communication Revolution
- Development Communciation
- Mass-Communication
- Models of Mass-Communication
- The 'New' Development Paradigm
- Radio Strategies for Development Communication
- Communication Strategy for Tribal Development

4. In the chapter of 'Tribal Development and the Broadcasting Media', three important subjects have been included.
   - Tribal Economy, Scope and Approaches to Tribal Development.
   - Socio-Cultural Changes and Identities in Tribal Life.
   - Roles of Broadcasting Media.

This is the last theoretical chapter in the book. Attempt has been made here to make a content analysis of certain important programmes.

5. While dealing with Area and Profile of Tribes in Ranchi and surrounding areas, following issues have been discussed.

   - ST Statistics beginning from national level to the field level with a detail description of Chotanagpur housing maximum tribals in the state.
   - The primitive Tribes
   - Details of the area of study (Geography, demography, literacy, economy and other infrastructural facilities including access to mass media).

6. The chapter deals with a detail account of the existing pattern of broadcasting in the country which also include certain important service rendered by All India Radio (AIR).

Ranchi, the only high power broadcasting center in the region.

7. The chapter 'Impact of Broadcasting on Tribals' summerises data collected at the field level under four different heads.

   - Background information,
   - Dimensions and source variables of different programmes (Listening Behaviour),
   - Awareness, and
   - Reactions on different function areas.

8. Findings, Concluding Observations and Suggestions is the last chapter of the book.

2

REVIEW OF LITERATURE

Communication in the new phase requires continuous adjustment to the requirement of mass oriented development strategy. This means having a keen perception of local specificities and peculiarities of problems, which vary from area to area, group to group and community to community. The new approach requires new communication strategies, which can generate as well as disseminate packages of information relevant to widely divergent local needs and requirements on a continuing basis. Such information packages can't be provided by a centralised network, which generates and transmits only standardised, undifferentiated and uniform messages from top to bottom. Such a centralised communication network is alienated from local needs and the local milieu and is incapable of sensitising the top level planners and policy makers about the perceptions of the people at the bottom layers of the economy and society (Joshi, 1989).

Communication technology is being altered at an extremely fast pace. Communication researchers, communicators, technologists, and educationists together have to design new systems to meet the new situation. The new technology offers the possibility of a new configuration to meet our needs. However, one has to develop a ground infrastructure and develop a system, which establishes the greatest number of linkages (Yashpal, 1986).

FM broadcasting is being adopted increasingly as it provides the listeners with high quality signals relatively free from interference; more over, it employs hitherto unused high frequencies in the overcrowded radio spectrum. FM broadcasting for local services is capable of expansion in a way which would relieve much of the present burden in the low, medium and high frequencies bands and thus improve conditions for national, regional and international transmissions. The introduction of FM broadcasting is, therefore, of special interest to developing countries and particularly tropical areas affected by solar interference. Keeping in view all this, All India Radio is keeping FM in a big way (Shrivastava, 1989).

There are areas in which we must investigate and discuss the need for setting up separate directorates for different departments for local radio networks. All these areas need massive and specialised software and programme inputs (Bali, 1989).

Radio has a particular value for reaching scattered audiences and has been extensively used in giving media support correspondence courses in many Third World countries. It is providing considerable support to distance education in China and Pakistan. Radio is going to be an important medium for distant education in future. The university of South Pacific has been using similar audio links between a number of islands served by it (Mohanty, 1989).

Radio can bring news to people who can't read news papers. It can bring instructions and advice to people who need help with farming or health improvement or community development. It can bring extension teaching to individuals and groups who are unable to get to school. It can carry the classical music and drama of a nation. And it can carry light entertainment, popular music, light comedy, serial dramas, variety shows, sports and the like (Schramm, 1964).

Professor Schramm (1964), boosted the intellectual field of development communication by providing a readable, useful text-book. According to him, a Third World nation could facilitate development by expanding the mass media, at least to the extent that information is a vital ingredient in moving a nation towards development. Schramm's book was very influential, convincing many governments to invest in expanding their mass media. Schramm's basic thesis was sound: 'We must share information, we must share it widely........ for development to occur.' While his 1960's model of development communication may not be completely valid today, it helped us to get where we are at present. He institutionalised the field of communication research by pioneering the study of mass media and development in Third World countries.

While at Stanford universely, he wrote his landmark book, Mass Media and National Development (1964), of which Professor Daniel Lerner wrote in a journal review: 'Wilbour Schramm has written a book that puts all students of communication and development in his debt..... what Harold Laswel did for the theory of communication and Paul Lazarsfield for it's research technique...... this is what Schramm has opened the gates for all of us to do for communication-in-development.'

In 1964, he headed a team of experts who were invited by the Indian government to advise on developing the infrastructure for mass media communication in India. His team recommended the establishment of the Indian Institute of Mass Communication in New Delhi which came into existence in 1965, and the allotment of satellite broadcasting time by the National Aeronautics and Space Administration's (NASA's) Application Technology Satellite (ATS-6) for purposes of the Satellite Instructional Television Experiment (SITE) that was conducted in India in 1975-76. Schramm was a personal friend of the two late Prime Ministers, Jawaharlal Lal Nehru and Indira Gandhi.

Davison (1966) looked upon communication as a link between man and his environment. From this point of view, the effects of mass media could be explained in terms of their role in enabling people to bring about more satisfying relationships between themselves and the world around them. Davison points out that there are four assumptions underlying man's relation to his environment. It must be assumed that all human activities, including changes in attitudes and knowledge, are in some way directed towards the satisfaction of his wants or needs. These wants or needs could be satisfied through the environment.

It is found that there is a close nexus between literacy and exposure to mass media. According to Lerner (1967), the citizen living in an urban area, who is a literate and who is exposed to the mass media develops into a mobile personality. He develops the capacity to identify himself with the new aspect of environment. He can empathise with others, that is, he can see himself with the situation of the other people.

One of the chief fraction, if not most important, which promotes economic development, is the mobilization of human resources. This is possible when the country promotes the education and health services so that every child, youth and adult is liberate and in good health. Through mass media, information can flow to the people. This is why the UN Commission on Human Rights looks upon information as one of the basic human rights. It should help the village people to discuss their problems with their fellow villagers. This will enable them to alter their practices. An important function of the information through the mass media is to arise the aspirations of the people, change their attitude towards themselves, the society and the future, individual development as well as national development is made possible (Kuppuswamy, 1976).

Attention may be drawn to a study by Damle, a few years back. He demonstrated that there is a rapid decline in the information as one moves away from the city. He found that in the village close to the city, there was high degree of information regarding some of the national problems. But in the villages situated about 80 miles away from the city, there was hardly any knowledge about the national problems. This was confirmed by the fact that information level of the people living' in the intermediate distance was higher than that in the remote parts but as good as those in the villages close to the city (Damle, cited by Schramm, 1964).

P.C. Chatterjee (1987) describes the demographic, economic and linguistic background against which broadcasting in India operates. In his book 'Broadcasting in India' he makes enquiry into the centrist and standardising trends inherent in the Government of India's policy and the pull towards autonomy inherent in the very nature of broadcasting in a democratic polity.

Jaiswal, Vittal, Jaiswal & Ramchandraih (1981) in their book 'Development Communication–Process and Impact, A micro-study in Mahbubnagar Dist., Andhra Pradesh' discuss about various channels of communication at village level supported by case studies. The book is a practical guide to all communication researchers.

Mehra Masani (1976) suggests several ways to improve the performance of our radio services. 'Broadcasting and the People' is an analysis of some of the complex issues of Indian broadcasting. The author has assessed the potential utility and the practical difficulties of effective management and programming.

'Mass communication functions in relation to actual events, policies and programmes are in terms of the needs and objectives that the nation sets before itself', says R.K.Chatterjee (1978) in his book 'Mass Communication'. The objectives of the mass media follow closely the developments in various fields, informing people, reacting to policies and creating the social climate in which development and nation building programmes can take place. They can't operate in a social and political vacuum.

Dr. Shyam Parmar (1975), an eminent media expert and creative writer believes on the fact that no mass media can exist in cultural vacuum. In his book 'Traditional Folk Media in India', he opines that two important factors that obstruct communication in India are the high rate of illiteracy and inadequate spread of mass media.

Vivek Ranjan Bhattacharya (1976) is of the opinion that in a world of turmoil and tension, stress and strain, conflict and dispute, free flow of information is quite indispensable.

'Mass Media and Village Life' assesses the actual and potential contribution of mass communication media to the process of development in the third world in general and India in particular which is authored by Paul Hartmann, B.R. Patil and Anita Dighe (1989). The authors are of the opinion that despite the faith placed in the power of the mass media to promote desirable social change, the impact of mass communication on development in India has been limited.

S.C. Sharma (1987)'s work 'Media Communication and Development' admirably brings out the role of communication and media in the development. It shows how media can be effectively used for increasing literacy and socio-economic status in rural and urban sectors. The success of communication depends on effective use of the media. It emerges as a powerful mechanism of emotional integration of different sections of society based on religion, cast, language and regional sentiments.

Rahudkar (1958) found that the neighbour to neighbour communication was a greater means in the diffusion of farm innovations than any other communication channel. Though the mass media pour out information and make it available to all, it is personal communication between pairs of individuals and the direct observation that are still basic for diffusion of innovation. New thing and new ideas often look complicated. Therefore, people watch, ask questions, and try out new things before they understand and adopt the innovation. Once a person is interested in the new product or the new process, he can go to his neighbours and friends to ask them questions to discuss the utility and the feasibility of the new process that the personal information from peers is important.

'The ideology and reality of development communication through various mass media and interpersonal channels present political, economic, cultural and technological challenges. The evolutionary scenario of development communication globally in general and India in particular presents paradigm changes both in development and in development communication', says Uma Narula (1994) in her book 'Development Communication – Theory and Practice'. In her book, Uma Narula (1994) discusses the conceptual moves in human communication for the last four decades.

Dr. Arbind Sinha's book 'Mass Media and Rural Development' is a complete account of the village life and the effects of mass media. It is based on a five year longitudinal study, where in the holistic approach of anthropology was used to trace successfully the communication process, decision making, other related factors, and finally the effects of SITE on the life of Ismailpur village in Jharkhand. The book raises some partinent questions regarding the limitations of communication. If the agents of development donot assume higher responsibility, the communication input may lead to distrust and dissatisfaction towards the message as well as the media. He is of the opinion that if these two factors are supplementary to each other and go hand in hand, the pace of development will be hastened (1985).

The work of Krishan Sondhi (1980), 'Problem of Communication in Developing Countries' tries to define our basic concepts in communication from an Indian point of view. The work is divided into six parts. Parts I deals with the problems of communication in atleast three development areas : health, agriculture and education. Part III solely devoted to developing the understanding about the relationship between social phenomena on the one hand and art and communication symbols on the other. Part IV discusses the impact of revolutionary developments in modern communication media while Part V deals with organisational problems of Indian mass media. The last part highlights the need for a national communication policy.

Two types of tape are used in All India Radio; the brown tape which records programmes for broadcast, and the red tape of bureaucracy : one a vehicle for creative enterprise, the other a symbol of rigid formalism. No wonder, the two are always getting into a triangle. This is the central theme of the book 'Tangled Tapes' authored by K.S. Mullick (1974).

After 1984, when the system of taking radio (and TV) license was abolished, there has been no longer any authentic count of how many receiving sets are in operation. According to the estimate of Department of Electronics, which in September 1987 put the number of radio a point to be noted. 62 million is a big figure and provides a great base on which to build the hope that the 'sound only' medium can't but have a positive future. What is needed is to exploit radio' s potential fully and build up the listening habits through attractive programmes backed by vigorous and intelligent publicity. In an effort of economy, the Ministry of Information and Broadcasting abolished all its programme journals in 1986-87 forgetting that making listeners aware of which station broadcast which programme when, and at what time and on which wavelength, and the basic purpose for which the department itself exists (Luthra, H.R., 1989).

In this context, it can be mentioned that right now news papers are bringing out AIR programme highlights but in a very precised form. In village-India, accessibility to newspapers is still restricted.

In a seminar on 'Future of radio in developing countries', Mr. Sindhe, Ex-Director General, All India Radio said, 'local radio stations are going to be very important centres of communication in future. They will bring information to the doorstop of the listeners. He saw a very important role for radio in the field of functional literacy. He pointed out that in Karnataka, 15,000 persons registered for a programme of social forestry with the Forest Department of the Karnataka Government. There were 13 lessons and 12,000 persons who appeared for the open examination. Later the state government broughtout cassettes of those programmes at a subsidized rate. Now there is a demand to publish those lessons in book form. Along the same lines, another programme was put out by the Bangalore station on agriculture. Similarly in Delhi, a programme was introduced for the youth and 6,000 people registered for the programme (1989).'

Rural broadcasting has demonstrated the linkage between the radio and the social change. Since the vast majority of the people are illiterate, the only mass media that could reach them are the radio and the TV. Rural programmes generally consists of talks; dialogues and discussions on agriculture, rural health and other problems. Film music is one of the features of the programme.

Man has another fundamental need beyond the physical requirements of Food and Shelter : the need to communicate with his fellow human beings. In the process of development, communication plays an important role. The success of communication depends on an effective use of emotional integration of different sections of society based on religion, caste, language and regional sentiments (Sharma, 1987).

The effectiveness of communication could be enhanced by using a mix of the following mutually reinforcing channels, for the effectiveness of the subject matter of the broadcast : (i) the subject matter should be related to the felt needs; (ii) the dialogue should be able to create a mental picture in the minds of the listeners regarding the subject matter; (iii) clear summaries should be given at the end of the radio talk (Prasad and Rao, 1976).

According to Pye (1963), it was the pressure of communication, which brought the downfall of traditional societies. Mass media channels, such as television, radio and movies can be used effectively to remove illiteracy, to control popuation, to increase production, and to advocate health practices.

Bertrand (1971) described the procedures involved in the pretesting of communication material for radio, poster, pamphlets, TV, and movies and classified the contents of the media for presenting it's effectiveness as follows :

(i) Attraction,
(ii) Comprehension,
(iii) Acceptability,
(iv) Self-involvement and
(v) Persuasion.

Mani (1974) pointed out that cultural factors can pose obstacle in the process of decoding signal into message and stressed the need to involve the audience and field workers in communication material production.

In his book, 'Mass Media and Mational Development (1964)', which achieved the status of a blue print for development communication, Schramm wrote, "Social change of great magnitude is required. To achieve it, people must be informed, persuaded, educated. Information must flow, not only to them but also from them, so that their needs can be known and so that they can paricipate in the acts and decisions of nation building; and information must also flow vertically so that decisions may be made, work organized and sklls learned at all levels of society."

According to Kakar (1987), 'Family planning communicators have relied heavily on what comes to them from their headquarters. This naturally results in presenting to the people software which may not exactly be in tune with their cultural ethos, needs, perceptions, preferences and a host of other factors inherent in a communication situation.' Kakar while reviewing the communication strategy, has given the description of message conveyed by mass media.

There is an urgent need for careful diagnosis of the motivational determinants of listening behaviour in order to design the content of the communication materials. Lalithmbal (1976) emphasized that motivational compaigns for women should emphasize health motives of family planning. The purpose of communication is to motivate people to act, change, adopt and achieve the desired results. The real purpose in communication is to get people to understand the message thoroughly and act accordingly. Establishing commonness through communication does not come naturally. There are many barriers, which make difficult for the communicator to reach his goal. The sender must know his audience's background.

'Traditional Change Agents among Rural Communities' authored by H.K. Ranganath which appeared in the book entitled 'Communication and the Traditional Media' (1981) emphasizes on the fact that message, medium and masses are the three major factors in the context of communication. Failure of effective communication in India has been traced to ineffective use of the message, improper handling of the medium (mass/electronic/folk) and/or inadequate understanding of the wants and needs of the masses. All the three M's need to be studied and treated with painstaking care in order to make communication draw the desired results in terms of practical achievement.

The Chanda Committee in radio and television has reported that radio rural forums had their genesis in a survey carried out at the Poona station of All India Radio in 1956, to ascertain whether farmers would derive any benefit if programmes specially designed for them were broadcast. An experiment was conducted to establish small forums of 15 to 20 persons in a village who would listen to the programme, discuss it among themselves and formulate questions, which needed clarifications what could be sent back to the AIR stations. The purpose of these forums was to establish a two-way-contact between the forum and the radio station, and help to bring the villages into closer association with the planning of the programmes. It was also the aim of the experiment to see whether the members of these forums would transmit their new knowledge and attitudes to other members of the village. The results of the survey were found to be encouraging and the radio rural forums became the integral part of the Poona station (Chanda, 1966).

An unguided or unplanned communication revolution is bound to have unintended consequences, resulting in the subversion of our social priorities and national goals. A wisely designed communication revolution, in contrast can enhance the beneficial consequences. The Ministries of central and state governments engaged in nation building and development tasks seem to create neither any communication awareness apparatus within their own Ministries nor do they make demands on the Ministry of Information and Broadcasting for information and communication support adequate to the needs of policy formulation and implementation (Joshi, l986).

Till now, the urban listener has received far more attention although in the cities, people have access to other media, such as the press and the cinema. Instead of local broadcasts of immediate concern to the rural community in local languages and dialects, the programmes are broadcast from one center covering a large area. The only solution is a local radio service (Mehra Masani, 1976).

To provide a worthwhile service for each of the tribes on our north/east frontier may require many more studios and transmitters than what we have. The choice is to have either no service at all or a satisfactory service in English, Hindi, and one or two of the major dialects. This requires a firm decision on the part of the political leadership which is not available because whatever be the decision, it would be unpopular with some of the tribes; so there is compromise of broadcasting in five dialects from Gauhati, eight from Dibrugarh, ten from Imphal and thirteen from Kohima for ten minutes in each tribal dialect once, or twice a week. The service does not and can not attract any listening and scarce funds are thus wasted merely to sustain a claim that there is broadcasting for most of the tribes in the region. Ultimately, there is no substitute for clear thinking to make a satisfactory plan of development (Masani, 1976).

Masani's observation is somewhat similar with the existing position in Chotanagpur where there are nine major dialects spoken by the original inhabitants of this part of tribal Jharkhand. Although AIR, Ranchi played a key role in recognising nine regional languages through its regular transmission of programmes, there is much scope for both qualitative and quantitative improvement of programmes.

'Tribal Development in Bihar : An Appraisal' authored by K.B. Saxena in the year of 1983 which appeared in the Bulletin of Bihar Tribal Welfare Research Institute (Ranchi) speaks of the marked deterioration in the condition of poor tribals who are now fighting a grim battle of survival. He takes a critical look at our development strategy towards the tribal people. He makes a systematic analysis of the problems of the poorer sections in the tribal population of Bihar and steps taken to solve them under different heads.

'Land and People of Tribal Bihar' authored by Narmadeswar Prasad (1961) is a systematic study on integration of tribal people in Indian society and undivided Bihar tribes, their homeland and different tribal communities. In last chapter of the book, attempts have been made to discuss their racial composition, economic organisation, religion, education, language and effects of social change on their life.

History of Indian Anthropology, Tribal India : A Dimension of Indian Civilization, Socio-cultural life of Tribals and Cultural change in the tribes of India are some of the important chapters of the book entitled 'The Tribal Culture of India' which is authored by L.P.Vidayarthi and B.K. Rai (1977). They also discuss different approaches, planning and programmes for tribal development in India.

Monographic works on Munda tribe by Soma Singh Munda (1993) and on Oraon tribe by Prakash Oraon (1993) are important literature which discuss the socio-cultural, economic and religious life of Munda and Oraon tribe respectively in the context of Chotonagpur.

The poor urban and rural masses are excluded from the national communication system just as they are excluded from the market economy thus creating an information poverty, which combines with economics disadvantage (Pasquali, 1975).

One can't blame the foreign influence alone for consumerism and cultural dependency. The elites as well as the social structural constraints thus imposed are equally to be blamed. To sum up, the mass mediated communication model operative in developing countries is a Linear Model. It is having 'effect' on the targeted audience. In Latin American countries who allow foreign mass media ideologies of developed countries, the 'effect' is reinforced consumerism which exacerbates social inequality (Narula, 1994). The tribal society's basic needs are two-fold. They want to get rid of poverty. Poverty has been their plight for the last several years. Whatever is done to alleviate their poverty is acceptable to them. The tribal land situation has become worst today. They have had very little land with them since the beginning. The process of fragmen-tation has reduced it today to a minimum. For most of the tribals land holding are not viable. Their problem today is to seek good-bye to agriculture and seek employment in off-the-farm occupations. The second need of tribals is to maintain their ethnic identity and at the same time integrate themselves in the main line of regional and national culture. This is the manner Mr. U.K. Verma (1993) broadly classifies the tribal society's basic needs.

The tribals of India are divided and sub-divided into a large number of sub-tribals which are mutually exclusive even they have common features like living in forest and hills, speak tribal dialect etc. There are few other classification of the tribals based on cultural assimilation, stage of economies etc. All these classifications bring out that they are at different stages of cultural assimilations and economic development and in general, they are at low level of living for which the government has initiated a number of welfare measures to improve their level of living and quality of life (Sinha U.P., 1986). The studies conducted by Aggarwal (1978), Sachchidananda & Jha (1980), indicate that the channel of communication is still not seen as a powerful force for change or as a means of passing the know how more economically and effectively. Much information is lost and or distorted in the process of travels from top to bottom.

Generally it is assumed that many rural development projects proved to be unsuccessful are due to the absence of appropriate communication strategy. Most of the projects are usually planned by technical specialists who are not trained in social communication. One reason for this failure is that communication message used in this process is not receiver oriented (Singh, 1993).

The book *Tribal Festivals of Bihar* (1992) authored by Dr. A. K. Singh deals with the different tribal festivals in detail where as doctoral work of Smt. Kaushal Sharma (1993) entitled "Mass Communication and the Tribal Society : An Impact Study" deals with exposure of tribals residing in Bisunpur Block of Chotanagpur to mass media.

Although there have been a number of studies on mass media, no specific study has ever been made on the potential role of the broadcasting media for tribal development in this part of Indian subcontinent. It is, therefore, intended to take up a research study in a place like Jharkhand at a time when this potential medium is being decentralized and the challenges are innumerable.

3

COMMUNICATION AND DEVELOPMENT

Meaning of Communication

Communication has several distinctive but related and mutually reinforcing roles and purposes. It must first of all provide the basic information which is economically useful to the individual and which gives him a better understanding of his civic rights and obligations and deepen his judgment. Then it must strengthen those forces in society, which will promote the resolution of conflicts through peaceful, constitutional means. Beside such economic, potential and intellectual functions, communication has also a cultural and aesthetic role that of improving taste and enlarging a sense of life's worthwhileless. In short, communication continues where formal education begins. The media are the people's lifelong university. They award no degrees but enhance the individuals relevance to the nation and the world. In our country, there are two main social hurdles to nation building *i.e.* the assimilation in the national mainstream of the lowest castes and tribes who had been so far left out of the polity and the reconciliation of linguistic and regional animosities. In our country, there are millions who can't read but who still are interested in right and wrong and in good government and social justice. The common method of measuring a nation's development by counting number of radio or television sets owned or newspapers bought per thousand of the population is not always very pertinent. An affluent nation may be politically lazy and culturally unenterprising and economically struggling (Prasad S., 1988). Basically, the word 'communication' means 'sharing' or 'common'. Schramm (1964) treats communication as the exchange of knowledge, skills and attitudes among persons or among 'social groupings'. Steinberg (1958) defines communication as 'the process of relaying or transmitting a sign or symbol (verbal, written or pictorial) from a specific source to a specific audience or receiver by means of any one or all of several media that act as channels'. According to Laswell (1960), a convienient way to describe an act of communication is to answer the following questions:

Who/Says what/In which channel/ To whom/ With what effect?

Leagans (1961) describes it as a process by which two or more people exchange ideas, facts, feeling of impression in ways that each gains a common understanding of the meaning, intent, and use of message.

In the simplest sense, communication means a sender and a receiver tuned together for a message. Communication is the process of transmitting meaning between individuals. This process is of great importance to human beings because the ability of communicate with others enhances the chances of success of individuals (Singh, 1993). Until and unless the message is encoded by the sender and relayed by the use of the signals and subsequently decoded at the destination, no communication can be expected have taken place.

Communication with India's tribal masses is of crucial importance. It not only informs and educates, but also motivates the people. People's involvement is possible only if the message of development reaches the tribal people in concrete terms and in simple and clear language and symbols. The Government of India's declared policy, programmes, and development strategy are for more stress on rural and tribal development. Banks, financial institutions, research organizations are now evincing increasing interest in tribal area development. There are innumerable welfare schemes of Government for the poor tribal people and the need of the hour is to reach them with adequate information.

As per the sampling survey, in Chhotanagpur remote tribal villages, the number of people possessing radio sets do not exceed 10 percent of the total households.

The fact, however remains that our communication media including radio have not yet succeeded in carrying development plans and programmes to every Indian home in the language and symbols of the people-an objective set in the First Five Year Plan.

Communication has different connotations in developing countries. The developing societies within themselves as well as compared to developed countries conceptualise communication differently. Therefore, it needs priorities (role defined) and the functions ascribed to communication in a variety of ways. This is true of developing countries in general but applicable to Indian society in particular. Developing societies are strongly vertical societies where government and elite groups control decision-making in particular (Narula, 1994).

Communication is described as a linear process in developing countries. What is significant in this conceptualisation is that communication is having effect and people are reacting in particular ways, may be by discontent or by making demands. But the discontents or demands are not conveyed back to the source for two reasons :

(i) Source is not interested in the feedback because the communicator in this case, government or elite group considers itself supreme as in the Aristotelian concept.

(ii) The receivers may not have the means and access to give feedback. Thus the sources (government) is the active communicator but the people remain passive receivers. This supports a mechanistic view of top-down communication. There is horizontal communication among the receivers (people) but it is not given any significance or conceptualized in this communication model (Narula, 1994).

The earlier liner process concept of communication and the concept that communication is natural tool to inform and persuade is fast revising. The need is being felt to take an interactive view of communication process. Communication is an interactive process of social relationships where both vertical and horizontal communication is subsumed. It is being felt that unless source and receivers communicate among themselves in an interactive process, no effective communication can occur. Therefore, communication should be multi-ways and multi-directional, vertical and horizontal at every level of hierarchy. It is assumed that diffusion of innovations and subsequently development will occur in a dialogue with the masses. This will occur when they are able to identify their needs; when they engage in problem solving activities; and when they are self-reliant and use their own sources and calls for innovations.

Dialogic communication has certain limitations though inevitable for development. The social structure in developing countries is incompatible for dialogue. There is a viewpoint that so long people are economically impotent and voiceless, educational programmes are better than the dialogic strategies. But in such situations, if dialogic strategies are not adopted; the government of the elites will always remain the supreme communicator and people will always suffer from communication effects gap (Narula,1994).

In developing societies, low media reach and access is compensated by strong interpersonal-ties which at times function as mass line to take the message. Communication through interpersonal channels and folk arts is considered as micro form or community level communication. The factors influencing micro form communication are social structure (caste and kinship), cultural norms, hierarchical institutional arrangements.

All development oriented communication is labelled as 'communication' in developing countries. In India in 1950's, it was synonymous with publicity and propaganda. At present, this is labelled as communication. In developing countries, due to this factor the communication priorities are set in the development framework (Narula, 1994)

Elements of Communication

Schramm (1964) mentioned that any process of communication required at least three elements; the source, the message, and the receiver. Edwin, Philip and Ages (1975) have included channel as the fourth element. Shanon and Weaver (1949) described the process of communication as consisting of five elements. According to them, there is need for a source, a transmitter, a signal receiver and a destination. Leagans (1961) went a step further when he described an effective communication process in rural development ought to have six elements, *i.e.* source message, channel, treatment of message, audience and the audience's response.

According to Leagans (1961) the success of rural development programmes directly depends on the transfer of useful ideas from a reliable source to the people who need them. The transfer must be made in such a way that, when received, the idea results in action. Handled well, the communication process can enable millions of rural people through their own effects from a state of poor living to one of economic and social well-being.

Access of Communication

Vittal (1980) argues that the access to communication channels governs people's participation in development programmes. Mass media interpersonal channels carry development messages for people, which suggest the necessity for accessibility of mass media and interpersonal channels for development communication.

Khan (1973) has argued that the availability of mass media institutions in a country itself is no guarantee that media will be used by the people (i) Mass media are usually not available where they are needed the most for development purpose, (ii) whatever media are available and are received usually don't carry the kind of information that might aid development, (iii) The mass media content may not be situationally relevant enough to aid development, and (iv) Even if functionally relevant information is available, the infrastructure and input may not be.

Problems in Communication

The essence of communication is getting the receiver and sender oriented together for a particular message. For tribal development, nothing is more important than the transfer of useful ideas from one person to another. In this process of communication lies the potential for millions of villagers to overcome ignorance. Each episode of communication has at least three phases : expression, interpretation and response. There are few crucial points in communication. If the expression is not clear, the interpretation inaccurate and the response is improper, hardly there can be an effective communication process. In more clear terms, if the message is not encoded fully, accurately, effectively in transmittable signs, if these are not transmitted fast enough and accurately too, despite interference and competition to the desired receiver, if the message is not decoded in a pattern that corresponds to the encoding and finally, if the destination is unable to handle the decoded message, so as to produce the desired response, then obviously, the system is working at less than optimum efficiency (Singh,1993).

Ranjit Singh (1993) opines that communication problems are generally of three types *i.e.* Technical problem, Semantic problem and Influential problem.

(i) *Technical problem* : These types of problems are concerned with the accuracy or transference of information from the sender to the receiver. They are inherent in all forms of communication, whether by sets of discrete symbols (written speech) or by a varying signal (telephone, radio) transmission of voice or music, or by a varying two dimensional pattern (television). In the process of transmitting the signal, it is unfortunate that certain things, not intended by the information source, are added to the signal. These unwanted additions may be distortions in the shape of shading of a pictures (Television) or error in transmission. All these changes in the signal are called 'noise'

(ii) *Semantic problem* : Such type of problems are concerned with the interpretation of meaning by the receiver as compared with the intended meaning of the sender. This is a very deep and involved situation, even when one deals only with the relatively simple problems of communicating through speech. In the restricted field of speech communication, the difficulty may be reduced to a tolerable size, but never completely eliminated by 'explanations'.

(iii) *Influential problem* : The problems of influence or effectiveness are concerned with the sources with which the meaning conveyed to the receiver leads to the desired conduct on his part. It may seem at first glance undesirably narrow to imply that the purpose of all communication is to influence the conduct of the receiver. But with any reasonably board defination of conduct, it is clear that communication either affects conduct or is without any discernible and provable effect at all.

Another method of classifying these problems can be according to their nature, such as : physical problem, psychological problem and cultural problem. Entropy and redundancy, noise coupling channel, capacity, network are some of the problems which can be added to this list as visualised through information theory.

Resistance to Change

It is important to know why people resist change. According to Watson (1971), all the forces which contribute to stability in personality or in social system can be perceived as resisting change. When the objectives are not clear and there is mystery and ambiguity in the purpose of change, people hesitate to participate. Lack of communication is another reason for people's reluctance for change. Resistance is often marked among people for the fear that they actually don't possess the strength or skill, which is required for the contemplated change. If people are satisfied with the present situation, they will not be willing to make efforts for change. Further, if the profits and benefits are marginal or less than the efforts involved, people will not care much for the new programme.

These barriers to change can be overcome to a great extent if there is an efficient communication system to inform people not only about the technology but also to motivate them for change. At present, information about most of the development, does not reach the majority of the rural people, specially weaker sections of the society. There is a need to develop human resources because development means rural transformation. It is not the change in production or of economic institutions only, but also of social and potential infrastructures which will lead to transformation of human relationship and opportunities. Mass media specially radio and popular litearetureshould be used to provide knowledge and entertainment.

Feedback in Communication

Feedback is the reaction given by the receivers in response to the stimulus, *i.e.* message. It helps the rate of adoption, because free feedback promotes understanding, acceptance and retention of knowledge by revolving errors in transmitting. Feedback plays a very important part in communication because it tells us how our message is being interpreted. If one receives no feedback, it means that no communication has taken place. Communication effects often fail, because there is no proper feedback. An effective free feedback promotes understanding, encourages acceptance and persuades the adoption of the message.

Ranjit Singh (1993) categories few roles of feedback which include the fact that it removes communication barriers, facilitates proper action, rectifies transmission errors, increases accuracy of the message, enchances confidence, improves learning and improves the process of communication.

When a sender transmits a message and the receiver returns feedback to the sender, there is effective two-way communication. There is a complete communication circuit, because there is a message flow from sender to receiver and back to the sender. This two way flow of communication is also called a feedback loop or communication loop.

Even when the receiver receives the message and makes a genuine effect to decode it, there are a number of interferences that may limit the receiver's understanding. There are three types of barriers to communication, *i.e.* personal barrier, physical barrier and semantic.

The truth is also applicable in the case of electronic media.

More Exposure–More Development

The speed of social change has picked up momentum in recent decades only as a result of rapid industrilisation, urbanisation and westernisation in almost all sectors of human endeavour.

A nation can change only when the people belonging to that nation change. Thus national development in the modern times depends upon social mobilisation. It involves an awareness in a large number of the citizens about the problems of development and an involvement in national development. Thus national development depends on the knowledge, the skill and the attitudes of the people, what the people know, what the people can do and what the people can aspire for the hope to get. This is why socialisation, education and mass communication play an important role in modern societies. They help the mobilisation of human resources for national development (Schramm, 1964).

In his study of the Middle Eastern Countries, Daniel Lerner found that modernisation and economic development involve urbanisation, literacy and mass media. He found a close relationship between literacy and exposure to mass media. According to Lerner, the citizen living in an urban area, who is literate and who is exposed to the mass media, develops into a 'mobile personality'. He develops the capacity to identity himself with the new aspects of the environment. He can empathise with others, that is, he sees himself in the situation of the other people. He is the man who is the cash customer, the radio listener and the voter. He accepts and advocates change. Thus the personality style of modern or civilized man is urban, literate and participant. This is why Lerner looks upon the mass media as the 'mobility multiplier' (Schramm Lerner, 1967).

Roles of Communication

According to Thayer (1968) the basic functions of communication fall under four broad categories : (a) the information function, (b) command and instructive function, (c) influence and persuasive function, and (d) integrative function.

T.V. Lakshmana Rao classifies various roles of communication into three categories : (i) Communication in the economic sphere, (ii) Communication in the social sphere and finally, (iii) Communication in the political sphere.

(i) Communication in the economic sphere

– It helps a person find alternative ways of making living.
– It reduces the pressure on land.
– It helps raise a family's economic status.
– It creates demand for goals.
– It motivates local initiative to meet rising demands.
– It broadens the entrepreneurial base.
– It helps economic development become a self-perpetuating process.

(ii) Communication in the social sphere

– It aids in the process of status change from heredity to achievement.
– It motivates the illiterate to become literate.
– It helps shift influence from age and traditional status to knowledge and ability.
– It helps in influencing parents to send their children to schools.
– It helps bring about greater equality and greater respect for human dignity.
– Communication makes cultural and social change a self-perpetuating process.

(iii) Communication in the political sphere

– It helps in the process of power change from heredity to achievement.

– It motivates traditional leaders to define their power by raising their information level.
– It helps the mass recognise their own importance in the power structure and acts as a stimulus to political participation.
– It helps the Government learn the needs of the public and plan its programmes.
– It helps the public know of Government plans and programmes.
– It helps bring about greater equality and human dignity in the political arena.
– It makes political growth a self-perpetuating process.

There are four goals of development communication to motivate, to inform, to reach and to change behaviour.

Functions of Communication

Six functions are assigned to communication, *i.e.* information, education, communication within the cultural matrix (Known by the acronym IEC), motivation, entertainment and discontent. The IEC functions implies motivation to seek process, and assimilate information. People need motivation for attitude and behavioural change and acceptance and adoption of innovations. Development community, even UNESCO has recognised IEC as the main community functions. But over a period of time, the communicaion through research, monitoring and evaluations have come to the conclusion that motivation is the most important and basic function of communication in developing countries. The communication will not be effective and meaningful unless people are motivated. The other implied function is creating discontent in the public about the existing situations by various development effects.

Such discontent is being recognised as the essential feature of communication by the communicators. Entertainment is implied through various functions but given a low-key role only.

The government and masses perception of communication functions is not co-ordinated well. Therefore, it results in 'learned dependency' among the masses as government assumes total responsibility in the communication situations and the masses turned to be passive and dependent.

In Latin American countries, free flow of information by multi corporate through mass media creates cultural dependency.

The Communication Revolution

In the 18th and 19th centuries, western countries were hit with two successive waves of revolutions, revolutions separated in time but tied in logic. The first was the industrial revolution which recognised the nature of work and the structural basis of class and community. The second was the revolutions in communication and popular culture which recognized the basis on which art, information, and culture was made available.

The most explored, though still dimly understood, dimension of this revolution was the rise of national mass media or communication-media which cut across structural divisions in society, drawing their audiences independent of race, ethnicity, occupation, region, or social class. Modern communication media allowed individuals to be linked for the first time, directly to a national community without the mediating influence of regional and local affiliations.

A second, and equally self evident dimension of the communication revolution was the development of the specialised media of communication located in ethnic occupation, class, region, religion, and other special interest segments of the society. These minority media, while virtually unstudied, are in many ways more crucial forms of communication because they are building blocks upon which the social structure is build up.

The third and least explored dimension of the communication revolution was the development of a new social order (role), the professional communicator.

A professional development communicator is a broker in symbols, one who translates the attitudes, knowledge, and concerns of one speech community into alternative and understandable terms for another community. The role operates in two directions: vertical and horizontal. Vertically, professional communicators link elites in an organisation or communities with general audiences, where as horizontal professional communicators link two differentiated speech communities at the same level of social structure.

The clearest example of a professional communicator is that he is a language translator who stands between two different linguistic groups and converts one language into it's general equivalents in another. While this is a pure manifestation of the role, many other communicators such as reporters, editors, artists, public relations men, public information officers, specialised writers in science, medicine and law, engineering and technical writers and ghost writers function as brokers or links between elites and masses and differentiated speech communities. The professional communicator takes the message, ideas of a source and coverts them into a symbolic strategy designed to inform or persuade an ultimate audience. The degree of independence of a communicator, the relative freedom of a communicator in creating a new message, the degree to which he is tied to the source, the number of mediate positions between a communicator and the ultimate source and ultimate audience, all are important ingredients of communication effectiveness.

Development Communication

A definition of development communication must rest on the meaning of 'development' which can be described as 'a widely participatory process of directed social change in a society, intended to bring about both social and material advancement (including greater equality, freedom, and other valued qualities) for the majority of people thorugh their greater control over their environment (Roger, 1976).

The exact behaviour changes that are the goal of development in various nations today, range from the one-child family in China to decreased pesticide use in the Philippines, to creating a 'Computer culutre' in Singapore, to combining infant diarrhoea with ORT (Oral Rehydration Therapy) in India, and many developing nations. Development in any particular nation actually consists of such development programmes and projects, and it is the top priority of the national government in every Third World Country (Rogers and Singhal, 1989).

Development communication refers to the uses to which communication is put in order to further development. Such applications are intended to either further development in general way, such as by increasing the level of mass media exposure among a nation's citizens in order to create a favourable 'climate' for development, or to support a specific development programme or project (this type of development communication is often termed 'development support communication' or DSC) (Rogers and Singhal, 1989).

Development refers to the complicated pattern of economic, social and political change that take place in a community. These changes include political consciousness, urbanisation, division of labour, industrialisation mobility, literacy, media consumption, a broad general participation in nation building activities.

The development of a society involves the diffusion of innovations so that new ways of thinking and new ways of doing become common in the society. All cultural changes are initiated by individuals and they are diffused in a social system through communication from one individual to another. Thus diffusion of innovation occurs through time. An innovation is an idea that is perceived by the individual as new. Diffusion is the process that helps spread innovation.

The development strategies and policies depend on three factors. Development communication has been defined in several different ways by economic development experts, sociologists and communication experts. The terminology 'development communcation' gained currency only in 1960's in India.

A contextual analysis of the traditional social research shows that in 1950s and 1960s, communication and development was a Lasswellian policy in which research was conducted on Third World people and societies for achieving policy objectives of the US Government. Development communication is described as the systematic use of communication in support of national development. The individuals who conceived development communication/journalism in 1960s believed that there should be better trained and informed economic specialists among the communicators. National development depends on economic growth to cover fully, impartially and simply the myriad problems of developing nations. Development communication has to deal with two types of audience (Uma Narula, 1994).

(i) The communicators comprising development bureaucracy, media practitioners, and professionals, and
(ii) The people.

The effectiveness of the development communication depends on the type and kind of audience, image of development bureaucracy, and the interpretation of media practitioners which affect the interpretation of communication and its persuasive efficacy. Wilbur Schramm was one of the first to recognise that communication could play an important role in the national development of the Third World Countries. He believed that mass media could better the lives of people by supplementing the information resources and exposing people for learning opportunities (Lerner and Schramm, 1969).

'Development Communication' is a technical term used by development planners and is often referred to as 'Devcom'. The general noting refers to the dynamic process of bringing development plans to the people for whom they are intended. The general role of Devcom is to create the human environment necessary for development to succeed. The specific concept of development communication identifies it with information, education and communication (identified by the acronym IEC) about development plans. In recent years the dimension of 'motivation' has been added to the concept (Uma Narula, 1994). Development and communication are linked together in symbiotic relationships where each feeds upon the other, stimulates and nourishes the other, suggests interaction between the dynamics of development and communication. According to various interpretations and definations, Devcom is purposive, goal-directed, educative and always is associated with some programme and desirable planned change. It is action oriented since it helps people in gaining better control over their environments by the use of appropriate technology for communication. Devcom negotiates to change attitudes towards development rather than to convert and persuade. It either supports a competent approach to development programmes as advocated by the development practitioners and theorists. More and more development theorists and practitioners are being convinced that 'development threshold' is significant for development communication. This concept suggests being receptive to development to certain point. For example, there is a marked difference between the development threshold of rural and urban society, between elites and masses, men and women within the urban and rural society. These differences in the thereshold are termed as 'development gap'. Development gap suggests that people in different development thresholds need different development communication for effective development (Uma Narula, 1994).

There are three central themes in development communication. Development communication like development has to be propoor, pronature and prowomen. We tend to brush aside the poor by saying that the poor are ignoramus, they lack dexterity and skill and they are incapable of managing their own affairs. The struggle for survival, their sweat and tears impart a new meaning to their existence. We have so much to learn and so much to emulate out of their rich treasure of experience. Much more than this, the poor have a sensitivity, a warmth which is entirely their own. Development media and communication should bring out these examplery aspects of the character and personality of the poor instead of dismissing them as of little or no consequence or reducing them to guineapigs of development. It should project the poor as human beings, 'the finest and best species in creation' (Mishra L, 1996).

Development communication must drive home the truth to planners, policy formulators and implementers that there are enough to work for the disadvantaged. It must bring out with full force and conviction the nexus between environment and development. It must open up an outlet for freedom of information for the people. Nothing could be more relevant than this at a time when there is so much of distrust and suspicion towards tribal dominated areas and tribal life, economy and culture, when there is no natural desire to visit rural areas.

Development communication has necessary a mass dimension. It is not a propaganda. It concentrates on needs, problems and demands of the people. In our country where atleast seventy five percent of people live in villages are still deprived of basic development input. In spite of a number of efforts, the movement taken by government and voluntary agencies to free them from the clutches of poverty, ignorance and illiteracy, much remains to be done. Development communication propogates ideas which motivate people for doing right things the very first time. It works for the attainment of certain objectives by spreading awareness about different schemes.

The successful practice of frank and honest development communication in any country depends much upon the state of public awareness and the value of the freedom of the mass media because communication is a two way process. But there can't be much appreciation of the value of the freedom of the media if the communicators don't exercise, with responsibility and such freedom as they may have in any given situation. Development affects fundamental, social and economic changes. It brings large majorities of people into the full stream of social and political processes, from which they have been excluded since centuries in many developing countries. Development communication is an ally of these revolutionary changes.

Tribal areas in these days have become dwelling places of anti-social elements, nauxalities and poverty may be attributed as number one reason of such kind of situation.

Development effects the lives and the problems of their mass, their wages, the price they get of what they buy, the value of the money in their pockets, their rights to education and equality, etc. This is also the stuff of development communication and if these themes are discussed and broadcast can make radical revolution in human consciousness and freedom. In any developing country, one of the primary ingredients of development is the dissemination of information; information about new fertilizers, seeds, insecticides, cropping patterns and other development input and so on. The process of education is basically related to an information-transfer process. For the rapid and sustained growth of developing countries, the urgent need to disseminate information to masses is obvious. While understanding role of communication in rural development, the term development means the betterment of the standard of living, educational level, level of employment, increase in gross national product or in per capita income which are the basic ingredients of development. Thus it is a type of social change in which new ideas are introduced into the social system in order to produce higher per-capita income. Besides the economic aspect, cultural and social development also take place through communication.

Mass Communication

From the inception of community development and extension services in the developing countries, significance of mass media as a method of communication has grown manifold. Literacy campaigns in the rural areas have increased the number of literate persons, thus the use of printed matter has became possible for disseminating the desired changes. Similarly, improvements in economic conditions and desire to live a better livelihood have increased the number of radio sets from a nominal to a significant higher percentage. In very few places television antennas are also observed. We have unlocked a new social force of incalculable magnitude in mass communication. In comparison with all previous social means for building the world, this force looms as a gigantic instrument of infinite possibilities of good or evil. It is of foremost importance, therefore, that we understand it's nature, it's possibilities and it's limits and the meas of harnessing it for human purposes. With the opening of overseas broadcasting, use of satellites for communication and international system of news gathering, the mass media has become an inseparable part of human life (Singh, 1993).

According to Schramm, a mass medium (1960), is essentially a working group organised around some device for circulating the same message at about the same time, to a larger number of people. Learner (1957) identified two main types of public communication systems; 'media' and 'oral'. Oral system of communication is more common among traditional societies, where literacy is low and primary groups are more. As a society modernises, the use of media system become more and more common because people become literate, individualistic, and cosmopolitan. Increase in urbanisation tends to be accompanied by an increase in the production and availability of communication media. A society where literacy and industrialisation is high, is likely to depend upon mass media chains of knowledge, entertainment and decision-making.

Mass communication comprises the institutions and techniques by which specialised social groups employ technical devices (Press. Radio, TV, Films, etc.) to disseminate symbolic content to large heterogeneous and widely dispersed audiences. In other words, mass communication perform essential functions for a society that uses complex technology to control and regulate the environment. These functions of mass communication include transmission of a society's heritage from one generation to another, the collection of information for the surveillance of the environment, and the correlation of the various parts of a society in response to changes in the environment. So, the significance of commumication through mass media in equipping people with new information and skills and mobilising them for their willing participation in various development programmes and activities has been well recognised and emphasised in Five Years Plans, the blue print of the country's development strategies (Raj Singh, 1994).

Information generally plays three roles in a society; the watchman's role, the policy role and the teacher role. Social development is possible only when the members of a society have a wider vision of the society in which they live and of their role in the society (Kuppuswamy, 1976).

As Mathur and Neurath (1959) have shown, it is the group discussion on the basis of the radio broadcasts dealing with the farm practices that help in bringing about a change in the agricultural practices. According to Pye (1963), deeper analysis shows that the press and radio can have a profound influence in changing the ways of the people only if they are fully supported by the informal, social channels of communications which are intimately related to basic social processes. Rapid national development calls for the coordinated and reinforcing use of both the impersonal mass media and the more personal face to face pattern of social communication.

Laxmana Rao asserts that retarded economic development, low media consumption and poor mass consumption facilities go together. He found that in the village with communication and transportation facilities, there was greater social mobility and general feeling of self-confidence. He also found a significant difference in attitude towards future between the two villagers, one developed and the other undeveloped. In the village with mass media facility, the people looked forward to their future with confidence. The study also confirmed Daniel Learner's hypothesis regarding empathy. Empathy involves not only future orientation but also the cultivation of a self-image, which enables one to improve oneself and aspire to achieve something in life.

Rao also found a new trend with respect to opinion leadership. When people were asked to whom they go for advice in matters of health, politics etc., the people of the developing village said that they got the young man who reads news papers and is thus in a position to help them with advice regarding the problems they confront. On the other hand, the people in the stagnant village said that they go to the Patel who always takes care of their families. Thus a man who is well-informed can become an influential person in a developing village irrespective of his hereditary status, wealth, age and such other characteristics (Rao, 1967).

Development involves the giving up or the modification of a number of old habits, beliefs, attitudes and values and the cultivation of some new ones which are necessary to live in the modern times. Further, development involves not only economic changes and increased production to meet the demands of all sections of the people for a higher standard of living, but also the recognition of changes in social structure so that those belonging to the members of the under-privileged castes can make use of the opportunities (Kuppuswamy, 1976).

There should be a change in the outlook of the government regarding the expenditure on mass media, education etc. Such expenditure should be looked upon as an investment like the investment in agriculture, industry, transportation etc. It should be realised that an effective communication system is an essential element for development (Schramm, 1964).

Mass media are enormously instrumental in accelerating development in many areas of human endeavour. The potential of mass media in development was realised late in India. But since then multiple media exploitation in several development activities has taken up speed. In fact, development is the main motivating factor behind the introduction of modern communication technologies in developing countries, like India.

Today, we all are experiencing change due to information revolution taking place in each level of human endeavour. As somebody has said, we can send a man to the moon in less time than it takes for a post-card to travel from Old Delhi to New Delhi.

The communication scene in India is transforming in such fundamental ways that many social scientists speak of the dawn of 'Information age'. The communication system in India has steadily expanded during the past four decades and has become one of the largest in the world. As Prof J.S.Yadava opines, 'It is necessary to first clearly define the development objectives and then accordingly also define clearly the communication objectives, and specific communication tasks and inputs to achieve the development objectives in most cost effective manner'. He also points out that an overwhelming majority of the 'rural poor' was not exposed to any of the mass media and therefore, the mass media are of limited relevance to masses, especially those who are living below the poverty line (1994).

Models of Mass Communication

Different communication specialists have different opinions regarding the system of flow of information from source to the receivers in mass communication. A brief description of the common and important mass communication models is as follows :

(i) *Single-step flow of communication :* This model is based on the assumption that information reaches directly from the source to the receivers in mass communication. Troldahi (1967), on the basis of research findings proposed the model of one step of flow of mass communication. This step of communication is contrary to earlier model of two-step flow of communication. Single step model states that mass media channels communicate directly to the mass audience without the massage passing through the opinion leaders.

(ii) *Two-step flow model :* Lazers-feld, Berelson & Gaudet (1948) proposed that influences stemming from the mass media first reach 'opinion leaders' who in turn pass on what they read and hear to their day associates who are influenced by them. Opinion leaders are more exposed to the mass media than those who they influence. This model implies that opinion leaders are active and followers are passive which is not true in every situation. There may be many non-leaders in direct contact with mass media.

(iii) *Multi-step flow model :* It is not desirable to limit the flow of information to one or two steps. The number of steps differ from situation to situation and the flow of mass communication is far more complicated than two steps. As suggested by Rogers & Shoemaker (1971), the exact number of steps in the process depends on the intent of the source, the availability of media, the extent of audience exposure, the nature of the massage and it's importance.

The 'New' Development Paradigm

The new paradigm was pluralistic and it recognised many pathways for development. It was also less western in it's cultural assumptions. Key elements in the new development paradigm include : (Singhal and Rogers, 1989).

(i) General equality in the distribution of development investments, information, and the consequent socio-economic benefits of focusing on such weaker sections of the population including poor women and children, racial and ethnic minorities.

(ii) Popular participation, knowledge sharing, and empowerment to facilitate self-development efforts by individuals, groups and communities.

(iii) Self-reliance and independence in development, emphasizing the potential of local resources. Self-reliance became a key concept at both the national and local levels, implying that every nation, and perhaps every village, could develop in it's own way.

(iv) Integration of traditional and modern communication systems and the use of 'little' media along with that of 'big' media in order to facilitate development.

Self development approaches to developmente communication led to more popular participation, mass mobilisation, and group efficacy with greater responsibility for development planning and execution at the local level. The main roles of mass communication in such self-development are : (i) to provide technical information about development problems and possibilities, and about appropriate innovations, and (ii) to circulate widely information about self-development accomplishments by local groups, so that other such groups could profit from others' experiences.

The transistor set revolution brought about significant changes during the 1960s. Previously, radio receivers were quite big due to their bulky vacuum tubes. The transistor radio was only about one-tenth the size and cost of it's predecessor. As a result, a so-called 'transistor radio revolution' occurred in India and in many other Third World Nations, and the rate of radio diffusion increased rapidly during the 1960s and early 1970s. During this period, the Indian Government viewed the radio mainly as a luxury, and imposed a heavy import duty on the items, and collected an annual fee from every radio owner. Gradually, however, the Government of India began to change it's policy on radio, and considered it as 'magic multiplier' of development, a view promulgated by influential American communication scholars like Daniel Lerner and Wilbur Schramm. They argued that the mass media, especially radio could play an important role in development by conveying useful information, changing attitudes, encouraging nationalism, and by facilitating school instruction.

Radio has certain unique advantage under Indian conditions unlike the press, it can also reach illiterates. Compared to television or films, it is relatively cheap, making it possible for radio broadcasts to be localised to each community. The localisation allows radio broadcasts to deal with topics that are of special interest to local people. However, radio only appeals to the senses of hearing (Singhal & Rogers, 1989).

Radio Strategies for Development Communication

Open Broadcasting

This strategy encompasses a broad variety of experience. What distinguishes from other strategies is the primary emphasis it puts on the message. Gunter and Theroux (1977) have summarised many of the advantages of this approach. Their basic assumption is that the mass entertainment media of most of the countries attract and educate much larger audiences than do most typical, educational broadcast programmes. They suggest that development communications strategists adopt a more creative approach to their work, and devote more time and money for improving programme quality and attracting larger audiences for educational radio. They argue that many development objectives can be achieved without the expenses of organising an audience. They cite three examples of how radio might achieve valuable learning results.

First, the authors review advertising and it's possible application to education, which they call 'advertising'. Second, they talk of audience participation in programme production, and finally, of a specific example of an educational quiz show.

A radio programme on health in Kenya is reported to be one of the most popular programme on the air in 1975. Another rural radio programme in Guatemala (AED, 1976) seems to have made a clear contribution to knowledge, attitude, and behaviour change. The experimental project distinguished between organized and unorganised listening groups, and preliminary results indicated that open broadcasting had clearly superior results in comparison with controls, and showed even some relative advantages over the organised approach. The development goals to be achieved are a critical element in the choice of strategies.

Radio Campaign

The second strategy, is in between the open broadcast and the organised-listening-group approaches. It has a number of historical predecessors, including the organised discussion group in Sweden and the mass-mobilisation campaigns common to socialist countries such as the Peoples Republic of China and Cuba. There are few examples of campaigns in which radio has played predominant role. The Tanzanian case to be outlined has made a unique contribution in combining radio and discussion in campaign format. Some of the distinguishing features of a radio campaign are the following : it's concentration of effort into a relatively short period of time; it's focus on the achievement of one or a few well-defined goals that have broad appeal; it's effort to motivate and involve a large portion of the population in it's activities; the organisation of a listening audience during the campaign period; the long preparation for the campaign and the need of coordination of many institutions for it's success; and the role of public support for the campaign goals. The experience of Tanzania with campaigns is impressive. On both criteria of reach and impact, the radio campaign strategy seems to have succeeded quite well. There is evidence for low drop-out rate, a high participation rate and adequate learning.

Regular-Listening Group

The regular-listening group strategy consists of a combination of radio messages broadcast on a consistent schedule, usually with some printed support material, and a group organised to listen to the broadcasts together and, subsequently, discuss them or share some common learning experience.

The Radio Schools

The radio school was a form of organised listening in Colombia fifty years ago, and that spread to many nations of Latin America. The radio schools began when the originator, a Catholic priest, began to broadcast religious and educational messages to his disciples. Gradually he began to send out written materials and finally to pick and train a group leader or monitor to handout support materials. The important element that, distinguishes the radio schools from the other listening groups-strategies, is it's continual commitment to teaching literacy and non-formal-education-skills. Although radio schools also later included farm practice and agricultural innovations in their goals, like the farm forums, they remained primarily dedicated to their original educational goals (Jamison and McAnany, 1978).

The Radio Animation Group

The strategy again is a form of organised listening groups. The technique of animation grew out of a French tradition of group dynamic that was applied to development projects in the early 1960's, especially in Africa (Colin, 1965). The animation approach stressed the participation of community in defining it's own problems, the non-directive nature of the social animator's role, the degree of awareness necessary for the community to recognise it's own problems, and the self-help nature of it's development action.

It may be worthwhile to review one case of the animation approach. Cassirer (1977) has prepared a rather lengthy description of Senegal's rural radio project. In 1968, Senegal, through UNESCO sponsorship, began radio broadcast for rural groundnut framers in the regions of Thies, Diourbel, and Sine Saloum. Fiftyseven radio clubs were established for the pilot area, but many more were informally created during the following years. The very severe conditions of the peasants in the groundnut area during 1968-1970 provided an important historical backdrop for the farm in which RER (Radio Educative Rurale) evolved. A creation of joint efforts by various Ministries conceived of a two-way system. Two-thirds of the programming in this period (1969-72) contained materials recorded in the field, and thus allowed input from the peasant audience itself. In addition, President Senghor backed the creation of a written feedback system called Disso (or dialogue in the national language), which solicited letters from rural people concerning their problems. These letters were translated into French, printed and distributed to relevant government officials every three months. In the first two and half years of the project, 2300 letters from 500 villages were received. The project is now fully funded with national resources and has expanded into other areas with locally adopted programming is an indication of it's success in Senegal (Janison and McAnany, 1978).

Janison and McAnany (1978) draw three reasons, from their experience: a rural broadcasting system like the RER takes a great deal of effort as well as political help to create (given in this case by the President of the country) a project of this kind is not excessively costly and can be economical if it functions to it's capacity and the programming that allows audience input and encourages dialogue is more important than the content of broadcasts. The strategy faces four problems. First, the non-directive nature of the animation approach can mean endless dialogue and little action. Second, local participation must be defined for each radio project and examined for it's feasibility and it's eventual impact on rural life. Third, participating with the government may contain serious dangers of cooptation by the power holders who are inclined to short-term solutions. Collaboration of confrontation is often a serious strategy question for development project leaders who solicit and gain popular participation of large masses of rural people. Finally, the desire of localisation manifested means that radio often losses some of it's advantage as a mass medium and becomes more like a local telephone system or a community radio station.

The Radio Farm Forums

According to Rogers and his colleagues (1977), a Radio forum is a small listening group that meets regularly in order to receive special radio programmes. The radio farm forums are usually decision groups geared to a group action; the radio schools, are usually learning groups, but sometimes they make common decisions for action as well. The other way in which these two types of radio listening groups have distinguished is by their origin. Historically, radio forums began in Canada among farmers and were spread through the sponsorship of UNESCO while radio schools were begun and have spread primarily in Latin America and have been usually sponsored by the Catholic church. The basic idea about farm radio forum is that with it's multimedia approach of 'combining the mass medium of radio with the interpersorial communication of group discussion and feedback through the monitor, it aims to benefit the mass.

India's use of forums began with a highly successful experiment in Poona where forum members learned significantly more than individual listeners or those who did not listen at all. When the forums were spread nation wide shortly afterwards, the experience was not as positive probably because the new forums didn't experience the same national attention. A similar experiment was tried in Ghana where similar positive results were found during the initial period.

According to Janison and McAnany (1978), there is not sufficient evidence to prove that forums are an effective strategy in every case, but certainly this combination of interpersonal and mass communication can bè effective, especially in increasing knowledge. What seems evident from the experiences of India, Benin, and Indonesia, where large field tests of forums were made, is that the problems associated with capitalizing on the potential are formidable. Essentially, it is much easier to organise the radio message than the audience. Feedback often failed, and groups whose sole contact was the radio message itself often disappeared quickly after formation.

Communication Strategy for Tribal Development

Adoption of new technology by the tribal or rural people is one of the important prerequisites to substantially improve their life. Economic and human developments are the most significant pillars of rural development. Economic development improves the quality of life and better human resources play a significant role in generating more wealth. Mass media when used in it's full potential for reaching, motivating and instructing large number of people to take specific kinds of constructive action has a vast scope : (Singh, 1993).

(i) A greatly enlarged supply of learning aids especially print materials, radio and television programmes can spread the message more effectively, quickly and accurately. There is a need to pay more attention to create good educational software for both print and electronic media.

(ii) Greater collaboration among organisations in creating and transmitting high quality educational content is also essential.

(iii) Market places and other popular meeting grounds can be used for creating successful teaching-learning situations. Traditional forms of folk entertainment can be employed as communication channels.

An appropriate communication strategy through the broadcasting medium can play significant role in dissemination of information and in healthy entertainment particularly for the tribal people who live in diffecult circumstance.

The objective of any tribal development programme must be for the provision of food, clothing, shelter, education and health services for every one, under conditions, which provide for universal dignity. The goals of development should not be considered simply as agricultural and economic growth in the narrow sense but as balanced social and economic development with emphasis on the suitable distribution as well as the creation of benefits. Rural or tribal development calls for a massive and multiprolonged effort, not simply to boost production but to create and spread employment and to root out the fundamental causes of poverty, disease, ignorance and injustice.

Development does not start with goods, it starts with people and their education, organisation and discipline. Without these eliments, all resources remain latent, untapped potential. People are the primary and ultimate source of any wealth whatsoever. If they are left out, then nothing can ever yield real fruit (Singh, 1993).

The Seminar on Rural Development and Communication Polices, organised jointly by the Indian Institute of Mass Communincation (IIMC) and the International Institute of Communication in February 1979 at Hyderabad, examined the inter-relationship with regrad to rural development.

The following issues and problems which pointed to the inadequacies of current practices in regard to rural development communication were discussed :

- Quantitative shortcomings with regard to the availability of and access to communication and information facilities in respect of origination, transmission, and perception of messages.
- Qualitative shortcomings with regard to the content of information and messages.
- Imbalance in communication between urban and rural areas, between regions, between groups in society, defined in terms of social classes, power, sex, or age.

These and other factors have led to a situation where development message often do not reach those for whom they are intended. Even if they reach their target auidences, they are often not used. Information losses are considerable both within the development agency systems and between these systems and the users.

Communication can't be seen in isolation but as a part of total development system. Thus communication can't be dealt with by itself but only in relation to the political and socio-economic structure and cultural patterns. It is, therfore, important to avoid a simplistic relation between communication and the development effort.

There is a need for the formulation of communication policies on the basis of the adopted plan for rural development. The purpose of such communication should be :

- To promote change ; – To avoid alienation;
- To encourage participation; and
- To foster social justice and equity.

Communication policies should be based on clearly stated priorities in terms of investment, training, etc. for rural/tribal communication needs. Changes in structures of communication agencies, particularly those in the public sector, such as the grant of autonomy to the broadcasting service, should provide for access and participation by the disfavoured groups in the rural sector so as to promote communication 'from below'. Special strategies are required for this purpose as well as for reaching these groups with information.

Communication policies and planning should take into account the variety of message required for different auidences. Here again, decentralisation and localisation is necessary. In terms of priorities for rural communication, it is desirable to make intensive use of telecommunication and broadcasting facilities in the rural areas. There is a crucial need for adequate recruitement and training of rural communication and of rural development personnel. A number of specific recomendations were put forward in the seminar. These include the following :

- Experiments in 'densification' of communication in order to establish the role and impact of communication in rural development;
- More efforts towards establishing audience profiles;
- Consideration of separate broadcasting channels for rural programmes, and broadcasts by agricultural universities and other institutions for development;
- Consideration of all available technologies with regard to their adaptation and use in terms of the social and cultural circumstances in different societies and communities;
- The means of establishing an information system to aid rural development and industrialisation.

Attention was also drawn to a number of factors and pitfalls

- Incorrect and partial information plus the danger of loss of credibility, which in turn implies a waste of major communication resources.
- More attention should be paid to the process of communication, implying *inter alia* that the task of the communicator extends to the adoption and acceptance of the information provided.

Communication problems of rural India can't be solved through technology transfer. Indian reality is multidimensional and will not yield to a single point approach. We have high density, sparsely populated, and remote areas. Social institutions, traditions and ethos of people also differ. Each of the major media available to reach the rural India has it's own potentialities, skills, limitations, and possibilities. Since our information needs are diverse, no single medium can adequately meet the rural communication needs (Mehta, 1992).

In the recent years, there has been a definite policy shift in favour of adopting more of new communication technologies to accelerate the pace of development and change. The country is on the threshold of a new communication revolution of which satellite computer, television, radio, radio-FM, radio-paging and now internet are major manifestations. Radio is by far the most extensive network. Technically, the radio signals cover almost the whole country.

Rural programmes are broadcast from almost all AIR stations in regional languages and local dialects. In 1966, AIR set up Farm and Home units in selected AIR stations to provide relevant and problem oriented. Farm information to the farmers of a small homogeneous area with similarity of agro-climatic conditions. This marked the beginning of a new era of farm broadcasting in the country. The main ingredients of Farm and Home broadcasts are hints on day-to day agricultural operations, scientific methods of agricultural and livestock farming, soil and water management, fertilizer application, plant protection measures, storage and marketing etc.

The duration of broadcasts for rural audience from each station varies from 21 to 45 hours a month. The programme for special audience include those of the armed forces, women and children, youth, students, rural and tribal people and industrial workers.

It is an indisputable fact that communication is very important for an individual, a society and a nation. It is a process, which involves planned effort for human development. It is an act by which people share knowledge, ideas, feelings and information to gain common understanding of the meaning and use of the message. It occurs through speech and other senses like audio, visual, touch, smell and taste.

Mass-communication in the form of hardware and software have brought significant changes in the information scenario. Various researchers have made attempts in finding out the relevance of different methods, approaches and presentation modes. As science has been influencing our life and it's impact upon our society is quite remarkable, a need arises to look forward an effective mode of imparting scientific information to the people. It will be quite appropriate to search for a mode which enhances the insight of the beneficiaries into the basic nature of each social phenomenon so that the problems related to broad human concerns like monotony, poverty, malnutrition, pollution and ignorance can be controlled for better life.

The introduction of radio has obviously affected village life and brought about changes in the use of leisure time and other social processes. The modern media, particularly Radio and Doordarshan (Television) have affected the behaviour pattern of the village youth, who have a different orientation towards community life. Knowledge on external affairs is highly valued by the villagers and young people who acquire such knowledge gain considerable importance in village life. Many of the old villagers now accept that their own opinion, are worthless because they lack knowledge of external affairs. It is a fact that relative power of the older, traditional knowledge givers have gradually shrunken and these are being replaced by a class of young and more knowledgeable people as village life becomes more modern and complex.

The communication needs in India are much greater than the resources we have today to meet them. No communication can exist fully in a cultural vaccum. Cultural norms and attitudes of the people are sensitive issues and they act as a vital force. No one can afford to ignore them in planning communication strategies. For rural communication, broadcasting through radio can play a very crucial role. Any communication network unfamiliar to the masses, which does not function close to their cultural predispositions and institutional values will have little impact and significance. Studies have stressed that no mass media can exist in cultural vaccum. After all, communication is fully realised when it passes through the attitudes and behavioural patterns of the people. It is shaped by cultural heritage and common ties of existence of the people. Communication pattern of any society is a part of its total culture and can only be understood in the context of its social values. Thus the heritage, caste and creed based barriers and cultural complexity with the illiteracy among the population furnish a backdrop with which the cammunicators and electronic media have to reckon with while working. Effectiveness of communication, however, is influenced by several factors including distortion. The process of communication is influenced by many factors such as source's attitudes, encoding, receiver's attitudes, decoding etc.

All India Radio is a government operated monopoly within the country. It has a good number of regional stations from which programmes are broadcast preferably in regional languages and more or less confined to the regional culture. The Hindi language and other programmes are broadcast from Ranchi AIR station whose output may be seen benefiting its non-tribal audience. But since there are sub-regional, ethnic, religious and other cultural differences within it's broadcasting zone, it is difficult to serve such a large area of tribal population. There are about thirty tribes in this tribal belt of Chotanagpur and area-wise people speak different languages. Kurukh (spoken by Oraon tribe), Mundari, Khadia, Ho and Shanthali are some of the major tribal languages. The tribal languages broadcast form All India Radio, Ranchi is quite inadequate in terms of duration and format too. It's zone of broadcast almost covers entire South Jharkhand. Besides high power transmitter at Ranchi, there are also local radio stations in Hazaribagh, Chaibasa and Daltanganj and one low power radio station at Jamshedpur.

Here in the land of Chotanagpur, where the broadcasting medium has been playing quite an important role in promoting music, dance and culture since its inception in 1957.

Through participation in radio folk songs, invited audience programmes, the tribals of this region have been immensely benefited. Getting auditioned in a radio station matters because of it's social recognition. Radio has got very limited chunk to accommodate artists frequently because the number of groups auditioned in AIR have become quite high in recent times.

All India Radio now provides coverage to almost 100 percent of the country's population. The transistor revolution has taken radio to the cowherd, the Kisan and the small shopkeeper. It is the primary source of news for the people in large parts of the country. It may be mentioned that my three field areas show different degree of listenership. It is minimum in Hatma existing in center of Ranchi city and goes on increasing as one leaves city and approaches to rural area. The listenership in Mandar is moderate while it is maximum in Rania, a place about 85 kms away form Ranchi city.

The various rural uplift schemes like Integrated Rural Development Programme (IRDP), Training for Rural Youth for Self Employment (TRYSEM), Jawahar Rozgar Yojana (JRY), the programme for the Development of Women and Children in Rural Areas (DWCRA), Mahila Samridhi Yojana and PM's Social Security Yojana etc. are given adequate coverage in the electronic media. People in Rania are more curious to listen programmes in AIR than the other two field areas. But people have got lesser number of transistor sets in this remote area.

The awareness level particularly in Rania is the minimum as per observation in the field. The tribals having higher socio-economic status do have higher awareness about things happening in their surroundings. They have got access to both print and electronic media. There is another truth which speaks that in Rania, Two-step model of communication is more prevalent which implies that opinion leaders are active and followers are passive because of the influence stemming from the mass-media first reach opinion leaders 'who' in turn pass on what they read and hear to their every day associates. Sometimes, the number of steps differ from situation to situation and the flow of mass communication is far more complicated than two steps. The exact number of steps in the process depends on the intent of the source, the availability of the media, the extent of the exposure, the nature of the message and it's importance. The degree of curiousity for the broadcasting media is higher in Rania because of the fact that people do not have adequate access to print media and TV channels. It is minimum in Hatma, which is located in an urban heartland. Here in Hatma, Single-step f.low of communication is much more prevalent. It states that mass media channels communicate directly to the mass without the message passing through the opinion leaders.

The barriers to communication with the out side world are immense in Rania. The village level workers (VLW) and the extension workers even with the best of their efforts can reach out only to a limited despondent clientele of morbed villages. The villages in the block of Rania are in dire need of exposure to the modern methods of production, appropriate fertilizers and technology, soil and water conservation methods, cropping patterns, seeds and plantations, dairy development and animal husbandry etc. It is noticed that in Rania, tribal people cultivate with their traditional know how.

Development as a continuous qualitative process is aimed, at bringing about changes in every sphere of human life. Particularly in Rania various governmental schemes and programmes for the planned development of the tribal areas and the different strategies adopted for eradication of mass poverty have failed to bring out a corresponding change in the quality of living.

Interpersonal channels are important means most heavily depended upon by people of this part of Jharkhand for information on development related issues, particularly by the small and marginal farmers, artisans and farm labourers in Rania.

The essence of communication is getting the receiver and the sender tuned together for a particular message. In a remote place like Rania, people are happy with one source of information. They don't take initiative to make further enquiry. On the otherhand, in fast developing areas, people check the credibility of the message from different reliable sources. For, development of tribal dominated areas, nothing is more important than the transfer of useful ideas from one person to another. In this process of communication lies the potential of millions of village people to overcome ignorance and to attain social well being. Much misunderstanding results from faulty communication. What is needed is more people saying the right thing at the right time, in the right way and to the right people. This is the formula of effective communication. As one moves from the city towards remote countryside, it is observed that gradually people encounter lesser access to scientific communication. In Hatma, a number of respondents are found to have access to both electronic and print media whereas the story of Rania is entirely different. Moreover, the respondents in Hatma are having their busy life either in school, college, business or service.

Radio is a powerful medium in the transfer of technology to the people. At the same time, radio is also considered as a passive medium. It is observed that only with imaginative and interesting programmes, radio can attract it's listeners. Radio enjoys a sense of very high credibility as a source of farm information in all the field areas. It has been observed in Rania that farmers who are more close to extension workers and specialists are better listeners of farm radio programmes. A radio station can best serve a community only if its programmes relate to the interests, needs and problems of the people within its area of coverage and if it uses the language or dialect spoken by the people. Chapter 7 deals in detail about the impact of broadcasting on tribals.

4

TRIBAL DEVELOPMENT AND THE BROADCASTING MEDIA

SECTION-I

Tribal Economy : Scope and Approaches to Tribal Development

Simplicity and self-sufficiency are the twin characteristics of the economic life of a tribal village in Jharkhand. Tribal economy is mostly a subsistence economy. Agriculture is the most important occupation for the tribals of Chotanagpur. The importance of cattle and other livestock in tribal economy is considerable. Due to relative isolation and self contained nature of the tribal society, a mutually complementary and interdependent, self-reliant economy and simple life style become a reality. In Chotanagpur, the tribal society is not a homogeneous monolith; there are strong variations and diversities among various tribes. Depending upon the techno-economic status, L. P. Vidyarthy (1970) classified the tribal society into the following categories :

(i) Settled agriculturists,
(ii) Artisans,
(iii) Shifting or Jhum cultivation, and
(iv) Hunting and collecting stage.

On the basis of five indicators namely, (i) ecological, (ii) ethnicity and technology, (iii) literacy level, (iv) nutritional level and (v) income level, K. B. Saxena (1983) has identified following as poorer sections of the tribal community :

(i) Nomadic/semi-nomadic groups/food gatherers and hunters,
(ii) Shifting agriculturists,
(iii) Artisan groups,
(iv) Landless agricultural labourer,
(v) Urban/industrial wage labour in unorganized sector, and
(vi) Small and marginal farmers.

Saxena also identifies indebtedness, low literacy, malnutrition and disease, social exploitation, corruption in bureaucracy, poor return from produce, unemployment and under-employment, squeezing of rights and low asset base are some of the reasons of backwardness of the tribals of Chotanagpur.

Das (1967) has given a five fold division of tribal economy: (i) Nomadic food collectors and pastoral, (ii) shifting cultivators, (iii) plough cultivators of plateau, (iv) tribes who are partly assimilated with the Hindu social system, and (v) totally assimilate tribes who have gained a good social status among the Hindus. J. H. Hutton (1931) is of the opinion that there are three economic types of Indian tribes : (i) the tribes who collect food materials from the forests, (ii) the tribes who are in pastoral stage, and (iii) the tribals who live on agriculture, hunting, fishing and industries.

In spite of differences in problems between different zones, there are a few common features as listed by the National Committee on Development of Backward Areas headed by B. Sivaraman.

(a) Difficult terrain with primitive transport system,
(b) Agriculture and forest produce are the major source of income,
(c) No profit motivation, natural growth of crops,
(d) Barter system, unorganized market and private money lending system,

(e) Extra-vagance in social and religious ceremonies,
(f) Vulnerability to the unscrupulous hands and ignorance.

Tribal culture in India is passing through a phase of economic change with the rest of the country. The tribal economy is too witnessing a continuous impact of the new modern economies which is evident from the fact of the emergence of new typologies among them, *i.e.* lower type and white collar type. In 1958, when the typology of Bihar tribes was first formulated by Vidyarthy, it was only of four types in Bihar. Just after ten years, in 1968, Vidyarthy came up with seven types. This is the result of economic changes in the tribals. The modern economic activities are changing the traditional tribal economy. The following modern forces need mention in the changed context of new economy of tribes, *i.e.* (i) Education, (ii) New link of tribal markets with big markets or urban markets, (iii) Cooperatives, (iv) Commercial Banks, (v) Labour unions, (vi) Land Mortgage Act and it's knowledge, (vi) Concept of saving, (vii) A shift in consumption patterns, (viii) Changed situation in the international border line and the impact on the fontier tribals, (ix) Emergence of commercial attitude among the tribals like, (a) Emergence of tribal money lenders, (b) Change in cropping pattern from cereals to cash crops, and (c) Open sale of minor forest produce as a means of cash economy and (x) Reservation in Government and semi-government establishments (Vidyarthy and Rai, 1977).

The education has received a grand welcome by the tribals and the elites among the tribals are fast moving towards urban and industrial fields for white collar jobs in public and private enterprises and business. Major tribes like the Santhal, Munda, Oraon, Ho, Bhil, Gond and converted tribals of these groups are taking up new jobs according to their educational qualifications. The tribal markets have been linked to big markets and this has introduced many innovations in tribal life. The cooperative movements have also introduced a new economic trend. The agriculturist type tribals are accepting new seeds and fertilizers from the cooperatives (Vidyarthy and Rai, 1977).

Vidyarthy and Rai (1977) sum up the change taken place in tribal economy in the following manner :

(i) From forest hunting economy to forest,
(ii) From hill cultivation to settled agriculture (cultivation),
(iii) From simple agricultural economy to multicrop agricultural economy, labour and white collar job and commercial economy, and
(iv) From artisan type to artisan plus marketing and so on.

About 90 per cent of the people in the tribal area are engaged in agriculture. There is less shifting cultivation here. Almost 60 per cent of the holding are less then 1 ha. Most of the cultivable area is cropped in Kharif with about 90 per cent cropping intensity leaving about 26 per cent for Rabi and summer. Rice, wheat and oilseeds are primarily grown in the low and medium land. On the upland, maize and pulses are cultivated. Vegetables are grown intensively on household plots both for domestic use as well as for commercial use.

In general, small farmers supplement their income through wage labour and selling forest produce. Off-farm employment for men is common and includes supplying labour to larger land owners, as well as migrating to work elsewhere after the harvest. Although some work in the local mines and industries, most of the tribal people prefer agricultural work in more developed states, such as Punjab and Haryana, and are efficient labourers in the brick-making kilns in Calcutta.

The infrastructure base in Jharkhand is poor, and more so in the tribal areas. Most of the villages are without electricity and access to health service, drinking water etc. is inadequate.

The origin of the conflict between the Adivasis and the state can be traced to colonial times. The advent of the British brought about major changes in the pattern of resource use as the natural wealth of India became cheap raw material for British industry. The setting up of 'reserved forests' led to the loss of tribals control over natural resources. The 'right and privileges' of tribals under the Forest Act of 1927 was reduced further to 'rights and concessions' by the Forest Policy of 1976. The latest Forest Policy promulgated in December 1988, retained the concept of exclusive state ownership of forests. While industrial requirements were termed 'national needs' in the new policy, the rights of the tribals and other forest dwellers were reduced to 'people needs' rendering tribals encroachers in their own havitat. This crisis has been acknowledged by the 29th Report of the Commission for SC and ST.

Tribals constitute a unique stream of our society and form a very important part of our national heritage. Dr. Kumar Suresh Singh, an eminent expert in tribal affairs and well known for his pioneering work on People of India, asserts in an article, '...However, India is not the best example of a plural society, because while pluralism stresses cleavages and discontinuities between sections of people differentiated by race, ethnicity, religious or culture, there have been in India an all pervasive sense of cultural unity, a wide ranging sharing of idiom and symbols in spite of diversities.'

During the last few decades, a large number of tribals have suffered displacement and forced migration because of industrial, power and irrigation projects. The topography and the terrain and also the low density of population have attracted big projects. The process of rehabilitation has become very slow and improportionate. The on-going development process and the dominant consumer economy and the resultant overgrowing craze for short-term immediate gains have put tremendous pressure on the resource base of the tribal population. The tribals who once used to protect their forests are now competing with each other's vested interests, how to make immediate gains out of cutting of trees etc... It has led to almost uscrupulous loot of the forest products.

A detailed appraisal by K. B. Saxena notes, 'Instead of benefiting them, the increasing development of their areas is accompanied by a marked deterioration in the condition of the poorer tribals who are now fighting a grim battle for survival.....Official reports and non-official studies in varying degrees substantiate this conclusion. The tribals in varying degrees, in these areas have been displaced in a big way through loss of land, loss of occupation and growth in unemployment resulting from various factors.

The majority of the scheduled tribe population in the state of Jharkhand is concentrated in Chotanagpur and Snthal Pargana regions. Their major concentration area can be categorised in the following manner.

(i) Tribals living in those blocks where their concentration is of 50 per cent and above are spread over 17250 villages in 112 blocks of Chotanagpur and Santhal Parganas. These blocks are divided into 14 Integrated Tribal Development Projects (ITDPs) funds.

(ii) Special attention are attached by the Ministry of Welfare for the development of those pockets, where tribal population is more than 50 per cent and falling outside the TPS and MADA area. Deputy Commissioner of those districts are directly responsible for the development of those pockets.

The Tribal Sub-Plan

The Tribal Sub-Plan in the state of Jharkhand, is envisaged as an area development plan of scheduled area with special emphasis on tribals inhabiting the regions where there are 50 per cent or more of them are living. The delineated area and strategy of approach already started during the Fifth Plan period is being continued during the subsequent plan periods also. In order to optimize the socio-economic development of the tribal people and ensure their safeguard against continued exploitation by external forces, the approach to the development and welfare strategy is an on-going process of refinement with an ultimate object of free and full participation by the target group in plan formulation, implementation and maintenance.

Protective measures

(i) A number of measures have been taken to protect the tribals from various kinds of exploitation particularly at the hands of money lenders. These measures are in the form of tenancy laws and special regulatins including (a) Chotanagpur Tenancy Act, 1908, (b) Santhal Parganas Tenancy (Supplimentary Provisions) Act, 1949, (c) Scheduled Area Regulations,

1969, and (d) Excise Policy etc. By these measures security to tribal land is taken care of.

(ii) In matters of excise policy, the existing law prohibits commercial vending of country liquors where the traditional population is more than 50 per cent. In these places, tribals are, however, allowed to have their traditional system of brewing pachwai for domestic, social and religious purposes.

(iii) So far as the question of bonded labour in the tribal community is concerned, the position is comparatively better than the rest of the state. Till the end of 1993, 770 tribal bonded labourers have been identified in the TPS area of undivided Bihar as against 1331 tribals identified in the entire state who have been fully rehabilitated.

(iv) Tribals traditionally enjoyed concessions and privileges of minor forest produce. Concessions are given to villagers to collect dry and fire woods, fruits, flowers and twig leaves from the forest for their domestic needs. In pursuance with the New Forest Policy Guidelines, participation of the tribals particularly in the afforestation and forest management has been taken up in a large scale since 1992-93, and the result is encouraging.

Special Central Assistance

The Special Central Assistance (SCA) is one of the main sources of funding the Tribal Sub-Plan (TSP); the main sources being the state plan supplemented by centrally sponsored schemes and institutional finance. SCA is allocated to the state in addition to the flow of funds from the other sources.

Scope of Development

K. B. Saxena holds the views that the traditional society characterized by a greater degree of homogeneity, group action, community feeling has received severest jerk in the process of development which has disintegrated their solidarity and diluted their cultural values. His view has invited controversy because of the fact that the tribals of Chotanagpur, in particular, have remained backward mainly for two reasons: their long isolation from the general society and their exploitation by non-tribals specially the zamindars, the money-lenders, contractors on the one hand and their own brothers on the other. The need of the hour is integrated development which is sustainable, cultural, eco-friendly and finally holistic.

(i) Growth with equity has been acknowledged as the motto of planning for development. The hopelessness accentuated day by day by the present systems of technology pose a serious threat to development and it is a great challenge to generate technology systems, which can help and benefit the poor sections. If employment is to be generated in a tribal region, it is best possible by promoting and strengthening the existing mode of production with the inputs of modern science and technology.

(ii) To redress the situation both Government of India and the Government of undivided Bihar in the Eighth Plan have modified and prepared 'felt need' objectives designed specially for the development of tribal areas which include : (a) creation of employment, (b) decentalization of planning, securing involvement of the people and strengthening the village administration through panchayati raj and NGOs, (c) increased investments in rural areas, (d) self-sufficiency in food grains production, (e) reducing poverty and improving education, (f) infrastructural development, such as irrigation and communication, and (g) efficiency in government expenditure. The goal is to achieve these broad objectives without upsetting the ethnic identity of the tribal people.

(iii) An effective media can yield much dividend in terms of efficiency utilisation of development input. Particularly in tribal villages of Chotanagpur. People are ignorant because of their low awareness level. Media should report less about party polities and the corporate world and more about what concern to people at the grassroots level. This kind of reporting should be indepth and continuous. Events happening in villages and smaller towns, particularly development news ought to be given adequate coverage. Radio has got edge over other media because of the fact that in remote tribal area, hardly any body is a subscriber of a daily newspaper. Weekly markets (Hats), radio, government officials, voluntary workers and the people having frequent contacts with near by towns are important sources of awareness.

The poverty induced life cycle affects most of the people here in tribal Jharkhand. South Chotanagpur having tribal concentration of about fifty per cent of the total inhabitants are a impoverished lot. Nutritional deficiencies, ill health, growth retardation, slow learning, small body size, low productivity, excess of illpaid and unorganized work, low earning capacity, unemployment, less facility of communication and transportation etc. are some of the common features of tribal life.

Communication technology can play a significant role in developing human resources particularly living in tribal areas by motivating the masses for adopting the new technology. It has the potential to widen the horizons, to focus attention, to raise aspiration and to crate a climate for development. Multimedia approaches are best suited to reach the large number of people quickly and it is, therefore, essential to plan a multimedia strategy for communication development.

(iv) For alleviating poverty, it is essential to ensure full participation and involvement of the beneficiaries. The panchayatiraj institutions should be further strengthened. Voluntary organisations have to reach remote parts of this tribal belt and concentrate their attention in different problem areas.

(v) Chotanagpur is quite rich in natural resources. Therefore, the need of the hour is for an integrated policy of all the indicators of development sustainability. The uneducated masses with a poor economic base need to be strengthened through various programmes that integrate functional literacy, food for work, information, training in income generating skills, subsidised packages for production, market economy, storage and credit facilities etc. rural energy, biodiversity and forest conservation, water projects for human and animal use and irrigation are some of the areas which need more attention. The development of human resources, to analyse problems, formulate policies and evoke popular participation based on local issues and initiatives will continue to need special attention. The development works in tribal areas may be carried on an area basis. This will cover areas of major tribal concentration as well as tribal pockets. According to L.P. Vidyarthi and B.K. Rai, the broad framework for the purpose may cover area, *i.e.* (a) micro area, (b) meso area, (c) macro area, and (d) tribal pockets isolated and comparatively backward tribes, for smooth and all purposive development programmes.

(vi) This area has been neglected since long. The functioning of JAAC (Jharkhand Area Autonomous Council) comprising eighteen districts of Chotanagpur and Santhal Paragana, which started from 9th of August, 1995 was almost defunct. After grant of statehood things have started to change. There has been more social and political awareness among tribal people who consider that statehood of Jharkhand is a long awaited victory for people of Jharkhand. There is every good reason to believe that out of the present chaos, confusion and political uncertainty, if calm and equilibrium will be restored, the tribals will be able to assert their distinct rich and cultural identity in all its splendour to ensure that the society is enriched by their contribution. At different levels, sports and cultural activities are being organised spreading more consciousness towards the activities in these days. Growing political and social consciousness are certainly going to influence the human development index (HDI) in this region which has already taken up an onward trend.

It is true that tribals are poor because they are ignorant and superstitious. They believe in witch-hunting. So far little has been done to curb the abuse and killing of innocent people. Even educated and relatively well-to-do tribals, and most of the tribal leaders belonging to the various factions have desisted from fighting the menace for fear of hunting sentiments and losing votes. It has been acknowledged for the first time that the evil can't be fought until organised opposition to it comes from within the tribal community. The killing of a witch is usually preceded by sudden deaths, specially of children in the village. In remote tribal villages, living conditions are miserable, health facilities do not exist and deaths due to infection from water are quite common. A tantrik is preferred to a professional when a person is ill in most of the cases in remote part of this pleatue region.

Here, witch-hunting is convenient way to settle old scores. Where the dian killings are concerned, there is no age bar. The widowed women are the favourable target. Amit Khare, Deputy Commissioner of West Singhbhum, and V.H. Desmukh, the Superintendent of Police, had the conviction that the dian killing is a cover-up for something else. The more the illness, the more are the killing. West Singhbhum has the highest record. According to Desmukh, in 1991, there were 14 incidents, in which 15 women, 8 men and one child were killed. In all, 64 people were accused, of which 55 were arrested and chargesheeted. In 1992, the number of incidents mounted to 15, in which 15 women were killed. In 1993, the number reached a stunning 18 with 26 people killed (19 women, 6 men and one child). The rate came down to 12 in 1994, when 15 people were killed (Sarkar, Nov. 26, 1995).

This uncivilized act is due to under development. The tribals are abysmally poor and uneducated and therefore, superstition-prone. A desperate administration is battling with the slender resources at it's command in tackling the menance. It is organising rallies with NGOs and social outfits to create mass awareness against witch-hunting etc.

Approaches to Tribal Development

The Government even during British times, had realised the need to take concrete measures aimed at the development of tribal populations. But there was no unanimity on the specific steps to be taken. Historically, there have been three main approaches, each with its merits and demerits. They were : (a) Segregation, (b) Assimilation, and (c) Integration.

The policy of segregation was followed by the British rulers by isolating the tribals from the general population, maintaining communication in the tribal areas in a primitive way etc. Verrier Ellwin, a famous British anthropologist supported the establishment of national parks, for tribals, in which their contact with the out side world would be reduced to a minimum. But this segregation policy had the effect of encouraging exploitation by landlords, money-lenders and middle men in the tribal areas. The Government of India in the post-independence period too had supported segregation in some ways, by conceding the demand for tribal home lands like Nagaland, Mizoram etc., and by declaring a few particular areas of tribal concentration as Scheduled areas and tribal areas. Separate funds have also been allocated for tribal development and welfare.

The policy of assimilation foresees that culture contact with neighbouring populations will lead to acceptance of mainstream culture, religion, value system etc. resulting ultimately in assimilation in thc general population. But this policy has been criticised because it means the end of tribal culture, arts and crafts, and the loss of potentially useful knowledge of traditional medical systems. Tribals themselves face the extinction of tribal identities.

The third approach has been labelled integrationist. Based on the principle of unity in diversity, this policy aims at tribal betterment through the introduction of new schemes, technologies and projects with the full consent and participation of tribal populations while preserving their native cultural forms, and after full consideration of the susceptibilities of the people. Anthropologists and tribal experts have been co-opted into this programme, so that an integration approach can be adopted towards tribal development.

Constitutional Safeguards

The Constitution of India provides, 'The state shall promote special care for the educational and economic interests of the weaker sections of the people and in particular, of the Scheduled Castes and Scheduled Tribes and shall protect them from social injustice and all forms of exploitation. Several articles of the Indian Constitution are specially relevant to the protection of the weaker sections. Article I5 prohibiting discrimination on the grounds of religion, race, castes, sex or place of birth, Article I6 guaranteeing equality of opportunity in matters of public employment, Article 17 abolishing untouchability, Article 23 prohibiting traffic in human beings and forced labour, Article 29 protecting the interests of the minorities, and so on.

In addition to these general safeguards, there are specific articles dealing with tribal interests. Article 46 promoting the educational and economic interest of tribals, Article I64 providing for the appointment of a Minister to look after tribal interests exclusively, Article 244 providing for special administration of Scheduled areas and tribal areas, Article 235 providing for grants from the Union to the states, Article 330 and Article 332 reserving seats for the Scheduled Tribes in the Lok Sabha and the state assemblies respectively, Article 334 providing for reservation of seats and special representation, Article 339 providing for control of the center over the administration of Scheduled areas and the welfare of the Scheduled Tribes, and Articles 371-A providing for special provisions for Nagaland.

The Constitution holds the President of India primarily responsible to safeguard the interests of the tirbals and He has been empowered to appoint a Commissioner for Scheduled Castes and Scheduled Tribes at the national level to protect the right of tribal people. The Commission submits its report annually to Parliament through the President. Under Article 244 of the Fifth Schedule of the Constitution, the President of India can declare any area in the Indian union predominantly inhabited by tribal groups as a 'Scheduled Area'. At the state level, besides the government, several voluntary agencies, social work organisations, religious groups and non-official organisations are also active in tribal welfare.

Planned development has aimed at expanding and strengthening national economy through industrialisation. One of the foremost objectives of planned development has been raising the socio-economic levels of the backward and the poverty stricken. Development which is considered as unsustainable in all sense will hardly ameliorate the despicable life of the impoverised. Large scale migration of young people to urban areas and to far off places has adversely affected the village economy as well as the life styles.

More than anything else, the most agonising trauma has been destruction of ancient handlooms of the tribals *i.e.* their common property resources, specifically their land and forest. A number of tribal groups in the country have their own lists of plants, herbs, seeds, flowers etc. used for treatment of disorders.

Keeping in view the special nature of the problems connected with the development of such sections of the community, the five fundamental principles have been enunciated by the then Prime Minister, Pandit Jawaharlal Nehru (Sahay, 1997). These are :

1. People should develop along the lines of their own genius and we should avoid imposing anything on them. We should try to encourage in every way their traditional art and culture;
2. Tribal right in land and forest should be respected;
3. We should try to train and build up a team of their own people to do the work of administration and development. Some technical personnel from outside will, no doubt, be needed, especially in the belonging. But we should avoid introducing to many outsiders into tribal territory;
4. We should not even administer these area or overwhelm them with a multiplicity of schemes. We should rather work through, not in rivalry to their social, cultural institutions; and
5. We should judge results, not by statistics, or the amount of money spent but the quality of human character that is evolved.

Understanding of Tribal Life and Culture

In view of the above, it is necessary to have a good understanding of the tribal life and culture *vis-a-vis* type of approach to their development. In this connection, the following aspects may be kept in view(Sahay,1997).

1. It is important to make a systematic personal observation of their social, economic, political, and religious groups and the beliefs, values and the material culture.
2. We must also be aware of the latest theories of social change, including the theories about the negative effects of irregular culture-contact situations and the three major steps involved in a social change situation: (a) innovation; (b) response to the innovation–either negative or positive; and (c) if the response has been positive, the integration of innovation into the pattern of socio-culture life.
3. The knowledge that the economic changes are often faster than the social changes would save us from disappointing and frustrating situations.
4. The realisation that we should not be in haste and be careful introducing new ideas could save from a situation of their coming in clash with the 'hard core' of culture. The understanding of the tribal people, their relationships in various groups, needs as perceived by them, institutions, beliefs, and practices, values and norms, and aiming at linking the new ideas of development with the tribal people's existing and past ideas would go a long way in obtaining the results of tribal development more successfully.
5. The picture of society as an integrated whole should always be kept in mind.
6. We have to be careful with regard to the 'hardcore' of culture.
7. Natural personal identification with the community is essential in making one acceptable to the community.
8. We should bear in mind that social change is a slower process.
9. The knowledge of social anthropology and it's methodologies can contribute a lot.
10. If the socio-cultural and economic aspects are properly studied, analysed, and exploited, the programme based on a scientific understanding with pragmatic approach, will stand a good chance of success.

SECTION-II

Socio-Cultural Changes and Identities in Tribal Life

The word 'change' denotes a difference in any thing observed over a period of time. Social change, therefore, would mean observable differences in any social phenomena over any period of time. According to Jones, social change is a term used to describe variations in, or modifications of, by society in social processes, social patterns, social interaction or social organisation. Yet another definition of social change is given by Mazumdar (1966), when he says social change may be defined as a new fashion or mode, either modifying or replacing the old, in the life of people or in the operation of a society by its very nature, social change is an universal phenomenon, social change results from the interaction of a number of factors. There are a number of factor that contribute to social change. These can be classified as biológical factors, physical factors, technological factors and cultural factors. Added to these factors are mass media, which play a pivotal role in social change of a nation. Everett M. Rogers (1962), well known sociologist and communication scholar is of the opinion that new ideas are diffused into a community through mass media and interpersonal communication. He argues that new ideas spread into a community slowly, and this follows a four step process. In his social diffusion theory, Rogers postulates that a series of steps are adopted by people in the process of trying out new ideas. According to Rogers, there are few stages which include : (i) Knowledge stage, (ii) Persuasion stage in which the individual gets persuaded about the new ideas, (iii) Decision stage in which a decision to adopt or not to adopt is taken and lastly, (iv) confirmation stage in which confirmation of earlier decision is taken. Rogers has carried out a number of research studies regarding diffusion of innovations largely passed on to third world contexts and his researches are particularly relevant to a country like India in the field of communication and social change.

(i) India is a large country with a huge population of over 900 million and more than seventy per cent of the population live in 600000 villages.
(ii) Our GNP and GDP are low in comparison with a number of developing countries.
(iii) Many of the social welfare schemes launched by the Government do not reach people.
(iv) In the fields of literacy, nutrition, health and awareness, we are even far behind small developing countries.
(v) Indebtedness, social exploitation, corruption in bureaucracy, low productivity, unemployment and low asset base are some of features of day-to-day life here.
(vi) The fruits of development don't reach the needy and the places where major inhabitants are tribals.
(vii) We are poor because we are ignorant and we still have many superstitions prevalent in the country, which impedes growth.
(viii) Right now, the picture in rural/tribal India is that the people and particularly the tribals are suffering from a culture of obsolescence. Poverty and backwardness are common features.

Radio is the largest and cheapest medium which can be made available to people at the grassroots level. The correct use of media becomes imperative particularly in our country where illiteracy abounds and there is need to bring about an awareness among the tribal population to accept the new ideas.

Impact of Social Change on Tribes

The tribals live in their day-to-day life with utmost simplicity. In Oraon areas, the population pattern of all villages is quite diverse. In Munda villages, there are a number of functional groups like the Panr (weaver), Lohra (blacksmith), Kumbhar (potters), Teli (oil presser) etc. Their presence is of vital concern to the village economic relations between different communities. The interaction is not only in linguistic plane but also on the culture and biological plane (Sachidanand, 1965).

The missionaries have been working in Chotanagpur for more than hundred years. There are a number of missions each competing with the other in social, educational service and proselytisation. All over the world, they have been one of the most important agencies of social change. Christianity introduces a new kind of leadership and new principle of social control. The prist becomes the all round leader, the path finder, the friend, philosopher and guide. The importance of sin and the fear of retribution is a powerful instrument of social control (Sachidanand, 1965).

By far the most important factor responsible for rapid change is industrialisation. The industrial potentialities itself of the tribal areas in Chotanagpur have increased by the work of the DVC (Damodar Valley Corporation), big industrial establishments in Jamshedpur, Bokaro, Dhanbad, Sindhri, Mosabani and Hatia near Ranchi which have opened up new avenues of employment. In the areas around these places, a large number of tribals have been displaced from their land as well from their traditional occupation and agriculture. Thousands of tribals have been transformed into busy industrial labour from quiet agriculturists. (Sachidanand, 1965).

The influence of education and social welfare activities by voluntary agencies are some fruitful areas of social change. Non-formal education by BEP (Bihar Education Project) and hundreds of non-governmental agencies have taken up the difficult task of literacy and education in this part of tribal area. Various awareness activities by missionaries and voluntary agencies need special mention in this regard. People are gradually acquainted with the modern communication channels.

Community development is another important agency for social change. This is different from other agencies. It is observed that status and prestige offer an important incentive for social change. Social change is marked in individual behaviour, food habits, dressing, rituals and festivals, folkways, mores, music, dance and in almost every aspect of their life. In tribal society, kinship is an important principle of social structure. Every person is not only a part of household, but every household is part of a series of wider groupings like clan, tribe and village. In recent times, kin groups have been widely dispersed as people moved in search of livelihood to distant places. The area within which kinship ties operate has contracted, though in some cases, the sense of moral obligation to a distant kinsman is not entirely dead. The forces of social and economic changes have influenced almost all institutions existing among tribes in Chotanagpur. Social mobility is much more evident today than before, one may attain social prominence without having been borne to rank. The old criteria for elevated social status still operate, but new criteria have also come into being. Prominence based on special skills and recognised competence enable individuals to achieve leadership status (Sachidanand, 1965).

In fact, the morals of tribal people who are famous for their simplicity and honesty, are in a state of flux. One set of value is superimposed on the other. Villages in tribal areas are no more self-sufficient. People have to rely more on outside for their requirements. There is more uncertainty in day-to-day life. People are no longer sure as to which action they ought to follow.

Migration of tribals to North-East, Calcutta and North India is another important reason of social change. According to Sachidanand, with the increasing pressure on land, hundreds of tribals, both men and women go out to work for a few months between the winter harvest and the summer sowing. This helps them to meet their requirements for cash money needed for payment of land revenue, buying cloths, etc. Most, of these people return during Sarhul festival, which is celebrated during the month of April. These people not only bring cash, but new fashions, new dresses, new ideas and concepts. They are well versed with the glib talks, which make their acceptance with the non-tribal people. Thus they try to upset the traditional power structure in the village. As a result of the interaction with the outside world, a tribal tries to settle in near by towns to maintain his *status quo* and earn livelihood for the family.

It is noticed that the number of tribals who are coming to settle in nearby towns *i.e.* Khunti, Ranchi, Lohardaga, Gumla, Chaibasa and Jameshedpur for the purpose of, earning bread or for giving better education to their children are constantly increasing. The primitive tribes are comparatively unfortunate.

It is also marked that economic backwardness is the prime reason for underdevelopment. In all the towns mentioned above, thousands of tribals daily labourers come from the satellite villages ranging up to a maximum distance of thirty kilometers in search of employment and most of the time, they return back to their villages in vain. It is also observed that there are equal number of non-tribals (Sadans) who meet the same fate and the story is painful. The payment made to a daily labour is not at all lucrative. When a labourer can earn maximum forty rupees for the whole day, he can't save more than thirty rupees for his family after lunch and conveyance. Equal number of female labourers are also found and, thus a number of tribals belonging to this group lead their life hand to mouth.

The change from traditional modes and pattern of leadership in some tribal villages were studied by Sachidananda (1964). The impact of change can be seen on traditional leadership behaviour and status, leadership roles and sanctions, leadership characteristics and on the nature of emergent leadership. Culture change has resulted new conflicts and stress. New leaders are rising to focal positions of power. New leadership roles are introduced as new concepts of education, public health and economic development take hold. Leaders are not solely derived from the upper strata of the social structure as was formerly true. The present system allows access to position of respect and power to more categories of individuals than earlier.

When the impact of a change on a social system is great, there is a conscious and organised attempt for a part of a society's members to revive the selected aspects of their culture. Linton calls this a nativistic movement. Such a manifestation always concerns itself with elements, never with culture as a whole. The history of the tribals of Chotanagpur from the middle of the 19th century has been marked by a number of such revitalisation movements. Unlike other areas, such movements acquired a political shape here. The Birsa movement was embodiment of the social, economic and religious unrest among the Munda. Beffeted by the waves of repressions and oppressions and torn by despair, the Mundas saw in Birsa a prophet and saviour. His religion is combination of Munda belief, Hinduism and Christianity. He was as much a rebel against the zamindars, money-lenders and missionaries as against the Government. So tremendous was the impact of the movement that for sometime, the foundation of British rule in Chotanagapur was shaken (Sinha, 1964).

Another movement which is still in force is that of the Tana Bhagats. The present Jharkhand movement is for political autonomy. For over 70 years, Advisasis of Chotanagpur and Santal Pargana belt of Bihar have lived with a dream for a separate Jharkhand state after countless tribals have suffered incarceration, braved lathi chares, untold atrocities inflicted on their kith and kin in their struggle for a tribal state, their dream realised on 9th of August, 1995 to certain extent when the Jharkhand Area Autonomous Council (JAAC) was formally inaugurated by the State Planning Minister, Mr. Tulsi Singh. Shibu Sorean, called Guruji by Adivasis all over the tribal belt became its first chairman. The JAAC with limited power and a small budget allocated to it by the Patna based state government, was a far cry from an autonomous state, which in due course led to the formation of a separate state. The original inhabitants of this tribal belt of Chotanagpur particularly the tribals because of their simplicity, have been continuously exploited by Britishers, their own brothern who are non-tribals, and the people of North Bihar who are continuously migrating to this beautiful land and making it their permanent home. In a nutshell, the tribals in this region have not been able to improve their standard of living adequately because of their low awareness level and attitude of obsolescence. Here, integration in terms of another type of structure is taking place. With the growth of education, the tribals are being drawn into the services and professions in large numbers. In literacy, the figure shows a definite upward leap. A tribal service class family living in Ranchi for a generation or two is indistinguishable from others as for as standard of living is concerned. Most of the tribals are bilingual.

Regarding the direction of change, all groups everywhere are registering socio-economic changes and the gaps between tribal societies and other communities are being filled up. Communities are becoming less homegenous as one passes from the interior to the suburb and from the suburb to the city. We see that the new industrialisation and modernisation forces have dethroned the old culture. Every new invention disturbs the old adjustment. The transformation of class structures, the breaking up of traditional family system and the disintegration of social nearness are some of the consequences. One most important influence on tribals is visible that is decreasing faith on superstitions and social evils which is a result of social change.

Social and Cultural Identities : The Roles of Language and Music

The most visible expression of the cultural identity and intgrity of a tribal community is its distirict language and a unique body of songs, with accompanying dance and drumming in that language. In some cases, the unique song repertories constitute only a portion of the tribe's overall song reportory. The Mundas, for example, perform reportories of song that are uniquely theirs. In Chotanagpur, people identify themselves and each other as belonging to the Munda jati, Oraon jati, Lohra jati, Bania jati and so forth. Every group officially designated as adivasis is not identified by a distinct language and music. Some such as Lohra and Mahali, are simply too small and scattered to maintain separate cultural identitics. Regardless of their official classification, they appear in their social and cultural relationships to be more like the caste artisan jatis of the same occupations. But for the large tribes, a distinct language and songs distinguish one from the other. Language and music are, no doubt, important expressions of cultural identify in Chotanagpur, whether that expression is directed within the group or outside. With whom a persion makes music, what music they make, and in what language they make it are reliable indications of that person's cultural references group. Groups that have a unique linguistic identify also have a unique musical identity (Carol, 1991).

Language and music are so important to cultural identity in Chotanagpur that both have figured prominently in cultural identity movements that have been launched in the area in recent times. Nagpuri is now spoken with pride in urban area too, and textbooks, and periodicals are available in the language in these days. The language has been successfully established as an independent language. Several cultural societies regularly publish collections of newly composed poetry and song texts as well. There are number of NGOs (Non-Government Organisations) which are functioning in the tribal belt for promotion of different tribal dances and Nagpuri songs. Musical cassettes are plentily available in the market and Nagpuri star singers are found to be very popular crowd pullers.

Department of Tribal and Regional Language of Ranchi University and All India Radio, Ranchi have the distinction to patronise four non-tribal and five tribal languages. Mundari, Santali, Ho and Kharia, all Austroasiatic tribal (single jati) languages and Oraon, a Dravidian tribal language have developed into literary tribal languages. In the non-tribal category, Nagpuri, Panchpargania, Kurmali and Khorta are all emerging Indo-Aryan, caste-based (multi Jati) literary languages.

Each tribe is a relatively homogeneous social and cultural group, a group of social equals, sharing a similar history, status, occupation (in village), and value. Their common language and music are reflections, outward expressions of the social and cultural identity they share. A caste based cultural group, like the Nagpuris, is a community of diverse social groups unequal in status, different in occupation, origins, history, race, custom, and values. Their common language, music and oral and written literature function to unify otherwise extremely hetero-geneous population (Carol, 1991).

Cultural Approximation

The boundaries between tribe and caste in Chotanagpur have defied clear definition by anthropologists in part because the settled village cultivators, whether tribes or caste, have developed a common base of shared cultured traits over centuries of co-existence. The anthropologist, R.P. Srivastav observing the process there and else where in tribal India has called it as cultural approximation (1966). Even a partial enumeration of traits that are shared by the tribal cultivators and Indo-Aryan castes, particularly those of lower status, suggests of the approximation. Such a list would include, for instance, some marriage customs; animistic beliefs focused around magic and natural and ancestral spirits; animal sacrifice; certain seasonal rituals and festivals; the decorative tattooing of women; and items of material culture such as dress, jewelry and implements. Some traits probably originated among the Munda speaking tribes, others among Indo-Aryan castes. The nature of such approximation and the character of the resulting shared culture depend on the particular cultural groups residing in a given geographic area. But common cultural features have developed to such an extent that the anthropologist, Surajit Sinha has suggested that the cultural variation in Chotanagpur may be primarily a factor of geography rather than linguistic or cultural group identity. The development of this shared cultural base of a regional Chotanagpuri culture is something that marks this as a cultural area, different from Bengal to the east, the rest of Bihar to the north. Cultural approximation here has been accompanied by a corresponding musical approximation. Approximation has been in the areas of performance, practice, instruments (drums and flutes), and drumming patterns, while the songs (texts, tunes) if each cultural group, or some portion there of, have remained distinct (Carol, 1991).

Many assumptions have been made by anthropologists about the nature of culture change in Chotanagpur, particularly regarding the tribes, on the basis of such enumerated observations of cultural approximation. Therefore, we should examine very carefully just what such observations do and do not tell us. To begin with, the identification of shared cultural traits indicates merely an approximation of cultural product. It tells us little about the use, conceptualization, or meaning of these products within a cultural group of village community. And it tells us nothing about the role of approximated cultural traits in either weakening or strengthening a sense of cultural identity within the group. The approximation of cultural product does not necessarily mean the loss of a group's distinct cultural identity. The features they share are not those that are important to them in identifying an individual's cultural reference group. It is rather their differences in customs, Beliefs, origins, language, saying, stories, and songs that define and express their cultural identity. On the other hand, cultural approximation among long time residents of this tribal belt has contributed to their perception of the cultural distance between them and the outsiders, the Hindus and Muslims (Carol 1991).

Linguistic Identities

The linguistic diversity of the Chotanagpur plateau is remarkable. The region is a meeting ground of the subcontinent's major language families, the Austroasiatic, the Dravidian and the Indo-Aryan. Of the three, the Austroasiatic has the longest history on the subcontinent. All the Austroasiatic languages, in the subcontinent, collectively called the Munda languages belong to the western branch of that family, the eastern branch of which includes the language of the Nicober island in the Bay of Bengal, the Khasi language of Assam and North-Eastern states and Mon-Khmer and related language of the Southeast Asia. The Munda language group should be distingiushed from the tribe of the same name. Mundari, the language of the Mundari tribe, is only one of the Munda languages. The others include Ho, Santhali, Kharia, Korwa, Juang, Saora, Korku, Gata, Remo, Gutub, Gorum and Sora.

The Dravidian language family is also represented by a large tribal group, the Oraon, the second largest tribe in the plateau after the Santhal (Mundas are the third). Their language, Kurukh, is related to Kannada, one of the literary Dravidian languages of southern India. It should be noted that not all the tribal groups of Chotanagpur speak Austroasiatic or Dravidian languages. Some, such as the Lohra, Bhumij, Mahali, and Turi, are Indo-Aryan speakers today, presumably having abandoned their own Austroasiatic languages generations ago.

Chotanagpur's Indo-Aryan languages are also many and are all related with each other and are more widespread like literary languages of northern India. The Tribal and Regional languages Department of Ranchi University has recognised four distinct Indo-Aryan language of Chotanagpur: Nagpuri, spoken in central and western parts of Chotanagpur which is also link language among the tribals and non-tribals of Chotanagpur; Khortha related to Nagpuri; Panchpargania, spoken in the eastern parts of the Plateau and related to Bhojpuri and Bangali; Kurmali, spoken by the Kurmi people in the eastern parts of the plateau and related to Bengali. The speakers of each of these regional Indo-Aryan languages are less homogeneous socially and culturally than the speakers of any one tribal language. They include jatis (Endogamous social groups) of different social status, occupations and religions. The local manifestation of Hinduism is by far the predominant religion among Indo-Aryan speakers; there are also small numbers of Muslims, Sikhs, and Jains. There are number of tribals who have embraced Christianity in this tribal belt of Chotanagpur.

Chotanagpur, like the rest of India, contains a mixture of racial types, and language is not necessarily a reliable indicator of race or religion. Most Austroasiatic speakers are descended from a racial type that has been called Proto-Austroloid, different from the Mediterranean type that characterizes much of the Indo-Aryan population. Still, at a time when Austroasiatic speakers were dominant and widespread across northern India, before the large scale influx of Indo-Aryans; small, marginal group of non-Austroasiatic speakers probably adopted Austroasiatic language and culture. In more recent times, the Indo-Aryan speaking communities have in turn subsumed small, marginal populations of Austroasiatic speakers. And while intermarriage between Austroasiatic race is rare and even rarer between them and Dravidian and Indo-Aryan groups, it does occasionally occur. Nevertheless, the physical as well as linguistic resemblance of Austroasiatic speakers to one another contribute to their sense of a common origin sometimes in the forgotten past (Carol, 1991).

Another fact which has influenced the linguistic evolution in the tribal belt of Chotanagpur is that the state language has deeply penetrated into the tribal languages spoken in the plateau. The absence of a written script and lack of tribal leadership to develop their language of this region have made them lose their language identity to certain extent.

The Oraon people who live in Chotanagpur close to the Santhals and Mundas are not different socially, economically and culturally from their Austric neighbours, Santhals and Mundas. For employment, purposes they have migrated to Assam, Orissa and West Bengal and are slowly merging with the locals of the respective states. But their language is quite distinctive and has got oral literature in which, it has been compiled by W. G. Archer in the form of poems and songs and published in Nagri script by the Government of Bihar and in English by the same author in London. This book gives in English version a series of beautiful traditional poems in Oraon with notes and commentaries.

Art and Culture

Art is the embodiment of human creative spirit. People generally believe that backwardness in the context of tribals is invariably associated with lack of education and that who is unlettered is uncultured. But this is not always true. According to Ananda Coomarswamy; 'there is no necessary connection between literacy and culture'. The tribals of India are a convincing proof of that. The tribals who live in inaccessible and remote areas of India where modernization has not made its impact on their life we find that the tribal folk have an integrated pattern of life where music, dance, art forms and well designed functional objects are necessary parts. In the absence of modern inputs and abundance of resources which are presently available with the modern-day man, the tribals have got great sense of indigenous-attitude, skill and creativity in making their houses, utensils, baskets and musical instruments. And every object of creation is not without a purpose.

Chotanagpur which houses about thirty tribes, both advanced and primitive, possesses a rich cultural heritage. The tribal arts and festivals are based on community participation and their preservation to this date despite the onslaught of modernisation in this tribal plateau, which is something miraculous (Gulati, 1993). The modernisation has opened up the tribal areas to influences of the outside world leading to the decline of their institutions. Their migration to urban area in the state of Bihar, Orissa and Assam and far off places of Punjab, Haryana, parts of Northern India in search of livelihoods has brought about noticeable changes in their skill, imagination for art and songs.

Cooperation is spontaneous among tribals and it has deep sociological roots characterised by kinship bonds and mutually reciprocal obligations. There is no monetary payment for cooperation rendered. Because of this reason, the tribal's social structure is generally egalitarian and the differential asset endowment does not affect inter-tribal social intercourse in the level of equality. Personal and marriage life is characterised by a great degree of personal choice and freedom, subject only to the tribal taboos. Except the power of inheritance, tribal women have an equal and assertive position in society largely because men and women both work and at times together. The community dance and a drink at the end of the day's hard work help them to relax and lend cohesion and solidarity to the group. The day-to-day life and the productive activities of tribal society are marked by a high degree of integration and cooperation (Saxena, 1983).

Linguistic Diversities

There is a great deal of diversity among the tribes, even among those who are related linguistically. The late anthropologist, L.P. Vidyarthy portrayed tribal Chotanagpur as a tableau of human evolution, with tribes at each stage of development coexisting side-by-side, hunters and gatherers such as Birhor; shifting cultivators such as Asur, Malpaharia and Hills Kharia; and settled peasant cultivators such as Munda, Santhal and Oraon (Vidyarthy, 1964, 1980). The broad cultural difference among tribal groups do correspond to differences in their patterns of subsistence, settled cultivators have more in common with each other than they do with hunters and gatherers, regardless of origin or language. However, each cultivating tribe still maintains an identity as separate, independent, self-sufficient social and cultural unit. The large tribes, such as the Mundas, Santhals, Hos, and Oraons are bounded linguistically and to some extent geographically. Regardless of what these groups may have in common, the separate identity of each is presented and articulated through tribal endogamy, a common origin and history, and unique customs and beliefs (Carol, 1991).

Saving the Language of Tribals

A significant proportion of Indian tribes have opted for the languages of the advanced cultural group. As a result, some of the tribal languages may vanish soon. In Chotanagpur, because of urbanisation and migration of tribals to near by or far off towns, tribal languages are dying out.

A language without any literary tradition may not survive in the modern age, because contacts between those speaking folk language and those speaking advanced and literary language are increasing. The new generations among tribal groups find that their languages are incapable of coping with the demands of modern knowledge. Such situation invariably leads to language shift. Had the teaching in their own languages been possible, such a situation wouid not have arisen. The survival of a language depends not only on its own literature but also on it being spoken by sufficient number of people. Sanskrit, though a highly developed and rich language, is considered dead while Santhali, a tribal language without any literary tradition is a lively one opines M. Ishtiq (Feb. 3, 1995).

All India Radio, Ranchi since its inception in 1957 and Tribal and Regional Language Department of Ranchi University have remained main promoters of five tribal languages and four non-tribal regional languages spoken by majority people in this tribal belt. The identification of linguistic area for each tribal is important for planning. The objectives should be to emphasise the development of their education and script for their languages.

The Role of Dance and Music in Tribal Life

An enunciation of the role of music and dance in tribal life is pretty difficult. There is appropriate music and dance for each occasion; birthdays and weddings and in almost all rituals and celebrations which act as a centripetal force for upholding tribal unity. The sweeter the melody, the more vigorous and spirited is the dance. Among the tribes of Chotanagpur, there are no dance without music. The full throated melody and the exquisite footwork are vitally connected. With their rich and vibrant traditions of dance and music, artisanal skill, and diverse ways of life, the tribals of Chotanagpur have added colour to our national culture.

Plate 1 : Tribal people enjoying broadcasting while work

Plate 2 : Tribal woman artist performing folk song.

Plate 3 : Tribal artists performing in an invited audience programme.

Plate 4 : Tribal woman artist performing folk song.

Plate 5 : Recording of OB (Outside Broadcast) based programme in a rural area.

Plate 6 : Tribal woman artist performing folk song in an invited audience programme.

Plate 11 : Tribal male performers in a moment of ecstasy.

Plate 12 : AIR sponsored Kavi-Sammelan of tribal and folk artists.

Plate 13 : Folk dance performance by a single artist sponsored by AIR.

Plate 14 : Folk dance by group artists.

Plate 15 : Folk dance performance by a single artist sponsored by AIR.

Plate 16 : Stage performance by folk artists.

The tribal and non-tribals of Chotanagpur share a rich cultural heritage from time immemorial. According to Dr. R.K. Tiwari (1994), there can be some broad classification about their song and dance.

(i) Tribal folk-song : Jadur nritya, Jatra nritya, Bisu nritya, Baroya nritya, Lujhari nritya, Jhumer nritya, Dasai nritya, Domkach, Angnai and Paika etc.
(ii) Non-tribal folk-song : (Sadani nritya) Ragin nritya, satriya nritya, Nachni nritya, Natua nritya, Agni nritya etc.

It is also learnt that there is much more commonality in observance of dance, music and festivals between tribals and non-tribals because of their physical proximity and staying together for a pretty long time.

Jhumar, Damkuch, Angnai, Daind-Dhara, Biyah, Jhanjh-in are some of the important ragas of folk-songs while Sarangi, Kendra, Tohila, Bansuri, Sahanai, Veri, Manjira, Kathwal, Dhol, Nagada, Mandar, Daf are some of the popular musical instruments among tribals (Table 4.1).

Almost all the tribals speak Sadani with some local variations. Hindi is also intelligible to all with some exceptions. Sadani, Sadri, also called 'Nagpuria' is the dialect spoken by almost all the tribal people in South Bihar. Sadani is sub-dialect of Bhojpuri as said by Grierson and thus it falls in the Indo-Aryan category. It is the lingua-franca of Tribal Jharkhand. It has become mother tongue of some tribal people such as Chik Baraik, Lohra etc. and in other places it is the second language for tribals. The Gawari, which is also spoken in Chotanagrpur, is a dilect of Magahi, varies from place to place. Gawari is also the second language of some Tribals. There are effects of neighbouring dialects of some of the tribals. The vocabulary varies from place to place but there is a structural uniformity with some minor differences. The main tribal dialect of Bihar are Santhali, Mundari, Ho and Kurukh. Kharia and Gondi are dying dialects in Bihar and are superseded by the Indo-Aryan dialects. The Dravidian dialects are greatly influenced by their neighbouring dialect (Prasad N., 1961).

Table 4.1 : The dialects of the 30 scheduled tribes of Bihar with their language affinities : as per information gathered

Name of the tribe	Dialect	Language affinities
Asur	Asuri	Austro-Asiatic
Baiga	Sadani	Indo-Aryan
Banjara	Sadani	Indo-Aryan
Bathudi	Mixed	Indo-Aryan
Bedia	Sadani	Indo-Aryan
Binjhia	Sadani	Indo-Aryan
Birhor	A dialect of Mundari	Austro-Asiatic
Birjia	Sadani and Bengali	Indo-Aryan
Bhumij	A dialect of Mundari Sadani and Bengali	Austro-Asiatic and Indo-Aryan
Chero	No language of its own but speak neighbouring Munda language (Austro-Asiatic group).	
Chik Baraik	Sadani	Indo-Aryan
Gond	Gondi	Dravidian
Gorait	Sadani	Indo-Aryan
Ho	Ho	Austro-Asiatic
Karamali	Karmali	Austro-Asiatic
Kharia	Kharia	Austro-Asiatic
Kharwar	Sadani	Indo-Aryan
Khond	Sadani	Indo-Aryan
Kisan	No language of its own but speak neighbouring Munda language belonging to Austro-Asiatic group.	
Kora	A dialect of Mundari	Austro-Asiatic
Korwa	Korwa	Austro-Asiatic (it is closely related to Asuri)
Lohra	Sadani	Indo-Aryan
Mahli	Mahle	Austro-Asiatic (It is a sub-dialect of Santali)
Mal-Pahariya	Malto	Dravidian
Munda	Mundari	Austro-Asiatic
Oraon	Kurukh	Dravidian
Parhaya	Sadani	Indo-Aryan
Santal	Santhali	Austro-Asiatic
Sauria Pahariya	Malto	Draviadian
Savar	Kharia	Austro-Asiatic (The Hill-Kharias are called Savars)

Of the 30 tribes, the major ones are Santhali living mostly in Santhal Parganas, the Oraon in Gumla, Lohardaga and Ranchi. People belonging to Munda tribe live mostly in the district of Ranchi and Ho in Singhbhum district of Chotanagpur.

The tribes of Chotanagpur ethnologically belong to Proto-Austroloid group but linguistically they don't have the same language affinities. Tribal languages of Chhotanagpur are preserved in spoken form. A few books have been written on tribal language using Devnagari script. Thus it is better to call them oral languages.

With the setting up of All India Radio at Ranchi in the year 1957 and Regional Language Department (Ranchi University) in 1982, major tribal languages and non-tribal languages spoken in the tribal belt of Chhotanagpur have got fillip in true sense. Right now, there are low power AIR stations in Hazaribag, Daltanganj, Chaibasa and Jemshedpur which need a mention in view of the fact that these stations are designed to boost local participation in broadcasting. Before few years, AIR, Ranchi was the only, station to cater to the requirements of entire South Bihar. Although this high power station has the potential to reach the remote part of Chhotanagpur, it has not been successful to utilise its full potential to promote regional language spoken in its broadcasting region.

Linguistic Classification

Looking at the linguistic map of Chhotanagpur, it can be found that there are about thirty tribals speaking different languages in different regions which can be grouped into three main linguistic families. No tribe here speaks Tibeto-Chinese language. There are a number of tribals who do not have dialect of their own and because of their lesser numerical strength, either they speak the language of the dominant tribe or Sadani, the link language of the tribal belt and the language belongs to Indo-Aryan family.

Sadri or Nagpuri is the link language among the tribals as well as non-tribals in this part of South Bihar. As one moves from urban area towards the country side, one experiences the fact that the tribals having close proximity with city either speak Hindi or Sadri more in their interpersonal communications while tribals living in remote villages speak their own dialect or Sadri, the link language.

In Rania, maximum people speak Mundari at home and similarly in Mandar, maximum people speak Kudukh at their home. It was observed that each tribe is having knowledge of at least three languages in Rania and Mandar (mother tongue, Sadri and Hindi) while in Hatma where people are comparatively well-off, the young people are found to have lost contact with their own tribal dialect. In Hatma, because of the social demand, more and more tribals are getting admission into English medium schools. The dominant languages with literary traditions have become much more influential among tribal communities particularly in a place like Hatma where most of the respondents are educated and belong to lower and middle-income groups.

In sheer monetary terms, the mass media are of limited relevance to the masses, especially those who are living below the poverty line, the tribal poor. They can barely meet their essential needs of food and clothing etc. Buying a transistor set, subscribing news papers, periodicals are certainly luxury items for them. In this circumstance, mass media are essentially class media. It is very important to decide useful communication channels for their greater participation.

SECTION-III

ROLES OF BROADCASTING MEDIA

Entertain, Inform and Educate

Entertainment is by far is the important service of All India Radio (AIR). This is especially true from the view point of millions of its listeners. The most popular medium of mass communication in tribal dominated areas where the majority of the inhabitants are illiterate is radio. Film music, tribal music, folk music, devotional music and light music are some of the musical programmes, which are regularly broadcast from AIR, Ranchi besides play, short story and poems. Particularly in tribal areas, radio is the most successful mass media.

Entertainment may be what the public want from the media, but information is probably their most important requirement. Perhaps the most important information of all is information about the government. For example, appropriate publicity campaigns on Nutrition support for Education, National Social Assistance Package, Rural Group Life Insurance Scheme, Indira Awaas Yojana, Employment Assistance Scheme, Jawahar Rozgar Yojana, Watershed Development Projects, PM's Rozgar Yojana and Mahila Samridhi Yojana etc. are given coverage in this potential electronic media from time to time.

A number of programmes aired in the medium have got immense educative value. There are a number of literary programmes both in Hindi and in local dialects which influence and motivate its listeners.

Broadcasting for National Integration

The idea of nation building through broadcasting has been evolving through the decades. The creation of national consciousness of national integration is a major problem in this country as diverse as India with its many languages, cultural traditions and ethnic groups. By presenting national programmes of drama, features, poetry, short stories and the like, AIR has attempted to project one part of the country to the others and this has been one step in the direction of creating national conscious-ness.

To deal with the developing schism between north and south, in which the fear of Hindi domination is a potent factor, AIR instituted the broadcast of south India language lesson from the states not essentially belonging to South.

The growing demands of linguistic minorities for programmes in their own language have constituted a major problem for AIR. In a place like Jharkhand where there is only one high power radio station, it is not possible to do justice to all regional languages spoken in this tribal belt. The major language in which there is maximum transmission is Hindi and, therefore, all the nine regional languages (five tribal and four non-tribal) are given lesser importance. Setting up Local Radio Stations (LRS) in tribal concentration areas or introducing separate language channels may be appropriate alternatives for ensuring maximum participation in language broadcast.

The situation is far more serious in the tribal areas of the North-East. Several stations are broadcasting in four or more dialects and the most extreme case, as we have seen, is found in Nagaland where AIR Kohima, with single channel, broadcasting in no less than thirteen dialects. Single channel broadcasting in several language leads to duplication. Fragmentation of transmission time satisifies no one (Chatterjee P.C., 1987).

The Indian concept of secularism, which is an important pillar of the state, does not imply skepticism of indifference to religion but rather an attitude of equal respect for all religions. Another aspect of secularism is the replacement of traditional beliefs and practices by information based on scientific knowledge. AIR's policy towards religion has been summed up in several statement in Parliament and in other fore. It has been clarified that AIR does not broadcast religious programme as such. However, coverage is given to public celebration of festivals of all communities. The vast majority of devotional songs broadcast are taken from Hinduism. Official enquiries showed that several stations in the South reserved particular days of the week for the exclusive broadcast of songs pertaining to different sects. A genuine problem for programmers is the paucity of hymns, the text of which can be divorced from the creed of the religion, which inspires them. But the fact remains that devotional programmes broadcast are predominantly Hindu in character (Chatterjee, l987).

Clause 2 of the AIR Code does not permit attack on religion or communities. The Constitution specifically empowers the state to limit the function of the religion if it endangers public order, health or morality. Unity in diversity is the spirit of Indian culture and heritage. Yet a stray spark may ignite in and its harmony may be disrupted. Particularly, when there is imposition of curfews or tensions runs high in a particular place, this media has a role to play.

Radio as Motivator

A communication system in a society is most often used to reinforce existing values, and behaviour patterns (such as popular cultural messages in radio soap operas), or to persuade to a new behaviour. Although there are congnitive elements in such messages, the primary thrust of the content is in the motivational area. Development communication is certainly devoted to this general goal, whether it is to motivate a country politically towards national unity, or to arouse the public against the common external enemy or to motivate a group towards self-development activity. There are numerous specific examples of radio which has been used to motivate people. Many of the Latin American Church related radio stations called radio schools, have adopted as one of their primary goals the task of consciousness raising among poor, rural audience (Jamison and McAnany, 1978).

Tanzania in its health and food growing campaigns, Cuba in its literacy campaign and India in its family planning campaign and more recently in Pulse Polio Campaign used radio as an important part of the motivation.

There are some of the ways where radio has been used to motivate its audience.

(i) Information in this context refers to a wide variety of things: local, national and international news, messages about the availability of social services; and announcements concerning an event of importance to the audience. One of radio's important functions is to inform it's audience about what is going on; it serves these roles in both high income and low income countries (Jamison & McAnany, 1978).

Radio has played the role of information provider and has even created in rural people the need for more information. In the literature on adoption of innovation, the stage of awareness or first learning about a new idea or method is often best initiated by some form of mass media (Rogers and Shoemaker, 1971).

(ii) Radio can be used to teach *i.e.* for non-formal education in both the basic cognitive-skill area and in the work-skill area. There have been, however, several examples of attempts to teach work skills by radio, and where proper supporting elements were included, some success has been achieved.

(iii) Radio provides the only reliable communication system that reaches large portions of rural populations in many countries. Hudson (1977) relates how a two way radio system among widely dispersed Indian villages in Canada was used for giving instruction, calling meeting, or settling business. Tanzania (Hall and Dobbs, 1977) used radio as the only feasible means of instructing rural dwellers on how to vote for the first time. Kreimer (1977) provides the most precise case, where a doctor gives health care instructions to a rural health aide in Alaska by two-way radio. A Radio spot in Ecuador (Manoff, 1975) announced to rural people why they should use iodized salt in their diet. Radio can more effectively provide exact instructions or directions for behaviour change when few people are involved and they have a two way capacity, but even where instructions are for large masses of people and the message is one way only, radio often functions for instructing people in certain behaviours (Jamison and McAnany, 1978).

Language and Culture

Language is the means of expressing oneself and communicating ideas to others. And when this language is developed and the folklife or lifestyle is expressed through a disciplined way, it becomes literature. To call a folk-speech a dialect or a sub-dialect is a deliberate plan to minimise it and crash the inner force that sustain it. The people of the so-called developed languages want to prolong this exploitation over folk-speech groups labelling them as dialects or sub-dialects (Mahata, 1991).

Nine major languages/dialects as recognised by AIR, Ranchi and Regional Language Department, Ranchi University have gained momentum to flourish as full-fledged literary languages in Jharkhand. Whenever a person thinks or whatever his ideas are can only be conveyed through a capable language and as such, the need of the hour is to promote important tribal languages in this plateau region.

For millions of Indians, especially those who can not read and write, and who can afford no more, the transistor radio is the main source of news. Regional language press has not developed here while radio is the only potential medium of mass communication and awareness.

There is no gainsaying that local languages are very much under-developed here and they demand our attention for developing them into modern language's which may become vehicles far advanced ideas of today and flourish. To achieve such a great goal, radio can play quite an important role.

The whole of Jharkhandi culture is to be found in the folklore of the land, but the folk songs, nursery rhymes, proverbs, riddles, folk tales, etc. are scattered all over the land. Very few of the Jharkhand people have felt any urge to collect them. The diamonds of Jharkhandi folk literature is very rich and invaluable. Whatever memorable works were done in the field were done in the pre-independence days by the western scholars, especially by the missionaries. Their translated works of tribal folk literature have gained worldwide acclaim. But the original language was neglected, though there are few exceptions in the Santhali and Mundari languages. After independence, the craze for collecting folklore materials could be seen. But these were mostly done by outsiders for self gratification, for their career oriented research degrees. So they toured the land in a haste and collected materials even more hastily (Mahata, 1991).

Very few tribals have been able to promote their academic interest in their mother tongues. The medium has got to combat divisive and disintegrating tendercies based on language, caste, community, region and other factors. It is true that well-conceived national efforts is yet to be mounted to wean away the educated youth from unproductive agitational activities, to provide them with a sense of close involvement in the nation's development efforts and to draw them into the mainstream of national heritage of life. The medium is required to promote an awareness of the value of nationhood, elements of unity in diversity, the heritage of harmony and emotional integration.

The most popular medium of mass communication in rural areas where the majority of the inhabitants are illiterate is radio. Where as regular education is imparted through reading, writing and arithmetic, the new methodology of training the masses without introducing the three "Rs" and without taking into consideration their ages is through radio programmes. People throughout the world thirst for knowledge and the easiest form of providing it without going into the details of regional programmes of teaching in class rooms is just by listening to the radio.

Therefore, as far as language and culture are concerned, the potential medium is blessed with immense potential for sustainable information dissemination.

Sustainable Agriculture

Environmental education is essentially a practical process equipping man with the knowledge, skills and commitment to improve his environment. Radio has great potentiality to spread awareness among people about adverse effect of pollution, cutting of trees, loss of top soil due to erosion etc.

Though full-fledged eco-development programmes are rare in India, there are many programmes which can be viewed from the point of view of eco-development. The impact of environment degradation on the socio-economic conditions of tribal communities has got to be emphasized to characterize the links between environment and poverty and the vicious circle created thereby. Indentification of ecologically sensitive areas where eco-development approach is necessary, can be taken up by the popular electronic media. Radio can be an appropriate medium to initiate debates on eco-sensitive areas inviting NGOs working at the grassroots level, the social activists, the government servants and the victims. OB (Outside Broadcast) based programmes will be more productive in this regard. A programme man can reach the tribal heart-land and collect first hand information from the tribal inhabitants and the block or panchayat level officials.

Because of a number of development projects, displacement problem has become acute here and most of the victims are tribals. The earth is on the verge of experiencing an alarming extinction of plant species unparalled in human history. Nearly 60,000 species or one in four of the world's total species could become extinct or near extinct by the middle of the next century. This could mean a tremendous loss to the world of medicine, both modern allopathy as well as the traditional systems of Aurveda, Unani and Siddha, which are heavily dependent on plant based drugs. As many as 75 to 90 per cent of the world's rural people rely on herbal medicine for their primary health care. Their role is all the more crucial in the gene-rich tropical third world countries like India where traditional medicine can form an important part of the health care system. Large development projects and prolonged exploitation for commercial reasons have resulted in many species becoming endangered. Several species are on the brink of extinction (Uma Ramkrishna, 1993).

Often development and ecological concerns are viewed as conflicting goals. The attempts to integrate these two views have not been very successful as they failed to incorporate the socio-ecolological aspects into the concepts of sustainability. The issues that need further discussion, in this context, include (i) awareness and attitude of the people at the grassroots level towards environment and sustainability, (ii) Sustainability within agriculture developed (green revolution) regions *vis-a-vis* fragile resource regions, and (iii) role of technology and its relevance in working towards environmental protection and sustainable agriculture. It involves not only the identification and application of improved technologies but the incorporation of ecological and socio-economic considerations.

With no iota of doubt, radio has proved to be friend, philosopher and guide for its agricultural listeners living in country side. Both media experts and social scientists have come to one conclusion that the medium has got immense potential to communicate various dimensions and components of sustainable agriculture.

Dr. M.S. Swaminathan, the eminent agricultural scientist, identified 14 major dimensions of sustainable agriculture covering the social, economical, technological, potential and environmental facets of sustainability.

(i) Technological appropriability,
(ii) Economic feasibility,
(iii) Economic viability,
(iv) Environmental soundness,
(v) Temporal stability,
(vi) Resource use efficiency,
(vii) Local adaptability,
(viii) Social accessibility and social sustainability,
(ix) Political tacitness,
(x) Administrative manageability,
(xi) Cultural desirability,
(xii) Renewability,
(xiii) Equity,
(xiv) Productivity.

Recently in AIR, Ranchi Radio Krishi Pathsala became a grand success in view of the overwhelming response received from the listners. The declining trend in the carrying capacity of land and other natural resources has drawn the attention of environmental, agricultural and social scientists as well as media policy planners in recent times to look for an alternative approach for sustaining the resources supporting human life.

The main reasons for degradation in the life supporting ecosystems, specially soil and water, are indiscriminate use of pesticides, excessive and improper irrigation and improper land and water use. The ecological degradation affects the agricultural production to sustain its growth for future generation. The major ecological problems affecting the sustainability in agriculture are water logging, soil erosion, soil salinity and alkalinity and pests and disease problems, which can be highlighted through media.

Media are great motivators. Once the people in rural areas are motivated by strategic, planned and regulated media exposure, change can be brought about in any aspect of human life. According to Evertt M. Rogers, media can facilitate change and bring in development among rural people if the messages disseminated help raise the aspirations among the masses, popularise need to education and literacy, stress need to seek information about new ideas, propagate ideas on innovativeness, remove superstitions and inculcate greater knowledge about people and the world, and stimulate increased contacts with urban areas. However, immigration to urban areas should not be the aim. What is important is that media should develop need for change. Change automatically leads to development, suiting to the environment. The impact may be slow but is sure. Radio with more OB based programmes and invited audience programmes in different tribal pockets, can certainly leave tremendous impact on farmers. The issue has been discussed in detail in Chapter 7.

Since there is a strong linkage between biodiversity and sustainability, the existing biotic resources of the forest must not only be conserved but the regeneration of the denuded forests should be the primary objective of any sustainable development plan. The sustainable dependency on the forest has developed through centuries of experience. For the economic development of the tribal people, emphasis should be led on cottage industries based on forest products and improving the marketing facilities of these products. Education should be imparted to village communities with a holistic approach for the protection, conservation, preservation and expansion of their resources.

Their knowledge of preparing harmless medicines from plants and herbs for the treatment of various diseases, their knowledge of raising cattle, piggery, sericulture and agriculture along with the pest control were in many respect more effective and less harmful when compared to present day practices. These indigenous methods have built in scientific approaches which ensure sustainable livelihood. The tribal people's sense of cleanliness can't be underestimated. Sustainable development refers to a development process which enhances people's capacity to create and consume wealth on a lasting basis.

In fact, there are a number of farmers in the developing countries who realise the negative impact of modern cultivation practices. Here there is an urgent need to revive traditional varieties and irrigation practices, which have several useful features. Our forefathers were using organic methods of cultivation, which were environmental friendly and cost effective. People should be adequately informed about the negative impact of Green Revolution such as costs of environment degradation, erosion of biodiversity and the ecological disorder. Thus there is a need to spread awareness on the fact that ultimate hope lies in organic cultivation practices. These practices preserve biodiversity and cause no damage to the ecosystem.

Therefore, information dissemination through the mass media particularly for the tribal people is of prime importance. The crucial issue facing the tribal people today in rural India is very simple. Does a poor, illiterate peasant, landless labourer, artisan and housewife have a right to demand from the government details of development expenditure carried out in their own village? Here dissemination of information through radio which is the cheapest modern mass media, helps in removing misconceptions and in promoting right perceptions, and accelerates the process of people's empowerment. This is how transparency and accountability in administration can be established.

Taking into consideration the changing forest policy of the government, since the British period, and it's economic impact on tribals, it can be stated that this particular electronic media can influence tribal people with it's awareness generating programmes. Before the advent of the British rule in India, forests were well managed by local tribals. With the Britishers came, the commercial exploitation of the forests took place in the name of scientific management. After independence also, the revenue-oriented approach of the government did not change. As of today, the forests have degraded to a large stage and the plight of tribals has also worsened. While the government blames the tribals for the degradation on the one hand, tribals feel that it is the government's policies that have alienated them from forests on the other.

Viewed in the context, an appropriate media policy has to be designed to stop deforestation and desertification in tribal belts.

Probably no other group is more affected by environmental destruction than poor village tribal women. Every woman brings with it a long march in search of fuel, fodder and water. As ecological conditions worsen in this part of Jharkhand, the long march becomes ever longer and more tiresome. Cought between poverty and environmental destruction, poor tribal women could well be reaching the limits of physical endurance.

Rural energy use, biodiversity and forest conservation, water projects for human and animal use, irrigation and food security ought to be important items for media coverage. Biodiversity, the variety of living organisms on earth, exists at three levels : genetic diversity, species diversity and ecosystem diversity. The world's heritage of plants and animals, biodiversity is increasingly being eroded. There is significant and growing scientific consensus that biodiversity is being lost at a higher rate in tribal areas. The main causes of this loss are habitat destruction and fragmentation, introduction of exotic species, climate change, pollution and other human economic activities. It is quite important for this electronic media to arrange wide publicity for this cause. There should be more programmes for preserving ecology and environment.

Panchayati Raj

One of the special characteristics of tribal societies is a well knit system of government and socio-political organisation within a strong democratic framework. Long before the appearance of Nagabansi Rajas in Chotanagpur region, the Munda-Manki system of village management was prevalent. Mundas were the administrative heads of the Khuntkatti villages formed by the tribals belonging to one Killi (descendants of one ancestor). For administrative purposes, a few villages were grouped together to form a *Parha*. A most influential village head of a *Parha* was elected as Padha chief. He was known as Manki. The Mundas and the Mankis were the custodians of the customary laws.

After independence, when the Constitution was made, special provisions were incorporated in the Fifth Schedule of the Constitution for the tribal areas in the main land. The superimposition of Panchayati Raj in the tribal areas systematically weakened the tribal system of self rule. The tribals of Chotanagpur region had emotional attachment with their indigenous form of local government. This is why Moghul empire had to rule the region through Nagbanshi Rajas allowing the tribals to enjoy their traditional system. The British empire also tried to establish their direct rule in the tribal region denouncing tribal system. As a result, it had to face a series of rebellions and revolt. Emergence of political association among the various tribal groups during the post-independence period took the shape in the form of 'Jharkhand Movement'. Nevertheless, the tribal panchayat had lost most of it's significance during Moghal and British regimes. At the time of independence of country, only few traditional village heads of Ranchi and Singhbhum districts survived enjoying the customary rights in village management.

There was no existence of Panchayati Raj System in the year 1998 in the region.

Since the Panchayati Raj System in defunct in tribal areas and the Padha system is struggling for recognition, the development work suffers because people at the grassroots level do have less contact with opinion leaders and social activists.

This broadcasting media can play a key role to strengthen the traditional institutions like Gram Sabha.

Child-Care, Education and Broadcasting

Ultimately children are the victims where there is no proper child-care, education. The first few years of a child being very important for its future life, the parents need sensitization.

Studies in psychology, sociology and anthropology have now shown the importance of childhood experiences to enable the child to develop into a free and responsible individual and contribute to social development. Adequate nutrition and warm mother-child relationship have been shown by recent studies to be very important for the physical, emotional and intellectual development of the child. The child who is brought up with protein deficiency and ill-care, not only suffers from physical defect but is also prone to emotional maladjustments and mental retardation.

Very recently, the most successful mass media campaign was initiated by Government of India to propularie pulse-polio. Almost all media units were involved to make it a grand success on 9th of December 1995, and 20th of January 1996 and also afterwards. At a time about 7 crores of children were given polio drops. Needless to mention that radio played the leading role in the mass media campaign particularly for the people inhabitating in tribal and rural areas. It was observed as a festival and millions of tribal children were given polio drops in their nearest centers. Important health care information including message of family planning are continuously aired in this potential media. As most of the programmes are transmitted in Hindi from AIR, Ranchi, the tribals in remote places having less knowledge of Hindi are a deprived lot. There are a number of possible areas where similar experiments can also be considered.

Radio as a Career Counseller

The expansion of television in India has significantly influenced the programme package of All India Radio, though both of them are controlled by the Government. The AIR has introduced several innovative programmes in order to attract listenership according to the requirement of the people. One such innovative programme was 'Problem Solution (Samasyae-Parihara)' which aimed at providing guidance on higher education and employment avenues broadcast by AIR, Dharward station. In consultation with various concerned government and non-government departments and based on their own experiences of youth section, the objectives of the special programme was formulated. It was observed during the discussion that the educated youth do not have or get the competent information about higher education as well as employment avenues. This was also realised by the station authorities when they broadcast a series of programmes helping the students to prepare for the competitive examinations on a previous occasion (Balsubramananya and Kakade, 1994).

Letters were invited from listeners who wanted information and guidance on higher education and employment. The response was overwhelming. Letters were broadly grouped according to the types of information sought by the listeners. Experts from Government and the Karnataka University, Employment Guidance Bureau were invited to provide guidance which were aired once in a month for two years during 1990 and 1991.

The evaluation of the data correlates the fact that a sizeable number of rural students require useful information on various aspects regarding their future. This type of experiment can be taken up for the tribals of Jharkhand also.

Role of Media in Science and Technology

When India attained independence, people faced gigantic problems of poverty, unemployment, social and economic backwardness and vast inequalities. The credit for revitalising and scientific traditions goes to Pandit Nehru. He said science alone can solve the problems of hunger and poverty, insanitation and illiteracy, of superstition and deadening customs and traditions, of vast resources running to waste, of a rich country inhabitated by starving people. The basic objective of our policies is to bring about a broad based improvement in the living conditions of our people breaking through the bonds of poverty, which still afflict majority of our population, and to put the economy on the path of accelerated growth, technological change and modernisation which is necessary, if India is to occupy her rightful place in the world.

According to Rogers and Shoemaker (1971), "nothing is more important for India's development today than the transfer of ideas from person to person. It is essential to discover effective channels of communication in rural India. A combination of media is the most effective way of reaching people with new ideas."

By far, radio has been the most powerful medium to cover the entire geographical area of the subcontinent. In rural India and in tribal pockets, it is the most popular electronic medium for education, entertainment and information. With its classical character, this powerful medium is potentially blessed to influence the IQ level of the people living in country-side through disseminating the achievements of science and technology in a planned manner.

In fact, the mass media perform a vital public service. They bring to the people an awareness of the entire range of activities and the wide spectrum of news and views. It is the credibility and reliability that count most. In modern democracy, the people have a fundamental right to get correct information on various problems and subjects. A Government which seeks to deny this basic right by suppression, loses it's credibility, and it's claim to be described as democratic. After all a well informed public is an asset to a democratic order.

It is relevant to note that the higher rungs of the judiciary in various democratic countries have laid emphasis on 'the obligation of fairness and objectivity' in providing information through state controlled media. The Constitutional Court of Austria for instance, made it clear that broadcasting is a public function that has to be discharged with objectivity and impartially. It also ruled that the sole broadcasting corporation in Austria must be available to everybody without discrimination. The Scotland Sessions Court directed the IBA (Independent Broadcasting Authority) of Britain not to relay four political programmes because they did not give parity of broadcasting time and treatment to persons seeking a devolution referendum. US Courts have also disapproved the trend to use powerful media to produce a nation of people who are submissive to the executive's notion of the public good.

A few small publics in various parts of the world have led the way in establishing the correct role of the mass media. Perhaps the most significant verdict in this arena came from Trinidad High Court which said that 'Radio and Television Broadcasting are part of the public domain and government must ensure free and fair flow of information over the air waves to the public from all legitimate sources. Persons entrusted with the electronic media are servants of the people, not masters, and their duty and only duty is to serve the public good which in this area of political broadcasting calls for a sense of openness and fairness'.

The authorities in this country tend to forget that the powerful mass media are expected to cater to the needs of the entire community and development in reality. The people's fundamental rights of information, speech and expression, which is the basic of democracy, should be fully respected. Particularly in the case of disadvantaged mass of our country, majority of whom are tribals, there should be positive discrimination. Radio should no more be treated simply as an entertainment media. The question may well be asked why the electronic mass media should be conducted in a manner totally at variance with the role of independent, credible and impartial sources of information? Why should the newspapers alone be regarded as the voice of the people and why should not the electronic media, which together have a far more extensive reach.

The need of the hour is to ensure the tribal people more accessibility and participation in the entire broadcasting process, so that benefit will reach to the grassroots level.

The Role of Media in Literacy Promotion

Media is undoubtedly lynchpin around which the entire literacy programme rotates. This is especially true of mass media due to it's special characteristics and it's revolutionary potentialities a few of which are listed below.

(i) Mass media act as watchman as it informs widely and effectively enough to move people.
(ii) The mass media can widen horizons to understand other people one has never met and gain insights into oneself and one's society.
(iii) The mass media can focus attention as it largely shapes the agenda for discussion. This charactertic is of primary importance in sustaining literacy programmes.
(iv) The mass media can raise aspirations both at a personal and national level reducing fatalism and fear of change.
(v) Mass media can feed interpersonal channels, thus helping change agents and influencing in their work.
(vi) Mass media can confer status on an individual, village, district of nation and is a strong motivator for social change.
(vii) Mass media can help form tastes as people tend to like what they hear and see over a period of time.
(viii) Mass media can effect tightly held attitudes but can only indirectly alter strong held attitudes.

Media can be an effective motivator and disseminator of information and public service messages. Media can be the catalyst in promotion of better quality of living. Media has also been characterised as 'hot' and 'cool'. This signifies the intensity with which it can attract people and promote them towards action for a specific cause like social upliftment or literacy (Mc Luthan, 1964).

In the era of privatization, electronic media, through installation of FM Radio and partial autonomy to the media, it will be possible for private producers to employ local field staff. This is of utmost importance for the huge 'tasks' of reaching out to every nook and corner of the country and promoting literacy for all.

According to Aldous Huxley, 'Every man who knows to read has it in his power to magnify himself, to multiply the ways in which he exists, to make his life full, significant and interesting'. This should be the guiding spirit in the promotion of literacy among the less privileged illiterate persons of the country.

Even when marching towards the 2lst century, the Indian society reflects a pyramid like structure, with the elite at the top enjoying the benefits of development, while the poor masses remain deprived of most of the opportunities like access to media and education. Thus, first challenge is to create easy accessibility of media truly to masses. Further, the importance is that of making media for the masses in terms of simplification and emphasis on local for ever.

The eradication of illiteracy is an issue concerning every individual. It is, therefore, necessary that the media professionals don't underestimate the 'experience', 'practical knowledge' or 'creative potentials' of the illiterate masses. Hence, for making concrete efforts towards promotion of literacy, the media specialists must come down to the grassroots level and understand the social and cultural ethos. This will help to promote effective developmental efforts by planning programmes based on the issues and needs concerning the target group itself. A bottom to top approach should be used, whereby the illiterates can be asked for the topic on which they would like to learn, for example, learning to read signboards or buses or information on packets of fertilizers, wage calculation, signing bank forms, and applying for developmental works in their own areas.

The programmes for promotion of literacy should be broadcast at times when the illiterates are free from their daily chores and wage earning activities and need some form of entertainment.

For this purpose, in a democratic country like India, the media producers need to develop the concept of 'Community Communication'. It is based on the philosophy, 'of' 'by', and 'for', the community. For promotion of literacy, it is necessary to apply the participatory, horizontal development communication approach, where people are helped to help themselves. It is worth mentioning that regular weekly broadcast in AIR, Ranchi with the association of Bihar Education Project was a great success.

Content Analysis

Content analysis is an important technique of social sciences; which has been utilized for evaluation of mass media messages and suggesting improvements. Content analysis instrument is developed for message analysis. The instrument has three major categories of items (Singh, 1994).

- (i) Items on substance (what is said),
- (ii) Form of expression (how the message was said), and
- (iii) Quantity(coverage).

The messages are encoded into signals, symbols, language, sketches, photographs etc. The receiver or the audience decode these signals into meanings. Signals, perceptions of signals and meaning are culturally patterned and learned. Given the same signal, people of different socio-cultural system may generate quite different meanings. Berelson defined the content analysis technique as, 'objective, systematic and qualitative description of the manifest content of communication'.

Berelson (1952) had reviewed the methodological aspects of content analysis in communication research. Bonnie etc. (1975) discussed the radio and television spots, announcements for family planning. He identifies fifteen obstacles for family planning. His central theme was that many of the most severe and critical problems facing the family planning programmes could be alleviated by the proper spot announcements. Dubey and Burdhan (1981) developed a module on content analysis of message and programmes in health and population communication, to orient and develop a greater appreciation and understanding of communication research among middle and lower level field workers.

The message must be timely, meaningful and applicable to situation. Even if all the barriers have been removed, communication could still be a failure without good presentation. Good presentation requires complete understanding of the subject and establishing relationship with the audience. Quantitative as well as qualitative assessment of the audience is always a pre-requisite to a good communication. The message and channels should be selected by keeping the nature of target audience.

The message contents of mass media materials may be produced locally so that masses in village can identify themselves with the family welfare communication. Considering the main role of the message in communication there is a need to conduct indepth studies on communication materials utilising content analysis technique relevant to rural/ tribal masses.

With the significant advances in farming technologies, speedy dissemination of those innovations became inevitable. The electronic revolution has made radio as one of the cheapest mass media channels having access to even the landless labourers. Releasing its great potential, All India Radio has designed several rural programmes to carry forward timely relevant and problem oriented messages to reach its rural masses and such programmes are designed in divergent formats covering all sectors of farming enterprises to cater to the information needs in varied farm operations.

Since in the remote rural area of Rania, Farm and Home programmes register highest listenership, it was desired to conduct a content analysis of rural programmes broadcast by All India Radio, Ranchi. All the programmes under Farm and Home of AIR, Ranchi for three months (From 1st January 1997 to 31st March 1997) were taken into account for the study of content analysis.

In the analysis of the format of presentation, straight talk was the most important mode of presentation followed by interviews. Straight talks on technical subject matter is considered to be a monotonous format in presentation which arouses low level of interest among the listeners. A content analysis schedule was used for message analysis of Farm and Home (F&H) programmes broadcast from AIR Ranchi.

'Hamari Dunia Khetibari' is a multilingual programme which is supported by bilingual (Hindi and Sadri) comparing. Here in this special audience programme which is meant for rural and tribal audiance of this tribal belt, programmes are usually aired in the medium of tribal dialects, Sadri and Hindi in between 6.30 p.m. to 7.30 p.m. from AIR Ranchi.

Besides the above there is also a five minutes programme known as *'Kheti Kisani'* which is broadcast a 6.05 a.m. and contains some useful tips about agriculture (Table 4.2)

Table 4.2 : Distribution of programmes (Jan.1997-March 1997)

	Duration in Minutes	Percentage	Rank
Agriculture	2250	41.6	I
Animal Husbandry	195	3.6	IV
Health	135	2.5	VIII
Nutrition	585	10.8	III
Developmental	315	5.8	V
Language & Culture	240	4.4	VI
Education	390	7.2	VII
Others	1290	23.8	II

The special audience programme which is broadcast from 6.30 to 7.30 p.m. has been considered for this purpose.

While making analysis of the above table, it can be stated that agriculture programme heads the table followed by folk songs and music. While there is more emphasis on developmental information (10.80), there is less emphasis on animal husbandry (3.6 per cent), health and nutrition (2.5 per cent) and educational (7.2 per cent) programmes.

It is observed that the listeners are more intimately and emotionally attached with this particular special audience programme. The total duration of OB (Outside Broadcast) based programmes during Jan 1997 to March 1997 is 7.7 per cent in this special programme, which is certainly not an encouraging trend. The OB based programmes usually involve more participation of the people at the grassroots level.

5

AREA AND PROFILE OF TRIBES

The Tribals

Majumdar (1958), a noted anthropologist, defines a tribe as a collection of families or groups of families bearing a common name, members of, which occupy the same territory, speak the same language and observe certain taboos regarding marriage, profession or occupation and have developed a well assessed system of reciprocity and mutuality of obligations. A Tribe is ordinarily an endogamous group or unit, the members of which confine their marriage within the tribe.

A 'tribe' is generally described as a group of people characterised by a common and distinct name, a group sentiment and a common and a specific territory. It is endogamous and has common institutional agencies for maintaining order in the community. A tribe follows it's own specific rituals along with other social, economic, political and cultural traditions of Hindu and Christian communities. Each particular tribe has it's own code of conduct and practices.

The tribals are believed to be the earliest among the present inhabitants of the country and their origin can be traced to such races as Negrito, ProtoAustraloid (Austric or Pre-Dravidian) and Mongoloid who came to India in early periods.

The tribals of India are divided and sub-divided into a large number of sub-tribes, which are mutually exclusive. Even then, they have common features like living in forest and hills, belonging to one of the three racial stocks of Negrito, Austric and Mongoloid and speaking tribal dialect with their brothern etc. There are few other classifications of the tribals based on cultural assimilation, stages of economies, etc. All these classifications speak that they are at different stages of cultural assimilation and economic development and in general, they are at low level of living for which the government has initiated a number of welfare measures to improve their quality of life (Sinha, 1986).

Scheduled Tribes

The Scheduled Tribes (ST) have been listed in each state, union territory separately under the Presidential Order. The Scheduled Castes and Scheduled Tribes Lists (Modification Order 1956) as amended from time to time, 67.76 million persons were counted in 1991. Scheduled Tribes in different States/UTs in India, excluding Jammu & Kashmir, constitute 8.08 per cent of the total population. The percentage of ST has marginally increased from 7.83 per cent in 1981 to 7.95 per cent in 1991. Only 7.39 per cent of the ST population of India live in Urban areas as compared to 25.73 per cent of the general population and 18.72 per cent of the SC (Scheduled Castes) population living in the urban areas (Census Report, 1991).

29.6 per cent of the ST population in the age group of 7 and above is found to be literate as per the 1991 Census. These figures are much lower than the corresponding figures for the total population in India. If we were to take out the population of North-Eastern states like Nagaland, Mizoram, Meghalaya and Manipur which have a predominantly tribal population and very high literacy rates, the literacy rate of the ST population in rest of the country would become much lower.

The work participation rate (total workers as per centage of total population) of the ST population is 49.30 per cent which is much higher than that for the general population (37.46) and also the SC (Scheduled Caste) population (39.25). This is primarily due to high participation rates among the ST women. In case of males, the work participation rate of the ST population is 54.74 per cent, which is some what higher than that of the total population (51.55) as well as SC population (51.48 per cent). But the female work participation among the ST category is 43.71 per cent as against 25.98 per cent for the SC and 22.25 per cent for the total population of the country. The female work participation is generally high in most of the states and Union Territories. 90.03 per cent of the main workers among the STs are in primary sector, 3.85 per cent in the secondary sector and 6.12 per cent in the tertiary sector. The corresponding figures of 1981 were 90.71, 4.57 and 4.72. Thus, there has been a very marginal increase in the primary sector, but there has been a considerable decline in the secondary sector leading to a substantial increase in the proportion in tertiary sector. There appears to be a clear shift away from the secondary sector to tertiary sector. Within the agriculture sector, 54.51 per cent of the ST main workers have reported as cultivators while 32.69 per cent have reported as agriculture labourers. This is in sharp contrast to both the SC population as well as the total population of the country (Census 1991).

The children in the age group 0-6 constitute 20.18 per cent of the ST population in India as against 17.94 per cent for the total population and the ST population has a relatively higher population of children than the general population. The sex ratio (defined as females per 1000 males) for the ST population is 972 as against the total population 927 (Census Report, 1991).

The Tribal people of India have for centuries lived their own secluded and traditional life. Because of their age old isolation, they have not been able to maintain good living conditions. They are at various levels of socio-cultural and economic development belonging to a number of linguistic and racial groups. They are scattered all over the country with concentration in some pockets or zones. Most of the tribals live in remote hilly and forest areas and have been at a very low level of development.

During the last eight Five Years Plans although rigorous efforts have been made for their development, the results have not been commensurate with the funds spent and efforts put on. Most of them are economically backward, poverty stricken, semifed, illiterate, semi-naked and have several complex problems. The story is also same in Chotanagpur where there is large concentration of tribal population.

Chotanagpur

Every Twelfth Indian is a Scheduled Tribe person. The term 'Scheduled Tribe' has a specific connotation both constitutional and anthropological. The ST are specified as per provisions in Article 342 of the Constitution. The two hundred fifty and odd tribes and tribal communities tend to confirm the norm sought to be applied consisting of (i) Geographical isolation, (ii) Distinctive culture, (iii) Shyness of contact with community at large, and (iv) General backwardness. The tribal situation in the country is indeed complex; some have described it as 'explosive' and some others as 'desperate'. It is basically the governmental effort, supported by massive administrative apparatus and vast legal enactments that has been instrumental in giving a fillip to their advancement as also arousing in them the urge for a better deal. It must be admitted that the state sponsored initiatives have own both acclamation and incrimination. Acclamation, for the efforts have resulted in increasing the educational and economic level of vast majority of the tribal people especially in the matters of governmental employment and developmental projects in tribal areas. Incrimination, because of creation of a sense of frustration in the minds of the tribals in many areas due to (i) displacement, (ii) land alienation, (iii) erosion of resources base etc. (Menon, 1993).

The poverty induced life cycle affects most of the people here in this remote area. Nutritional deficiencies, ill health, growth retardation, slow learning, small body size, low productivity, excess of illpaid and unorganised work, low-earning capacity, unemployment, least facility of communication and transportation etc. are some of the common features here.

The tribal population consisting of 8.29 per cent of the total population of undivided Bihar, is divided into thirty different tribal groups. Representatives of the Negrito, Proto-Australoid, and Nordic races are found in the population of Jharkhand. Certain Negrito features were noticed by anthropologists among the aborigins of the Rajmahal Hills. But the nature of evidence about their existence is rather hazy. The Proto-Astraloid features are found in the Kharwar Munda, Bhumij and Mal Pahariyas. They are said to have observed much from other racial stocks as well. The racial history of the Austric speaking groups is still shrouded in traditional antiquity and in spite of all painstaking researches, no clear picture of the origin and composition of these tribals have emerged. Austric speaking groups include Munda, Santhal, Ho, Birhor, Kharia, and others. There are considerable differences in between the Mundas and Oraons. The differences between Santhals and Sauria Pahariyas are significant as they are indicative of the differences between the Austric speaking and the Dravidian speaking people.

The agro-climatic region of Chotanagpur and Santhal Paraganas covers about 46 per cent area of Bihar and nearly 2.0 crores of human population. The Region forms part of zone No.7 called Eastern plateau and Hill region which is one of the 15 national divisions on the basis of agroclimatic conditions for planning total development of the area. The agriculture being the mainstay, it affords for their living hardly for five months. There is heavy migration of people in the villages to other areas in search of income and employment.

The region of Chotanagpur and Santhal Paraganas has about 78 lakh hectares of land area, out of which hardly 30 per cent is cultivated; about 23 lakh hectares is unproductive and barren; 90 per cent of the cultivated area is monocropped; about 92 per cent of the agriculture is rainfed, hardly 8 per cent has an access to irrigation. The terrain is undulating; the soil is mostly acidic and less fertile. The soil erosion and loss of soil fertility, deforestation and pollution are progressively increasing. The region has 90 per cent of the tribal population of Bihar with about 80 per cent of the forest area of the state with bulk of precious minerals below the soil. The yield of the crops including livestock continues to the quite low. The agriculture is consuming at present hardly about 30 per cent of the work force. (Dubey, 1996).

Tribals of the region are very rich in terms of cultural heritage. There paintings and dances have global recognition. Recent discovery of some ancient paintings in Chotanagpur plateau has established the historical importance of Gandwanaland.

Although nature has been generous in bestowing its bounty on Chotanagpur plateau, the people of this region have not been able to improve their socio-economic conditions. It is perhaps one of the richest mineral belt as well as store house of natural resources of the country.

The Chotanagpur region has the most advantageous situation in the country for the development of a sound diversified agro-industrial economy owing to abundance of forests, minerals and energy resources. Around 98 per cent of copper ore, 86 per cent of kynite, 90 per cent graphite, 50 per cent bauxite, 35 per cent of fire clay and 16 per cent of iron ore of our country is produced in this region. On the top of it all, Chotanagpur contains large quantity of national reserves of coal, the prime source of energy, and contributes almost one-third to the total national coal production. Besides the above, the availability of good quality limestone, mica, uranium etc. provides excellent advantages for the growth of industries (Majhi, 1995).

Rich forest resources and vast water resources provide base for agro as well as agro-cottage industries. On the other hand, this region is under the shadow of under development, with almost 50 per cent of the population living below the poverty line.

The majority of the city dwellers are non-tribals, and a significant proportion of those are wealthier, middle and upper class people who have migrated to Ranchi from outside Chotanagpur, mainly from North Bihar and from West Bengal Government offices, courts, banking, business establishments, and industry are dominated by people from outside Chotanagpur. The interaction between tribals of urban area and country-side is continuously increasing for a number of reasons. Annual sports and cultural activities, political rallies and festivals have become major attractions in this regard. A number of NGOs are involved in development work in the region.

The Primitive Tribes

Primitive Tribal Groups (PTG), who have been classified on the basis of (a) Pre-agricultural level of technology, (b) Low-level of literacy, and (c) Stagnant or Diminishing population, are spread over 20 districts of Bihar. The maximum concentration of the PTGs is in the Santhal Pargana and Chotanagpur plateau region. Though no official census figure is available for 1991 regarding the PTG population, as per survey conducted district-wise, the tentative PTG population would be approximately 2,00,000 (*i.e.* about 40,000 households). The PTG population figure for 1981 is 1,96,161. Out of 52 PT groups identified all over the country, 9 reside in Jharkhand. They are Asurs, Korwas, Birjias, Parhiyas, Mal-Paharias, Sauria-Pahariyas, Birhors, Hill-Kharias and Sawarns. Population-wise, Sauria Pahariyas and Birjias form the biggest and the smallest chunk, respectively.

Because of poverty, ignorance, economic backwardness and geographical reasons, the primitive tribes have long been leading secluded life. There are a number of state government schemes and centrally assisted projects besides the assistance given by World Bank for their development but little has been achieved in improving the standard of living of the primitive tribes. On the whole, it can be said that they are poor, because they are ignorant.

(Three blocks selected for investigation and the following data were collecting during 1997-1998)

(A) RANIA

Block Profile as per 1991 Census
(Source : NIC, Ranchi)

			Male	Female
No of villages	:	66		
No of households	:	6152		
Population	:	32105	Male	Female
SC	:	1953 (6 per cent)	949	1004
ST	:	22668 (71per cent)	11215	11453
Others	:	7484 (23 per cent)		
Literates	:	10118 (32 per cent)	6699	3419
Main workers	:	13263 (41 per cent)		
Cultivators	:	11003 (34 per cent)		
Agricultural Labourers	:	1264 (4 per cent)		
Health				
Hospital	:	X		
PHC	:	01		
PHC Sub-centre	:	10		

Education

Primary school	:	33
Middle school	:	10
High school	:	03
College	:	xx
Teaching/ Training centre	:	xx

Village Profile

Name of the selected villages : (i) Lohagara
(ii) Kulhei
(iii) Digri
(iv) Tangerkela

Location of the place : The place is about 80 kms away from Ranchi city. Situated in Khunti sub-division, the block is one of the most remote places in the whole state of Jharkhand.

Total number of households : 390

Total Population (Village-wise)

Lohargara	:	179
Kulhei	:	725
Digri	:	712
Tangerkela	:	505
Total	:	2121

Total tribal population of the villages : 1123 (52.9 per cent)

Ethnic composition

Name of the community	No. of households	Total population
(i) Munda	214	1042
(ii) Lohra	13	71
(iii) Chik Baraik	02	10
Total	229	1123

Literacy in per centage

	Tribal	Non-tribal
Male	38	52
Female	21	32

Health : In day to day life, people usually use traditional medicines (Jaddi-butti etc.) and elopathic medicines from the village practitioner. The researcher had made night hults with an elopathic medicine practitioner who could reveal the fact that he had no formal training in the profession. With his minimum knowledge of some medicines, he had to encounter no problem while dealing with his patients. For several health problems, very few can afford to reach Khunti or Ranchi for better medical care. A lot of people were marked to have malnutrition and ill health in the area. Drinking water is managed through deepwells and tube wells.

Transport : The only pacca road connecting Rania with the rest of the world is in hopeless state. With very limited bus services, the place is not well-connected with the rest of the places. From one village to another village, one can find narrow access through agricultural land and hill tracks. There is no permanent pacca road joining tolas of villages.

Electric Connection : There is no electricity in the whole block of Rania. This is due to continuous theft of transformers and electric wires.

Occupation : Majority of the adult population among triabals work as agricultural labourers. Very few are in Indian Army. There are also few people who move out of the village for engagement else where. Some are also engaged in construction work sponsored by government and private parties. Females are more active than males. Whether it is a weekly market or some cottage industry, a female workman seems to be more active. There are a number of women who sell 'Hardia' in weekly market and earn their livelihood.

Standard of living : Agriculture, animal husbandry and nature are important sources of livelihood. Each village consists of few 'tolas' and each 'tola' consists of 10-30 houses. Each area is difficult to locate. The tribal people inhabitating in the region are mostly Mundas and they are subject to evil forces such as ignorance, malnutrition and poverty. The people have no access to modern and civilized means of living. Most of the people are without work and are deprived of basic necessities of life. In such a situation, they can't think of education of their children. Long distance, poverty, teachers absence and apathetic attitude are few causes of low literacy rate among tribal people. The modern mass media can't be afforded by the people who are below the poverty line. They can barely meet their essential needs of food and clothing etc. Buying a transistor set, subscribing newspapers, periodicals are certainly luxury items for them. No household is having telephone connection. It is also observed that there is large scale migration of tribal population to far off places in search of employment. It can also be mentioned that depletion of forest resource here has affected village economy quite adversely.

Table 5.1 : Tribal Households in Communication Network (Rania)

(i) Name of the village : Lohagar

		Total Population	Radio	TV	Radio & TV both	News Paper
Total Households :	38	179	10	2	2	1
Tribal Household :	24	102	2	-	-	-
Munda :	22					
Lohra :	2					

(ii) Name of the village : Kulhei

		Total Population	Radio	TV	Radio & TV both	News Paper
Total Households :	121	725	15	2	2	-
Tribal Household :	91	424	09	1	1	-
Munda :	88					
Lohra :	3					

(iii) Name of the village : Digri

		Total Population	Radio	TV	Radio & TV both	News Paper
Total Households :	135	172	32	2	2	-
Tribal Household :	78	402	19	1	1	-
Munda :	72					
Lohra :	4					
Chik Baraik :	2					

(iv) Name of the village : Tangerkela

		Total Population	Radio	TV	Radio & TV both	News Paper
Total Households :	96	505	15	3	3	1
Tribal Household :	36	195	04	1	-	-
Munda :	32					
Lohra :	4					

Total Tribal Households : 229
Total Number of radio sets : 24
Per centage : 15 per cent

(B) MANDAR

Block Profile as per 1991 Census
(Source : NIC Ranchi)

			Male	Female
No. of villages	:	69		
No. of households	:	13719		
Population (Total)	:	78865	40567	38298
SC	:	806	373	433
ST	:	48108 (61 per cent)	24644	23464
Others	:	29951 (38 per cent)		
Literates	:	24723 (31 per cent)	17145	7578
Main workers	:	31859 (40 per cent)	19155	12704
Cultivators	:	25706 (33 per cent)	14968	10738
Agricultural Labourers	:	2878 (4 per cent)	1410	1468
Health				
Hospital	:	01		
PHC and PHC / Sub-centre	:	14		
Education				
Primary school	:	45		
Middle school	:	19		
High school	:	07		
College	:	01		
Teaching/ Training centre	:	xx		

Village Profile

Name of the Selected village : Ambatoli

Location of the place : The village is about 4 kms away from Mandar block in the north direction which is situated in Ranchi Daltanganj state highway at a distance of 30 kms from Ranchi city.

Total number of households : 240
Total population of the village : 1617
Total tribal populatin : 925

Ethnic composition

Name of the community	*No. of Households*
Sarana Adivasis (Oraon)	147
Lohra	02
Christian Adivasis	03
Ahir Mahto	18
Brahamin	01
Ansari Muslims	69
Total	240

Literacy in percentage :

	Tribal	*Non-tribal*
Male	54 per cent	67 per cent
Female	32 per cent	42 per cent
Total	43 per cent	54.5 per cent

(Non-formal education through Bihar Education Project has increased the number of literates).

Health : Here, health status of the people is not satisfactory. There is no medical facility available in the village. The nearest health care centre is in Mandar Missionary Hospital, which is located at a distance of 3 kms from the village. By simple observation, it can be stated that most of children' s health is not upto standard. Most of the children suffer from malnutrition. Drug addiction is not a problem here like that of Rania. But most of tribal males and females take liquor (Hardia) quite frequently. It is also noticed that the frequency is less than the villagers of Rania.

There are a number of deep wells which the villagers use for drinking water. Although there are few tube wells in the village, almost all are defunct.

Transport : Only half of the road that is about 2 kms from the Mandar block is of fine condition and the rest 2 kms road becomes difficult during rainy season. Public vehicles are easily available to different parts of the state from Mandar bazar which is a small marketing centre.

Electric Connection : There is no electricity. The story is almost repeated here like most of the villages in the state. Only one can find electric poles across the road side. Stealing of electric wires and transformers is also regular feature here.

Education : There are two primary schools and one middle school in the village. Besides, few non-formal education centres are also active in the village. The school drop-outs rate is high here which is mostly seen among the girls. Primary education facilities are no doubt satisfactory. As the poor parent need their young children to support them in their agricultural land and wage earning, the children have to leave the school on the half way.

Occupation and Standard of Living : Agriculture and business are important sources of livelihood here. The tribal people inhabitating in this place are mostly Oraon. Most of the people belong to low income group and below poverty line. A significant number of unemployed youth are quite visible. Unlike Rania, here in Ambatoli only few families subscribe local newspapers.

Since Mandar bazar is of walking distance from the village, people can easily move to the bazar to share information, for marketing and other useful work. The degree of isolation is not as that of Rania.

There is a tranquil ambience in Ambatoli village with a very cordial and harmonious relationship among the three different communities.

Each and every family in the village is engaged in agriculture activities. The main agriculture season starts from the month June (Aasar) *i.e.* Kharif and ends in the month of December. This is a rainfed area. During the lean period, the people having the additional irrigation facilities go for cultivation of Rabi crops and vegetables.

Most of the people here are marginal farmers and agricultural labourers. Some of the people also move to near by town Ranchi for work as daily labourer. The status of non-tribals, the Muslims, is somewhat better in the sense that some of them are otherwise engaged in business and services. Most of service holders here are engaged in the profession of police, and teaching.

Since the cash crops mainly vegetables are gaining the popularity in this area because of development of marketing infrastructure and availability of easy credit, people have shown more interest for vegetable growing. Truck load vegetables are being exported to neighbouring states and in the process, the middlemen are the gainers. The cultivators are being exploited and don't get their due.

Due to non availability of adequate irrigational facilities, growing of second crop gets set back. The root cause of low standard of living of this area in due to poor income from agriculture sector.

In this village only one household is linked by telephone. It is a tribal household.

Table 5.2 : Tribal Households in Communication Network

Name of the village : Ambatoli

		Total Population	Radio	TV	Radio & TV both	News Paper
Household :	240	1617	102	07	07	01
Tribal Household :	152	1060	35	06	06	-

Total Tribal Households : 152
Total Number of radio sets: 35
Per centage : 23 per cent in the village of Ambatoli

It seems that in the village of Ambatoli, radio is cheaply available electronic media among majority of households. In fact, people have got very limited access to TV and local news paper. All the TV sets are connected with battery sets which are charged in the nearest market place, Mandar. The individuals possessing TV sets are all service holders. Here also the people go to bed early, say about 9 p.m. As the people have contacts with the Mandar bazaar, most of them have also an opportunity to go through local news papers. Political news, crimes, accidents and development news are subjects of discussion in pan shops or near a confectionary. The information dissemination also occurs when one reaches his home and shares his days experience with his family. As observed, females don't have frequent turns to the market places.

In a nut-shell, it can be stated that listening behaviour depends upon several factors. Here radio listening of both CBS and Primary channel is quite impressive.

Here women and children are very passive listener in all field areas. Listening frequencies also varies from place to place and in different age groups. It also depends upon programme quality. When the programme is of good quality and audible on the set, the people take care to listen radio programmes. Students and agricultural labourers take keen interest in radio programmes in all field areas. Most of the agricultural labourers are illitetrate and majority of them live in Rania. They usually listen Farm and Home (F & H) programme, folk songs and films songs. News and news related items are more popular among educated mass, opinion leaders and aged people.

(C) HATMA (Ranchi City)

Hatma is a centrally located place in Ranchi city and here the inhabitants are tribals. The place is divided into two different Tolas known as Hatma Tola and Sarna Tola. Sarna Tola and Hatma Tola house most of the migrated population who ethnically belong to Munda tribe. Very few Oraon families also live here. Hatma Tola is a bigger place in comprison to Sarna Tola. Population of Hatma Tola comes about 7000 and that of Sarna Tola is 2800. Since no data was available from the Census Department the researcher had to make approximate estimation of the population figures. In comparision to Mandar and Rania here the population is much heterogenous in character. Here maximum people belong to below poverty line where as there are quite a number of people having moderate standard of living.

Ethnic Composition : In Sarna Tola, maximum inhabitants are tribals which is nearly 90 per cent of the total population. About 2 per cent of the total population are Oraon and all of them have adopted Christianity. Rest 88 per cent are Sarna Hindus (Munda). Here even though Oraon people speak Mundari dialect, Sadri (Nagpuri) and Mundari are important link languages. Here about 10 per cent of the total population belong to general and backward class. In Hatma Tola, tribal and non-tribal population ratio is almost 50:50. The SC population is about 40 per cent and rest 10 per cent constitute backward and general population. Here comparatively Munda tribe is dominant.

	Sarna Tola	Hatma Tola
ST	90 per cent	50 per cent
SC	02 per cent	40 per cent
General & Backward	08 per cent	10 per cent

Literacy : In Sarna Tola, the people seem to be more literate in comparision to Hatma Tola. The school drop-out rate is high here because of financial burden on the family. Since the place is centrally located, access to school is no more a problem. The tribals here belonging to even lower middle class send their children to public schools where the medium of instruction is English.

Health : Here, there is inadequate supply of water by PHD. The inhabitants mostly have to rely on wells for the purpose of drinking and bathing. By simple observation, it can be said that most of the children here suffer from malnutrition and ill health. There are also a few tubewells and most of them were not functioning at the time of field visit.

Transport : The pacca road joining Hatma Tola and Sarna Tola is not in a fine condition. The kaccha road within the Tolas is of bad condition. The city is not very far, and the inhabitants have to walk 1-2 kms to catch up motorable road running towards the city.

Electricity : It is noticed that the locality is not having adequate connections. Maximum households are having illegal connections. When one enters into the interior of the Tolas, it can be observed that no household is having electric connection. There is no facility of power supply. *Occupation and Standard of Living.* The tribals in Sarna Toli are comparatively well-off because most of the adult population are engaged in service and agriculture. In Hatma Tola, the inhabitants are comparatively poorer in the sense that most of them belong to labour class. There are also adequate number of rickshaw pullers and auto drivers who earn their bread. People are also engaged in small and petty business like shoe making etc. Some have also become owner of small shops.

Almost all the households are having radio sets irrespective of economic backwardness. A number of people also possess TV sets and two wheelers.

The recent award of statehood has brought about qualitative changes to some extent. The above observations on socio-economic status, health and educational status were made in the year 1997-98. There has been qualitative change in their daily life, access to resources and the basic amenities when the researcher visited the places in December, 2002.

6

EXISTING PATTERN OF BROADCASTING IN INDIA
A Case Study of AIR Ranchi

The Evolution of Broadcasting

Amateur broadcasting started in India in November 1923 with starting of a Radio Club in Calcutta. In June 1924, similar club in Bombay and Madras began transmitting programmes for some two and a half hours a day. Due to financial difficulties, the Madras club closed down in October 1927. But on 23 July of that year, the first regular Radio broadcasting commenced at Bombay and on 26 August, a station started functioning in Calcutta.

These stations were started by the Indian Broadcasting Company which had received a license from the Government. Lord Irwin, the then Viceroy who inaugurated the Bombay station, spoke of the needs which broadcasting could serve which remains true today.

'India offers special opportunities for the development broadcasting. Its distances and wide spaces alone make it a promising field. In India's remote villages there are many who, after the day's work is done find time hangs heavily enough upon their hands, and there must be many officials and others whose duties carry them into out-of-the-way places where they crave for the company of their friends and the solace of human companionship. Both for entertainment and for education, it's possibilities are great.'

The Indian Broadcasting Company commenced it's operation with a meagre capital of only one and a half million rupees. The revenue of the Company was derived from two sources. First, it received 80 per cent of its revenue from radio licenses. The second source of revenue for the Company was a ten per cent tribute on the invoiced value of imported wireless equipments such as receivers, wireless valves, electric wireless gramophones, which the company itself had to collect from the dealers. The monthly expenditure of the Company was considerably in excess of its revenue. The Company, therefore, reduced its expenditure. After a short life of three years, the Company went into liquidation on the 1st March, 1930.

The Government decided to acquire the assets of the Company and run the stations in Calcutta and Bombay on an experimental basis for a period of two years from the 1st April, 1930; and finally the Government decided in May 1932 to continue the Indian State Broadcasting Service under their own management; and placed it under the administrative control of the Department of Industries and Labour.

Then began a period of steady expansion. What was first being run as part of the Department of Industries and Labour, was in March 1935 constituted into a separate Department under a Controller of Broadcasting to work under the Department of Industries and Labour. In June 1936, 'All India Radio' replaced the earlier designation of Indian State Broadcasting Service. Besides the increases in the number of broadcasting stations at important centres, the activities of the Department also widened considerably. The Delhi station was opened on the 1st January, 1936. The staff position at the Headquarters was also augmented. There was also option for high power stations. New Departments, *e.g.* The Installation Department, Research Department and News Services Division were created. Broadcasting was transferred to the Department of Communi-cations in November, 1937 and was later transferred to the Department of Information and Broadcasting in October, 1941. This department was reconstituted as the Department of Information and Arts.

The name of the Department was again changed to the Department of Information and Broadcasting from the 10th September, 1945. New stations opened in quick succession at Peshwar, Lahore, Lucknow, Madras, Tiruchi arid Dacca besides the establishment of additional short-wave transmitters at Calcutta, Bombay, Madras and Delhi.

AIR at the Time of Partition

The total number of stations at the time of partition of the country was nine but with the partition of the country in 1947, India was left with only six stations at Delhi, Bombay, Calcutta, Madras, Lucknow and Tiruchi.

In 1947, AIR drew up a eight year plan for the development of Broadcasting in India at an estimated cost of about 364 lakhs as part of the post-war development scheme. Pending the implementation for the main scheme, an interim 'Pilot Scheme' was undertaken for the immediate setting up of pilot stations with low power transmitters. Under this phase of development, new stations were put up at twenty important cultural centres, *i.e.* Allahabad, Amritsar, Ahmedabad, Calicut, Cuttack, Dharwar, Gauhati, Jammu, Jullundar, Nagpur, Patna, Shillong, Srinagar and Vijaywada. Further, control of the five radio stations (Baroda, Hydrabad, Aurangabad, Mysore and Trivandrum) which had been functioning under the aegis of the erstwhile princely states was taken over by AIR during the period of 1946-50. Thus by 1951, when the First Year Plan was launched, primary broadcast service on the medium wave extended to about 12 per cent of the area of the country serving about 20 per cent of the population.

Thus the real break for broadcasting in India came with the World War II.

With about 200 broadcasting stations, AIR today serves nearly 100 per cent of the population in different parts of the country including difficult and far-flung places like Leh, Tawang, Andaman-Nicobar and Lakshadweep islands.

Home Service Programmes

In the Home Service, AIR broadcast programmes in 24 languages including English and 4 foreign languages and 146 tribal and other dialects. Immediacy, authenticity and objectivity are the guiding principles in all these broadcasts. The service includes a good deal of entertainment, informative and educative programmes along with news and current affairs programmes. The programmes put out by AIR stations can be categorised as follows.

(i) News and programmes of nation wide interest broadcast from Delhi,
(ii) News and programmes from the state capitals catering to the needs and interest of their respective areas,
(iii) Regional language services from individual stations catering to the needs of the respective regions.
(iv) Commercial Service.

AIR has a national channel, besides the regional and local channels.

National Channel

The National Channel of AIR came on the air on 18.5.88. It covers 70 per cent of the population and provides a judicious blend of information and entertainment (DAVP, 1993).

Regional Channel-Programme Composition : AIR stations broadcast classical, folk, light, devotional, firm and western music. The weekly national programme of music, the Annual Akashvani Sangeet Sammelan and the weekly Sunday night concerts are designated to provide the listeners the best classical music in Hindustani and Karnataki style. The national programme of music features well known exponents including old masters. AIR stations devote about 11 per cent of their total music programmes to folk music. A monthly programme of regional and light music on the national hook-up is also broadcast.

Spoken-word Programmes : The spoken-word programme includes talks, discussions, interviews, magazines, reviews, poetry reading, commentaries and memorial lectures. The spoken-word covers a wide range of subjects and provides support to several campaigns including national integration, communal harmony, environmental protection, energy, conservation, rural development, family welfare, eradication of social evils such as untouchability etc.

Plays and Features : Plays and Features including documentaries are broadcast from AIR stations. At the national level also a feature in English and Hindi is broadcast every month.

Programmes for Special Audiences : Farm and Home units set at various stations provide specific programmes about the latest scientific technology for increasing crop production and rural development programmes. These units provide information about subsidiary and agro based enterprises for improving the earning of farmers and about social programmes undertaken for the betterment of rural life. Under 'Home Programmes' these units arrange programmes regularly for rural women in support of different development and welfare programmes.

In addition to these, there are special audience programmes for senior citizens, women, children, troops, youth and industrial workers.

Educational Programmes : The Educational Programmes of AIR cover a wide spectrum. There are curriculum based programmes like school and university programmes. Radio support is also offered to correspondence courses of few universities. Radio Support to the National Adult Education Programme is also provided.

Central Education Planning Unit under the Directorate General, All India Radio has started in collaboration with various government agencies, nation wide broadcast on several topic. The first one is the broadcast of the 15 part serial entitled 'Vigyan Vidhi' oriented towards children in the age group between 10 to 14. The second one is the serial on social forestry entitled 'Nisarga Sampada' which was originally broadcast by AIR, Bangalore in Kannada. In collaboration with the Indian Council for Medical Research, a serial entitled Radio Date (Drug, Alcohol and Tobacco Education) was broadcast. A 130 part serial on 'Human Evolution' was also broadcast in different languages from various stations of AIR. In order to utilize the sound medium for the literacy mission, the project entitled 'PREAL' (Project on Radio Education in Adult Literacy) was conceived. Ten radio stations in Uttar Pradesh, Rajasthan and Bihar broadcast the programmes targeted towards adult women learners in the age group of 15 to 35 years. It was a collaborative venture with the National Literacy Mission.

Sports Broadcast : AIR arranges sports broadcasts on national, regional and on local levels. If due to certain reasons the live coverage of running commentary does not become feasible, in such a situation; the coverage through news bulletins, resume and radio report is provided. Generally, the live coverage of national events is done on All India National basis keeping in view the popularity of the game, listeners interest, technical feasibility and other programme commitments.

Yuva Vani : To provide a forum for self expression to the youth who constitute the majority, to give them a sense of partnership in shaping the destiny and to ensure their involvement in hastening the process of nation building, AIR stations broadcast programmes of varying duration using different formats. The service is open to persons in the age group of 15 to 30 years. Delhi, Calcutta, Hydrabad, Jammu and Srinagar stations broadcast these programmes on a separate channel. The service is of the youth, by the youth and for the youth.

Shramik Lok (Programme for Industrial Workers) : This programme is also aired from a number of stations particularly in areas where there is more industrialisation. Here also the programmes are broadcast in different formats for making the programme more interesting.

News Service Division : The News Service Division(NSD) came into being in September 1948. It was earlier part of the Central News Organisation set up on 1st April, 1937. Over the years, the News Service Division has undergone phenomenal expansion, leading to a vast network of regional news units.

NSD produces 88 bulletins in 19 languages which emanate from Delhi and are relayed by several AIR stations. In addition to these bulletins, the Regional News Units, 41 in all, located in different parts of the country, produces as many as 131 news bulletins in English and in a number of regional languages and tribal dialects. Spotlight in English and Sameyiki in Hindi broadcast everyday, deal with topical events/issues. The 'current affairs' programme is broadcast every Sunday in which experts, eminent academicians, legislators and politicians express their views on national and international issues across the table. A similar programme in Hindi entitled 'Charcha Ka Visai Hai' is broadcast every Wednesday. Major Hindi stations relay the programme.

The composite news programme called 'Samachar Pravat' and 'Morning News', in Hindi and English respectively, each of a duration of 15 minutes comprises a news bulletin, a commentary, and a look at the daily press at the capital. 'Samachar Pravat' and the Morning News are broadcast every day at 8 a.m. and 8.15 a.m. respectively. Apart from the hourly bulletins in the national network, 5 minutes hourly bulletins have been introduced in the national channel between 1 a.m. and 5 a.m. These bulletins are broadcast in English and Hindi alternately. News reels are broadcast daily carrying spot recordings or voiced despatches from correspondents on day to day developments. When Parliament is in session, NSD puts out commentaries on the proceedings in the Lok Sabha and in Rajya Sabha. The Regional News Unit in the state capital similarly broadcast commentaries in the proceedings of state legislatures in the regional languages concerned. To lay emphasis on developmental news a special news programme called 'Vikas Yatra' goes on the air everyday at 9.15 a.m. The programme schedule also changes from time to time.

Vividh Bharati and Commercial Service : A self contained service of popular entertainment known as Vividh Bharati was started in October 1957 to meet the growing demand of popular music and light features. Sixty per cent of the time is devoted to film music and the rest is earmarked for devotional music, light music and spoken word programme in the form of short plays, talklets, interviews etc. At present, there are a number of Vividh Bharati centres in different parts of the country. All these centres carry commercials. There are two short wave transmitters, one each at Madras and Bombay, which also carry the Vividh Bharati Service without commercials. Commercials on the national network were introduced from lst April, 1982.

The Commercial Service on the primary channel was introduced on 26 January, 1985. Spots, sponsorships are being aired in the rural programmes, women's programmes, and in film/light music, listeners' choice, plays and other popular programmes.

External services : AIR's external services developed under the impact of World War II and were initially part of the Central News Organisation. A number of languages are included in external broadcast now.

Radio Forums

In 1959, AIR started Radio Forums. It was felt that with the organisation of such forums; the rural programmes would have a greater impact. The Forums were modelled on the Farm Radio Forums of Canada. They are organised listening groups of fifteen to twenty persons who listened together in a community set to bi-weekly programmes, meant for them as part of the rural programme. After the broadcast, the farmers were expected to discuss the information and suggestions contained in the programmes and to decide on a plan of action. It was believed that such action oriented discussion in the villages could lead to many innovations. But the Forums too have become moribund. After the first flush of enthusiasm, the collective listening has dwindled. The reasons for the failure of the Forums are many. AIR lacked the resources to operate so ambitious a programme covering the whole country. The villages lacked the leadership to conduct the discussions intelligently and effectively and AIR could not be expected to provide it. The machinery for carrying the reactions of the Forums to the programme planners was weak. In Canada, the Forums were the joint responsibility of the Canadian Broadcasting Corporation, the Canadian Broadcasting Federation of Agriculture and the Canadian Association for Adult Education. Besides, it has been found that only Forums for a homogeneous membership can be successful (Mehra Masani, 1976).

Public Service Broadcasting

The aim and object of broadcasting since its inception has been to facilitate the functioning of society and to meet the requirements and need of the people by putting across useful, relevant and appropriate messages by which the listeners can derive benefits. Public Service Braodcasting (PSB) has the responsibility of providing a programme service which covers the whole spectrum of interests to its listeners. The aim is to arrive at a programme mix-a top quality service, both technically and editorially. The concept has been gaining popularity among the listeners throughout the world. In the event of natural calamities like flood, cyclone, earthquake, all the other media fail to operate effectively except broadcasting and the recent story bears testimony to the fact that this potential medium has enough to deliver at a time of crisis.

All the developing countries of the third world are facing innumerable problems of high magnitude. They are living amidst misery, hunger, squalor and disaster. The technological developments during the recent times have enormously increased the reach of the electronic media. We are in the threshold of a new era in which expanding human imagination and advanced technology will free us from many of the physical boundaries which impeded the reach. In such a scenario, the effective Public Service Broadcasting will enable the underprivileged to ameliorate the economic and social conditions and cast off the age old bonds of economic slavery (Sharafatiyar, 1993).

Tax your imagination for the most dramatic presentation devisable for public service causes. The constant efforts by the public service broadcasters has proved encouraging not only in informing the people but also involving them in their own welfare and thus encouraging them to participate in ameliorating their own lot. Easy access to the broadcasting medium has expanded the mental horizons of the people and with that their level of the people and with that, their level of aspirations and expectations have also gone up.

The sound broadcasting has survived mainly as an utilitarian medium and by putting out programmes exclusive for the tastes of selected audiences. People look to it not for glamour oriented entertainment but for programmes which can cater to their specific listening needs. However, this has necessitated modifications and restructuring of the programmes. All India Radio is committed to development and therefore, its socially useful programmes take precedence over the commercial interests.

The communication technology is changing very fast. This imperatively calls for modifications in the modes and methods of communication. The broadcasting behaviour, therefore, has to keep pace with the dynamics of technological and social change. It has the prime responsibility to bring about desired changes in the attitudes, beliefs and behaviours of its targetted listeners for galvanizing them to take up the challenges of development.

Weather reports, market rates, information on different transport services, information about the special schemes launched by the Government, educational broadcasts, agriculture and Farm and Home programmes, school programmes, population education, health, nutrition and maternal and child care, programmes on popular science etc. are some the lists of Public Service Broadcasting.

(i) Public Service Broadcasting should aim at contributing at a new social environment, reaching out to people, enriching their lives and seeking communication that provides the warmth of human contact.

(ii) Freedom of broadcasting programmes has to go hand in hand with self restraint exercised by individual broadcasters in determining the suitability of programme content. Public Service Broadcasting standards should be aimed at : (a) Welfare of the public; (b) Develop-ment of culture and prosperity of industry and commerce; (c) Contributing towards the realisation of peaceful society; (d) Respect for social, political, cultural and traditional values; (e) Respect for the delivery of nation and ethnic diversity; (f) Handling religious matters with respect and sensitivity; (g) Programme should take into account the innocence, inexperience and credulity of children.

(iii) PSB should respond to the trust placed in them by the society, abide by the spirit of democracy, maintain respect towards human rights and public sentiments, defend freedom of speech and expression and respect law and order.

(iv) In practical broadcasting operations, PSB should emphasize

(a) Fast and accurate news reporting;

(b) Healthy entertainment;

(c) Advancement of culture and education;

(d) Programmes having salutary influence upon children and young adults;

(e) Moderate and honest advertising.

(v) PSB should pay attention to human rights, family and society, betterment of education and culture news reporting, responsibilities and restraint in handing violence and crime.

(vi) PSB must pay particular attention to services for women, children and elders and improve regional broadcasting services mailing of regional stories to national network etc.

(vii) PSB must realise that listeners have a legitimate right to accurate news. News editors and journalists have, therefore, to aim at professional packaging and presentation of news, clearly identify news sources, evolve clear criteria for news selection and relate ethics to journalism. A Public Service Broadcasting organisation must provide comprehensive information on the policies, plans and projects of the Government in power, take up campaign themes such as rural development, consumer protection, energy conservation, adult education, empowerment of women and young people etc.

(viii) PSB must accord high priority to national responsibilities. What is important is not development of mass media *per se* but the use of mass media to achieve socially desirable, socially relevant objectives. A PS broadcaster has to be concerned about the wider impact of mass media at the socio-cultural level in terms of social changes and developments. A commitment to use technological development for desirable ends require that PSB should think of its national responsibility.

(ix) PSB should address itself to empowerment of the socially disadvantaged, poor and the illiterate, more audience access to media development.

(x) PSB should be utilised as a resource for development, as a force for social transformation. It should have a clear concept of nation building.

(xi) In a PSB organisation, the radio station's overall accountability to the public in terms of broadcast practices, and operating within a legal framework is of great importance. PSB should at all the times remember that it faces sanction if it were to broadcast comments that are sexist, obscene and offensive to individual member of the institution or contrary to the wider interest of the institution.

(xii) Each mass medium has a brand image and PSB must strive to achieve credibility as its brand image (As 'Bahujan Sukhaya, Bahujan Hitaya' for All India Radio).

(xiii) The relationship between radio and its listeners is based on trust, a trust arising form credibility. This relationship can be easily broken if the listeners trust is betrayed by blatant inaccuracy or slanted news story.

(xiv) PSB Organisation is restrained from broadcasting the voices of members of banned organisations, in circumstances where their words may be construed as supporting or encouraging support for any of these organisations.

(xv) PSB Organisation is restrained from broadcasting information regarded as state secret, where the act of broadcast will breach official trust.

(xvi) PSB Organisation should keep a close watch on guidelines relating to national security

(xvii) Judgement on sensitive matters in PSB Organisation is motivated partly by a professional sense of self preservation and partly by a sense of responsibility.

(xviii) PSB Organisation is governed by self-regulation and professionalism.

Development Broadcast Unit (DBU)

In most developing countries, one may find exiting instances of use of media for development, but the applications of such experiences on a large scale are rare. Development Broadcast Unit (DBU), Kota, is one of the interesting examples of an attempt to take lessons of some successful experiments conducted in the country and apply these in an operational broadcasting condition. The DBU, aiming at integrating broadcasting as community service, was set up in January, 1989 at local radio station of Kota. The DBU adopted a novel concept and philosophy and therefore, differed in terms of both programme structure and it's organisation and management style.

The DBU is an excellent example of use of media for development. A DBU is a core group of professional broadcasters constituted to produce development oriented programmes for its audiences. First, the area of operation of DBU ranges to district level. Secondly, the DBU has a significant research input. This determines the contents of the programmes. As part of the programme development, scripts are written and tested; programmes are built and pre-tested and necessary modifications incorporated before the programme is actually broadcast. During the experiment period, programme specific feedback is given to the programme producers on a continuous basis. Impact assessment research studies are also conducted to measure the impact of DBU. A detailed and thorough research thus plays a very important role and is an integrated function of the DBU methodology.

Thirdly, broadcasters work at the audience level to produce field based programmes relevant to the people. The audience participation is ensured by motivating them to identify their own problems and they themselves write for such programmes brief/scripts. Talents for the programmes are also taken from among them. The programmes are recorded in their real life situations and therefore, these become relevant to people's needs in terms of issues, language and presentation. Fourthly, to ensure common goals and reduce duplication of efforts, the programmes are integrated with on-going developmental efforts of extension agencies, voluntary groups and non-governmental organisations. Lastly, much of theory and practice is built around the available experiences gained through special development projects like SITE, SCRC and Kheda Communication.

All concerned *i.e.* Programme Officers, Extension Officers, Researchers, Content Experts and the target Community, work as a team into the development of programming. Three young dynamic programme officers were transferred form other stations to join the DBU. This was in addition to the FRO (Farm Radio Officer) who was assigned to the DBU. The production workload was significantly reduced. Each of the four programme officers was to spend a considerable time in the field to produce only one development programme per month. The women in development, the human settlement and the environment constituted the developmental topics of this experiment. Within the same radio station building, a separate sitting arrangement was made for DBU staff and a jeep was earmarked exclusively for their field visits.

The DBU working is quite unique. For all operations, one of the programme officers act as a coordinator. After coming from the field, all the four programme officers are to sit together to discuss among themselves programme approach and it's style of presentation. The programme officers themselves have to do lot of research for their programmes.

In order to give an orientation on the concept and philosophy of development broadcasting to the DBU, orientation and field production exercises were conducted during the later half of 1988.The orientation workshop covered topics on development communication, communication research, working in a community and issues in environment, human settlement and women in development. Subsequently, the field production training was also conducted to improve their techniques of interviewing people for generating programme ideas. More so, these exercises were planned to provide insights to the programme officers primarily on the "why" and "how" of audience research and to convince them to the "imperatives" of field research for producing the actual need and problem based development programmes.

Programme Production

A wide variety of approaches were experimented for programme development; actual dramas enacted in the village; competitions arranged and awards given; campaign and problem solving approaches adopted, and in the process, radio programmes were produced. For several of the DBU productions problems, difficulties and grievances of the audience were recorded and the government authorities were asked to listen to these broadcasts. Follow up visits were also made to press them hard to solve their problems. The authorities did not appreciate the problem solving approach of the programme officers and reacted to their programmes only after several reminders. The role of programme officers in this business of partnership was to encourage dialogue between community and the development authorities. Whatever role the programme officers played and whatever formats they used, one thing was very clear that they deviated from their past habit of calling subject matter experts producing studio based programmes.

The programme officers mostly used field production techniques like "Discussions" rather than "Straight Lecture". The language used was very simple.

While all the DBU programmes produced under one title "Nai Kiran", the programme did not have continuity of characters/presenters. A separate identity of the programme could not be established. The programme officers to a very large extent used the research techniques in understanding the audience.

Feedback and Programme Utilisation

With the assistance of full time researchers at the station as part of DBU team, regular feedback was available to programme officers. Their own field research supplemented by Audience Research Report in terms of feedback yielded quite encouraging results.

Programme-specific utilisation efforts were made through in a limited manner. Sometimes, the field experts of the extension agencies and other groups were physically taken to the village for on the spot solutions and help. However, these efforts remained mostly restricted to getting a commitment and broadcast it. Programmes were generally aimed at mobilising the efforts and resources of only the extension agencies. However, no effort was made to mobilise local community resources ontributing to the efforts and services (in the form of Shramdaan) to their own cause of development.

The only requirement is to first involve the extension agencies in programme planning and reinforcing the messages. Listeners Information Centres need to be organised and a youth from within the village needs to be appointed as Coordinator between villagers and the programme officers. Some posters, wallpaper etc. need to be specially prepared and sent to such centres and as such a practical and multimedia approach to programme utilisation needs to be adopted.

However, some impact of DBU working was conspicuous. First, 65-70 per cent of the post-DBU programmes were field based as against 40-45 per cent in the pre-DBU stage. Secondly, the working climate had become quite conducive and 'Nai Kiran' programme still continued and it could easily become an integral part of the Kota radio station programmes. At the operational level also, the new administrative head no longer insisted for monthly programme schedule and avoided several formalities.

The DBU experiment helped in creating a good working climate. It also helped in convincing the programme officers as well as the Station Director the utility of research and field based production.

The DBU (Development Broadcast Unit) success at Kota can be experimented in tribal pockets of Jharkhand. It should take the shape of a PSB (Public Service Broadcasting) which is

Note : The above contents are the excerpts of a paper entitled 'Broadcasting for Development' written by Sham Behari who works for Systems Analysis and Project Planning Group, Development & Educational Communication Unit (DECU) of ISRO.AMBD. (Broadcasting for Development, authored by Shyam Behari and published in 'Communicator', Vol. XXIX, No.4, October-December 1994. Overall Project Review Report was prepared by Mr. B.S. Bhatia, Training Evolution was done by Mrs. Manjari Shah and the Operations study conducted by the author himself.)

governed by self-regulation and professionalism. In AIR, Ranchi, NAGAR DARPAN, one weekly programme of fifteen minutes basically a public grievance programme was received well by the listeners. Although it was a city based programme, maximum listeners were from rural areas. It is true that listeners have always attraction for specific programme which gives a balanced view of social reality and issues of day-to-day life etc. Monotonous and sterile programmes can't generate curiousity.

Concept of Local Radio Station (LRS)

Local Radio is a new concept of broadcasting in India. Each of the stations serving a small area will be basically utility service and reach right into the heart of the community which will use the microphone to reflect and enrich it's life and artistic expression. What distinguishes Local Radio from the regional network will be it's down to earth character, intimate and uninhabited approach and programme will be area specific. The Station will function as the mouth-piece of the local community. It will demolish the division between the broadcaster and the audience. Local authorities, police, emergency service, adult educationists, schools, transporters, farm scientists, entertainers will all look up to the Local Radio Station for a sustained community service. Comprising predominantly field based programmes, it will adopt a two-way communication system between the listeners and the extension agencies of various government departments. Local events and functions, games and sports, exhibitions and fairs, meetings and debates-cultural or literary, and fairs will find ample coverage. It will organise a number of 'Helpline' services for the listeners in employment, education, housing, law and even family problems (Sharafatyar, 1993).

Local broadcasting can alone ensure coordination with district authorities and with extension services to guarantee follow up action. It is hardly possible to encourage participation from the state capital or regional level broadcasting.

The Local Station must appeal to voluntary effort. In place of professional standards and bureaucratic rules and regulations, there has to be an unofficial atmosphere and a spirit of experimentation. When rural people begin to communicate within their community, they acquire self-confidence which encourages 'them to articulate their own needs and those of their community (Mehra Masani, 1976).

Working of Local Radio

(i) Flexibility in programming being the main characteristic of Local Radio, the station may take the Fixed Point Chart (FPC) as a broad guideline and make deviations as and when required.

(ii) The Station's main emphasis may be field based programme. It must be their objective to cover every village in the district by turn. Inadequacy of staff for OBs could be overcome by casual bookings.

(iii) The Station may devote broadcast effort mainly to programmes of farming, rural development, health, family welfare and education. The agencies engaged in these fields may be tapped for supply of materials, scripts and recordings .

(iv) Programmes may be presented in the local dialect, language by engaging, if required, casual compares who may present the programmes in a breezy, chatty conventional style.

(v) The Station may make provision for programmes of special audience like women, children, youth, labour, farmers etc. and groups, associations, organisations, engaged in their welfare may be encouraged to produce and present programmes.

(vi) The Station may relay only one news bulletin in the local language originating from Delhi and another from state Capital. Stations situated in the Hindi zone may take one Central Hindi bulletin. No other news bulletin is compulsory or recommended.

(vii) The Station will not relay any programme from Delhi/ State Capital except the broadcast of the President and Prime Minister. Mandatory relays will not apply to Local Radio Stations.

(viii) The Stations will be free to indent programmes from their Stations/DTPES and use them at their discretion keeping in view listeners interest in such programmes.

The main objective of a Local Radio Station is to use the broadcast medium for total development of it's zone particularly the impoverished lot, all those who are below the poverty line. It is through awareness and participation in broadcasting which will sensitize the mass for total development. It is a con inuous forum for analysis of people's interrelationships witn their environment (social, cultural and economic). Programmes are area specific because of the zone of Local Radio stretches over to 40 to 80 km only and here the microphone functions as the mouthpiece of the community. The programmer in LRS is conceived to be the part and parcel of the community as a friend, philosopher and guide. The sole aim of Local Radio Station is broadcasting by the people. The concept further embraces mission/orientation; a commitment; a stand for the people in need of development. The way of looking at 'expertise' can be extended to include other development professionals, government extension workers, NGOs and others who can work together with a community to make it a better place to live (Sarfatyar, I993).

Broadcasters and Social Responsibility

In order that AIR's programmes create social awakening, it is necessary that the national network and the regional stations identify social malaise including social tensions affecting the nation as a whole and the specific region in particular. Only if the problems are discussed in relation to the specific audiences, the treatment can be realistic and convincing. There are national problems in the social context and there are problems which are specific to certain regions. An inventory of these problems and a clear and bold approach to deal with them are essential.

Secondly, the broadcasting system has an ethical obligation to create among the people an awareness of their rights which are given to them under the Constitution. It matters whether the medium reaches the last man in the village or the remote area.

There are villages in remote and tribal areas which may not have any radio set at all.

The very first challenge is to make the underprivileged and the deprived sections conscious of their rights. The right may be of a fair wage or a status of equality as a citizen. The broadcast media need to be more bold in this regard, and should provide access to such persons to air their views and grievances to create public opinion in their favour. The second challenge is one of discrimination on the basis of caste, creed of religion. Any discrimination on any such account is against the Constitution and should have no place in our society. The broadcast media can't be indifferent or neutral in this regard. The third social challenge is from parochialism and narrow mindedness (Chawla, 1982).

A Character of Broadcast Journalism

Guidelines on news policy for the broadcast media have been drawn up by the Advisory Committee on official media headed by G. Parathasarathi in the year 1982.

1. There has to be a clear understanding of the difference between news and views. The reporting of news has to be factual, accurate and objective.
2. Each news story should be judged strictly on the basis of its news value.
3. In the selection of news received from wide ranging sources and in news editing, AIR and Doordarshan should be guided by the highest possible professional standards.
4. Apart from treating news factually and objectively, AIR and Doordarshan should provide where necessary background to the events and happenings in order that listeners in any part on the country are able to place events and happenings in proper perspective.
5. The broadcast news should satisfy the highest criteria of accuracy and responsibility.
6. In a developing country like ours, a special function of broadcasting should be the coverage of development news.

7. With the limitation of time, AIR and Doordarshan can't be expected to follow the pattern of news coverage followed by the newspapers. The range and scope of news gathering and selection will have to be suited to the media.
8. The style and method of news reporting should reinforce the fundamental principles on which national policies are based.
9. Ministerial statements on policy matters, particularly those of the Prime Minister are important as they enable the people to understand the national policies.
10. In reporting on political controversies, the broadcast media should be guided by objectivity and fair play. Due representation of differing view points shold be the aim.
11. In the choice of international development, the objective should be to keep the people well informed.
12. AIR and Doordarshan should aim at creating an informed public opinion on international events and developments.
13. The primary purpose of the current affairs programmes should be to enlighten the people on various aspects of political, economic, social and cultural developments. The treatment of the subject should be comprehensive projecting different view points. It should aim at providing adequate background for a proper understanding and interpretation of events and issues.
14. The current affairs programme should be broad based in the selection of topics and participants.
15. Internal evaluation of news and current affairs programmes after their broadcast should be a regular exercise.
16. The characteristics and potential reach of the broadcast media necessitates the drafting of news items in spoken style.
17. There should be provision for evaluation from time to time.
18. Professional training and appreciation of the role of media are very much needed.

A country's media give us a fair indication of the concerns of its people. In our country, there are millions who can't read but who still are intensely interested in right and wrong and in good government and social justice. The common method of measuring a nation's development by counting number of television sets owned or newspapers bought per thousand of the population is not always very pertinent. An affluent nation may be politically lazy and culturally unenterprising; an economically struggling one may be culturally and politically dynamic. Communication has several distinctive but related and mutually reinforcing roles and purposes. It must first of all provide the basic information which is economically useful to the individual and which gives him a better understanding of his civil rights and obligations and deepen his judgments. Then it must strengthen those forces in society which will promote the resolution of conflicts through peaceful, constitutional means. Besides such economic, political, and intellectual functions, communication has also a cultural and aesthetic role, that of improving taste and enlarging a sense of life's worthwhileness. In short, communication continues what formal education begins. The media are the people's life-long university. They award no degrees but enhance the individual's relevance to the nation and the world. In our country there are two main social hurdles to nation building, *i.e.* the assimilation in the national mainstream of the lowest castes and tribes who had been so far left out of the polity and the reconciliation of linguistic and regional-animosities. The first has to some extent been achieved by the process of elections. The traditionally deprived classes have found their political importance (Prasad S.1988).

Multi Media Campaign

In order to publicize programmes and policies of different Ministries, multi media campaign are launched from time to time by Ministry of Information and Broadcasting. Besides Field Pubilicity Department and Song and Drama Division, All India Radio stations through out the country take active part in multi media campaign. Stations build up on intensive campaign on Panchayati Raj, Jawahar Rozgar Yojana, Employment Assurance

Scheme, Integrated Rural Development including rural water supply and sanitation, Wasteland Development, Poverty Alleivation Schemes, Nutrition programmes and Literacy programmes. Along with the Local Radio Stations, the main radio stations participate in the campaign for the benefit of the rural and tribal listeners who are unable to listen because of non-availability of FM facility.

The Field Publicity Department usually takes the help of traditional media to convey development message to the people at the grassroots level. AIR teams supplement the campaign by using it's wide network of broadcast success stories and interviews with beneficiaries and district officials are included in the programme broadcast materials. Different formats are used while producing programmes for multi media campaign.

Farm and Home section in each AIR station takes the key role to disseminate information in the areas of family welfare, environment protection, crime against women, prohibition of drug abuse, national integration, new economic policy, agricultural and rural development etc.

A Description on AIR, Ranchi

India's oldest broadcasting network the All India Radio, has grown many fold from mere 26 stations at the time of first five year plan covering just half the population. Much of this growth has actually happened during 1990's. It's intensive reach has ensured high listenership now. As many as 15 short bulletins were started on FM last year (1996) taking the daily number of AIR bulletins to 300. AIR has come a long way since 1970's and has now added 35 broadcasting centres to the External Service and has undertaken a massive computerisation plan for the Vividh Bharti Service and though it continues to be a public broadcaster, it's revenue drive has seen the income grow by 80 per cent in this decade alone. Direct rely of commercial and entertainment programmes recently from Bombay by regional CBS stations has not only improved reception quality but also earned good revenue in terms of advertisements.

Setting up of a Radio station in 1957 in this Chotanagpur plateau brought radical revolution in recognising the talents of tribal people and inviting the artists to participate in radio programmes. Once they face audition in AIR studio and get success, they become part time artists of AIR and of course in Doordarshan. Besides regular studio programmes, they are often booked for invited audience programmes. Booking for a programme fetch them handsome amount and this retain their motivation too. To me, this is the important service so far radio has done for tribals of this region.

Secondly, OB (Outside Broadcast) Programmes which are usually recorded outside the studio have brought about significant impact on listeners particularly in and around Ranchi city. A Number of development activities in the shape of workshops, seminars and exhibitions etc. are conducted through out the year in its broadcasting zone and coverage of these programmes bring immediate feedback to the listeners and the concerned people.

There are tribals who are members of different Advisory Committees of AIR in different sections. It shows that the participation of tribals in programme policy decisions is a continuous process. As per provision, in respect of AIR, the non-official members should represent the following disciplines (DG circular No. 9-l-96-P5 dated 27 Nov., 1996).

Music, Drama, Folk-lore, Art and Culture, Women and Child Welfare, Youth Welfare, Medical Science, Environment, Social welfare including welfare of SC and other weaker sections, Tribal welfare, Science, Sports, Literature, Linguistic Minorities (This is applicable where a station produces programmes in language other than the main language of the area), Humour, Agriculture and allied sectors.

Radio Krishi Pathsala and Krishak Gosthi

AIR, Ranchi set up in the year 1957 has a glorious history when radio listening was considered to be a privilege. With people having lesser number of sets and programmes being broadcast mostly on live that was perhaps the golden period of radio broadcasting. In Farm and Home (F & H) Programme, there are fixed programmes for specific purposes. Goan Kar Ek Saam,

Krishak Gosthi and magazine programme are destined to cater to various interests like culture, agriculture and literature of targeted listeners respectively.

The programme 'Krishak Gosthi' originally destined to involve farmers at the grassroots level. A programme person having knowledge of agriculture and animal husbandry has to rush to the remote villages, invite the farmers including the small and marginal ones for a discussion which has to be aired subsequently. The programme person may also invite opinion – leaders and government officials (B.D.O, Extension Officer or VLW as the case may), share with a group of farmers. It is a monthly programme which usually contains interactions of the farmers with one invited expert or a programme man or both. The purpose is to share the grievance of the farmers and provide useful farm related information.

Radio-Krishi-Pathsala recently started in 1994 has been very successful. Listeners have reacted overwhelmingly. It is a question answer programme where the listeners are involved. Each part is about thirty minutes duration and the programme is in an interview format. An expert on the subject is interviewed by a programme man. Questions are asked to the listeners and their response are included in the subsequent episode. Listeners are registered and certificates are also issued. Few attractive prizes are also given to the outstanding listeners.

The researcher was an eye-witness to the prize-giving ceremony of Radio-Krishi-Pathsala based on Tasar-Resam cultivation which was broadcast during April to June 1995. It was really a wonderful programme. The Director of Central Tasar Research and Training Institute, Ranchi gave away transistor sets to the outstanding listeners where as one booking each was given to the invitees by the host organization, *i.e.* AIR, Ranchi. Press people were also invited on the occasion and separately interviewed the awaredees. For this particular lesson, 210 listeners were registered and the result was excellent.

But the predicament is that continuity is not maintained. For this kind of programme, where participation of young farmers is unique, attempts should be made to popularise these kind of programmes. One question answer programme of twenty minutes duration is regularly broadcast in F&H

programme. The farmers and enterprenurs queries are replied by agriculture and animal husbandary experts.

Table 6.1 : Radio Krishi Pathsala

Item Covered	Time Period	Episodes	Beneficaiaries
(i) Paddy Cultivation	April-June 1994	13	Farmers
(ii) Tasar-Resam palan	April-June 1995	13	Farmers
(iii) Lah	Oct.-Dec. 1995	13	Farmers

An Introduction about AIR : Ranchi

Table 6.2 : Krishak Gosthi

1.	Name of the Station	All India Radio, Ranchi
2.	Date of Commissioning	27 July, 1957
3.	Areas of primary coverage (Names of districts covered)	Total 12 Districts (Ranchi, Lohardaga, Gumla, Palamu, Hazaribagh, East-West Singhbhum, Bokaro, Dhanbad, Chatra, Godwa and Girdih)
4.	No. of channels	Two (Main & CBS)
5.	No. of transmissions in each channel, with duration CBS – (Commercial Broadcasting Service) (i) 5.55 a.m. – 10.00 a.m. (ii) 12.00 – 5.30 p.m. (iii) 6.15 p.m. – 11.00 p.m.	Three Transmissions in each channel Primary (i) 5.55 a.m. – 9.40 a.m. (weekdays) (ii) 12.30–3.20 p.m. (Weekdays) 12.00 – 3.20 p.m (Sundays) (iii) 5.00–10.30 p.m. (Weekdays) 5.00p.m.–11.10p.m. (Saturday/Sunday)
6.	Frequency of each channel	Primary – MW-546.45 meter & 549 KHZ (Short Wave not functioning now) CBS – MW – 260.41 meter 1152 KHZ
7.	Main language of the Station	Hindi
8.	Other language in which programmes are broadcast	OtherLanguage/Dialects–Nagpuri, Mundari, Ho, Santhali, Kurukh, Kurmali, Sanskrit, Urdu, English, Bengali, Kharia, Panchapargania.
9.	Total population covered by the station	Total Population nearing 20 million

10.	Linguistic composition	Almost all understand Hindi and Nagpuri. In remote places, few among tribals donot understand neither of the two. They only understand their own tribal dialects.
11.	Power of the transmitter	Power of TR (MW) Primary – 100kW/10kW CBS – 1 kW (One kW)
12.	Total No. of stations in the state including Bihar	10
13.	Zone to which the state belongs	North Zone (Programme) East Zone (Engineering)
14.	Total hours of transmission (Monthly from each channel)	Total hours (Primary) :392.25 Hrs. (CBS):426.00 Hrs.
15.	Total no. of projects ready for commissioning	(i) 2×3 kW FM Transmitter
16.	No. of projects under different stages of installation	(ii) 50 kW SW Transmitter
17.	Introduction of weekly language bulletin	19 November 1994 S/C 178

Geographical data : Ranchi is situated at an altitude of 85.38 east and 22.30 north longitude. Climate is dry and semihumid. The place is situated at 271.48 meters above sea level.

Table 6.3 : Language-wise breakup of F&H Programme in AIR, Ranchi (June 1995)

Sl. No.	Name of the language /dialect	Duration of B'cast in a month	Per centage to total B'cast
1.	Hindi	720Mts./12Hrs.	33 per cent
2.	Nagpuri	480Mts/8Hrs.	24 per cent
3.	Oraon (Kudukh)	120Mts/2Hrs.	06 per cent
4.	Mundari	120Mts/2Hrs.	06 per cent
5.	Santhali	120Mts/2Hrs.	06 per cent
6.	Khardia	120Mts/2Hrs.	06 per cent
7.	Ho	60Mts/Hrs	03 per cent
8.	Panch Pargania	60Mts/1Hrs	03 per cent
9.	Kurmali	90Mts/1.5Hrs	3.3 per cent
10.	Kortha	90Mts/1.5Hrs	3.3 per cent
	Total	1950 Mts. Or 32hrs./30mts.	100 per cent

Morning Transmission 6.10 a.m. to 6.15 a.m. = 5 Mts × 30 days = 150 Mts.
Evening Transmission 6.30 p.m. to 7.30 p.m. = 60 Mts × 30 days = 1800 Mts.
Total 1950 Mts.

Coverage of Festivals and Anniversaries

Throughout the year at different intervals, a number of 'Kisan Melas' are being organized in different places within the broadcasting zone. There are also important festivals which are observed with traditional gaiety. The tribals of Chotanagpur are famous for their rich culture and heriage. They observe a number of festivals at different times which include Jatra, Makar Sankranti, Tusu Parv, Phagua, Sarhul, Jeth Jetra, Rath Yatra, Karma, Nawa Khanni, Dasai, Sohrai, Indi, Kartik Purnima, Pus Mela and Hariyari Puja etc.

There are important celebrations which commemorate birth anniversaries of a number of important personalities in the tribal belt. Birsa Munda popularly known as Birsa Bhagwan (Birth Day : 14.11.1875 and death on 9.6.1899), Siddhu Kanhu, Tilka Najhi, Biswanath Sahi, Sekh Vikari, Pande Ganapati Nath Ray, Tana Bhagat, Albert Ekka, Father Kamil Bulke and Diva Kisun etc. are important names to mention.

Electronic publicity given for different tribal festivals observed in Chotanagpur

January	Magh Mela, Murhu Mela
February	Makar Sankranti, Nagpeni Mela, Ram rekha Mela Tusu festival
March/April	Fagua, Holi, Sarhul (New Year of Tribals) (Worshipping of Mother earth and enivornment), Bah festival
May	Jeth jatra, Buna festival (Herod)
June/July	Rath Yatra (Jagannath Mela) Hariyari Puja
September	Karma (Worhsipping of mother earth and environment)
October	Sohrai, Dipawali, Nawa Khanni, Mundma Mela.
November	Ras Mela, Kartik Purnima
December	Pus Mela

The tribal people are famous for their dance and music and in all important festivals, they rejoice with traditional gaiety. It brings them immense pleasure. Now-a-days, music and dance competitions are also held in such festive occasions.

Besides the above, different occasions related to important personalities are also celebrated throughout Jharkhand now consisting of eighteen districts.

From time to time Parha Mela are being arranged in different parts of Chotanagpur. Th traditional Parha system is still prevalent in some areas of Chotanagpur region. Wide coverage is given to all such functions in this electronic media. Radio talks, Radio reports, interviews are some of the important formats. Simultaneously, news coverage is also available in the state hookup from RNU (Regional News Unit), Ranchi.

Plight of Folk Artists

Radio has been playing an important role in screening folk artists and inviting their participation in broadcasting media. The tribals and sadans (local inhabitants) of Jharkhand have not only immense potential to sing and dance for hours but they have got a rich cultural heritage of their own. Getting auditioned in All India Radio is certainly an important recognition for the group performers and individual artists.

Table 6.4 : *Lokgeet* Songs by folk artists

Name of the Lokgeet	No. of Groups approved in audition During 1997-98
Nagpuri	64
Oraon	23
Munda	48
Santhali	12
Ho	02
Khardia	06
Khortha	06
Kurmali	23
Panchpargania	42
Total	232

The number of artists in a party varies from five to eight. The groups/artists are graded as 'B' and 'B high'. With limited annual budget of about 2 lakhs, it is not even possible to book each group even once in a year. As per a rough estimation made by a Programme Officer-in-charge of folk songs, at least Rupees 7 lakhs is needed in the annual budget to book each party at least once in a year. The poor tribals have to come often to AIR, Ranchi for a booking but in vain. The folk artists need motivation for their songs and dance through this potential electronic media which is a point to be noted. There is enough to be done for the upliftment of tribal people in this part of Chotanagpur.

Besides the above, there are 25 instrumentalists who have been approved in AIR, Ranchi in different traditional music instruments, *i.e.* Flute, Mandar, etc.

Total duration of folk songs

Monday	70 Mts. (In addition, the duration of folk songs
Tuesday	50 Mts. is about 20 minutes in Farm and Home
Wednesday	40 Mts. Programme everyday)
Thursday	50 Mts.
Friday	40 Mts.
Saturday	50 Mts.
Sunday	35 Mts.

There is another monthly programme known as "Gunje Bihar" based on traditional tribal songs. The chunk is of 30 minutes. From February 1997, provisions has been made for a weekly chunk of 15 minutes for folksongs in Yuv-Vani.

It is observed that modern Nagpuri songs based on film tunes are getting more popular among youth and children. The artists sticking to traditional tunes allege that the songs based on film tunes should never be encouraged because this transformation will ruin the fragrance and richness of poetry. The issue being quite controversial, so far modern Nagpuri songs based on film tunes have not been included in studio based programmes. However, in invited audience programmes, the artists have been allowed to sing songs based on film tunes on audience demand.

Coverage of Sports

Ranchi is considered as an important AIR station as far as broadcast of sports is concerned. Besides national and international events, attempts have been made to give adequate coverage to state and regional level sports. Running commentaries, group discussions, radio reports, sports quiz and radio talks are some of the important formats used for highlighting sports activities in this region. The sports men and women who have shown excellence in the national and international level are invited to AIR studio. Jharkhand is quite rich as far as sports talent is concerned. In Hockey and Archery, a number of national and international players are from this tribal belt only. Tribal sports personalities are rarely booked.

Report of Audience Research Unit, AIR, Ranchi

The ARU (Audience Research Unit) of AIR, Ranchi came to existence in the year 1993. From time to time, surveys are conducted in different parts of its broadcsting zone to study listening behaviour of people. It was learnt that no such study has been taken up exclusively on tribals. Monthly reports based on listeners letters are also compiled and forwared to the Directorate. The letters usually contain appreciation, request for item, suggestion, query, quiz reply/solicitated letters, criticism and non-reply/non-playing songs.

Table 6.5 : Language-wise Distribution (Month of Feb. 1997)

Sl. No.	Language	Number	per cent
1.	Hindi	3614	89.67
2.	Nagpuri	416	10.33
3.	English	-	-
	Total	4030	100 per cent

Mostly the tribal people prefer Nagpuri language while writing for radio programme.

Table 6.6 : Series of invited audience programmes held in and around Ranchi during 1995 Calender year

Date	Name of the programme	Place
1995 Sept.	Special Balsabha	Ranchi city
1995 Sept.	Kabya Sandhya	Ranchi city
1995 Mar.	Folk music and Dance	Ratu (Rural)
1995 May	Workshop on Aids	Khunti (Rural)
1995 Nov.	Gajals	Ranchi city
1995 Nov.	Radio-Krishi-Pathsala	Ranchi city (function)

It is observed that maximum invited programmes have been conducted in Ranchi city itself which is contrary to AIR's own ideology. For maximum participation of tribal people, attempts should have been made to conduct invited audience programmes in small towns and villages.

There are few sponsored programmes, *i.e.* Gaon Vikash Ki Ore, Naya Savera, Aao Hath Badhayen, Hasin Lamhe, and Nai Rah Apnao Sasthe Me Sukh Pao which are broadcast in Commercial Service of AIR, Ranchi spread important development inputs for listeners. Right now, only the people in the city and in the satellite villages spread over 25 kms. radius are benefited of this commercial channel. Since such kind of sponsored programmes by different central ministries are qualitatively super than the ordinary programmes, attempt should be made to introduce such kind of popular programmes in the Primary Channel having high-power transmitter. This recommendation is based on the fact that the listeners of Ranchi city and Mandar are observed to be fan of CBS progammes and their duration of listening to this particular channel is all time high in comparison to primary channel.

7

IMPACT OF BROADCASTING ON TRIBALS

The question of impact is a complex one and needs careful examination. The exposure of radio has consequence both for individual and social groups. Radio listening is very common in all age groups *i.e.* children, youth, women, heads and aged people. In addition to closed ended questions, few open ended questions were also asked to the respondents to get their reactions about radio broadcasts and their relevance and effectiveness in terms of information dissemination, attitude change and finally their expectations from the potential electronic media. Four themes have been included in this chapter.

(i) Background Information
(ii) Listening Behaviour (Dimensions and source variables of different programmes)
(iii) Awareness
(iv) Reactions on different function-areas

The respondents have been decided broadly into five broad categories *i.e.* youth, heads, women, children and aged for convenience.

Attempts have been made to give representation to all households having radio sets. The minimum qualification of each respondent is that he or she should be a radio listener and possibly his/her house possesses a radio set. Care has also been taken to give representation to all age groups beginning from the teenagers to the aged ones. Almost in all households the male members function as head or guardian of the family.

A total number of 300 respondents were interviewed for the study, 100 each from Rania (a remote tribal area), Mandar (a rural area but growing rural marketing base) and Hatma (village of Ranchi city a tribal pocket housing migrants of the recent past). The tribals residing in the heart of Ranchi (Hatma), are well off status wise. Due to sanskritization they have adopted the life styles of higher castes and in some cases they are leading quite comfortable life.

The ultimate aim of media is to motivate people to take practical actions of the communication content. If the final objective of the communication is met, we say communication is effective, otherwise either there is communication failure or communication gap. Evaluation is done at three stages :

(a) Stage of Transmission,
(b) Stage of Semantics, and
(c) Stage of Effectiveness.

Here the whole process is based on evaluation on a single stage, *i.e.* stage of transmission. Since most of the development information are repeated in the electronic media, a regular listener is supposed to understand the received information in the same way as the medium wants him to understand. That's why while studying listening behaviours, a classification has been made for various dimensions for inviting response from the respondents, *i.e.* casual listener, regular listener and very regular listener. Thus it can be stated that the stage of semantics has been included to some extent. It is difficult to judge stage of effectiveness because of the fact that the respondents are surrounded by different communication channels. It is difficult to elicit information from the respondents on particular source of their change of behaviour or attitude or work effectiveness. Therefore, the researcher has omitted the stage of effectiveness from the levels of Communication Effect Evaluation (CEE).

BACKGROUND INFORMATION

In Chapter 5 (Area and Profile of Tribes), data beginning from state to the village level have been given. This part of the

Chapter (Background Information) contains detail account of the samples collected from three different places *i.e.* Rania (Remote), Mandar (Less remote) and Hatma (Urban). One hundred sample each from four villages of Rania block, one village of Mandar block and two villages of Ranchi city were chosen for the purpose.

Name of the area	*Name of the village*
Rania (Remote)	(i) Lohagara
	(ii) Kulhei
	(iii) Digri
	(iv) Tangerkela
Mandar (Less Remote)	(i) Ambatoli
Hatma (Ranchi Urban)	(i) Sarna Toli
	(ii) Hatma Toli

In remote tribal area like Rania, tribals usually prefer to speak in their own tribal mother tongue (dialect). In some cases the link language of the tribal belt which is known as Sadri (Nagpuri) is also used as mother tongue. In remote tribal areas, use of Hindi or Sadri is minimum. It is observed that the migration of people to urban areas in search of employment and the influx of Government workers and teachers to the interior areas in the reverse direction have influenced the communication potential of the tribal people. Sadri and Hindi are increasingly used in interpersonal communication. More and more people are using modern literary languages in these days.

Particularly migration of tribals to urban places has affected tribal dialect adversely. In some cases, perhaps this is the last generation to possess knowledge of three languages which include Hindi, Sadri and Mundari or Kudukh (Oraon speaking) as the case may be. The tribals having an optimum standard of living particularly in Hatma, have an inclination to admit their children in English medium schools. It is also observed that most of the tribal children of this generation in Hatma (Ranchi city) don't know their own tribal dialect. Sadri being very close to Hindi, there is no problem to learn this link language. Festivals, occasional trips to native places and the interaction with relatives and friends make the children aware of the link language and their culture. The younger generation is not keen to learn a tribal language.

There is more emphasis on the fact that the children should learn English besides Hindi. The influence of missionaries has brought about radical revolution in young people to learn English. Tribal dance and music have picked up English tunes and that of Hindi film songs. During fieldwork, it was observed that a number of tribals can speak English particularly in Hatma. Use of Sadri as the medium of interpersonal communication is quite common in Rania and Mandar. The position of Hindi comes next. Use of Tribal dialect is common in remote areas as observed in four villages of Rania Block. So with the process of urbanisation, a series of changes have taken place in the areas of attitude formation, thinking and grasping of modern languages.

A majority of the respondents are male attributable to the large sample of heads of households. A majority of economic decisions are known to be taken by men rather than women and even land is found registered in the names of men. Where women are heads of households, they are usually divorced, widowed or staying separate from their households. Although few such females were noticed during fieldwork in Rania and Mandar, it is interesting to note that none of them was possessing a radio set of her own.

It is also observed that in Rania and Mandar, it is either the monopoly of the head of the family or male young ones to retain the radio set more for personal listening.

Out of the survey of four villages in Rania (Lohagarda, Kulhei, Digri and Tangerkela) it was found that only 15 per cent of the total tribal households possess radio sets. Door to door survey was taken up in the four villages of Rania block and one village of Mandar and due to this reason the researcher was in a position to calculate the total number of radiosets possessed by all the tribal households. It is observed that the story of Mandar and Hatma is slightly better in terms of possession of radio sets while listenership is not as good as the inhabitants of Rania.

Sadri is the link language in each of the three field areas. In Rania, the major tribe is Munda and in the case of Mandar, the major tribe is Oraon. In Hatma (Ranchi city), there are equal number of tribals belonging to Munda community and Oraon community. In Hatma even the Oraon commuity know Mundari language. Here almost all the tribals use Sadri and Hindi as link language while interacting with the outside people.

Table 7.1 : Basic Information about respondents

Category	No. of respondents			
(A) Age groups	Rania	Mandar	Hatma	Total
(i) Children (12-15)	11	10	10	31
(ii) Youth (16-25)	25	28	27	80
(iii) Women (12-50)	20	19	20	59
(iv) Heads (26-50)	30	29	31	90
(v) Aged (Above 50)	14	14	12	40
Total	100	100	100	
(B) Education	Rania	Mandar	Hatma	Total (%)
(i) Illiterate	30	20	03	53 (17%)
(ii) Unschooled but literate	22	46	03	71 (23.6%)
(iii) Primary school	30	04	36	70 (23.3%)
(iv) Middle school	09	11	16	36 (12%)
(v) High School	08	09	23	40 (13.3%)
(vi) Above high school	01	10	19	30 (10%)
Total	100	100	100	
(C) Religion	Rania	Mandar	Hatma	
(i) Sarna/Hindu	100	97	62	
(ii) Christianity	-	03	38	
Total	100	100	100	
(D) Language (Knowledge of mother tongue)	Rania	Mandar	Hatma	
(i) Mundari	89	10	56	
(ii) Kudukh	-	60	20	
(E) Ocupation	Rania	Mandar	Hatma	Total (%)
(i) Agricultural Labour	35	15	10	60 (20%)
(ii) Cultivator	19	20	10	49 (16.3%)
(iii) Business (Small & petty)	01	13	10	24 (8%)
(iv) Service	06	08	35	49 (16.3%)
(v) Artisans/ Professionals	07	15	10	32 (10.7%)
(vi) Students/ unemployed and others	28	19	15	62 (20.6%)

Category	No. of respondents			
(vii) Housewife	04	10	10	24 (8%)
(F) Standard of living	MIG	LIG	BPL	
(i) Rania	03	13	84	
(ii) Mandar	18	40	42	
(iii) Hatma	39	21	40	
Total	60 (20%)	74(25%)	166(55%)	300

For classification of respondents into different income groups, the following criteria have been adopted.
MIG – Middle Income Group (More than 50,000 per annum)
LIG – Low Income Group (Less than 50,000 but more than Rs. 11,840 per annum)
BPL – Below Poverty Line (Less than Rs. 11,840 per annum).

The point to be noted is that majority of our respondents (55%) are from Below Poverty Line.

We have used certain variables in our study as independent and dependent. The variables are age-group, education, religion, language, occupation and proximity to urban centre. The dependent variables are (i) Listening Behaviour, (ii) Awareness, and (iii) Reactions on different functions and expected roles.

In each of the three villages, 100 respondents were interviewed which comprises 31 children, 80 youth, 59 women, 90 adults and 40 aged people in all. The head of household, in most of the cases, is a male who is either the father, the eldest brother or the husband.

(A) An attempt has been made here to gauge how far tribal people are linked with radio broadcast. The inputs of information, education and entertainment are of various degrees for different age groups and that is why data analysis for different age group has proved to be more convenient. Maximum respondents belong to the category of Heads (90) followed by Youth (80), Women (59), Aged (40) and Children (31).

(B) The cognitive processing of information depends on one's educational level. Table 7.1 (B) gives the status of respondents with regard to literacy and education. Maximum respondents belong to the category of unschooled but literate (23.6%) and primary school (23.3%). On the analysis of field data it is found that maximum respondents are illiterates in Rania while the interviewees of Hatma are more literate and educated.

In the subsequent section, attempt has been made to draw a relation between education and access to information media. The tribals of Hatma are not different from the general population as far as socio-economic status is concerned. With urban contact and with access to print media, Doordarshan and multinational cable channels, they have more exposure to the development world. The cognitive level of an illiterate ignorant person can't match with his urban counterpart who is literate, educated and having more exposure to things happening around him.

(C) Only two religions are represented here, *i.e.* Hindu/Sarna and Christians. A majority of the people as expected profess the religion mentioned first. In Rania, all respondents; in Mandar, 97 respondents and in Hatma 62 respondents belong to Hindu Sarna community while the rest are Christians. Although in Ambatoli village of Mandar the tribals live along with Muslims, the latter have least impact on the tribal population. The tribal people are culturally very rich and even if there has been conversion of Hindus into Christianity, all celebrate festivals in the same spirit.

Because of the missionary contact, the Christians among tribals seem to be more educated. Their exposure, awareness level and standard of living are better in comparison to their Hindu brothern.

(D) It is observed that as the tribals are having urban contact or more exposure to out side society and modern mass communication channels, their inclination to their own tribal dialect, say Kudukh, Mundari etc. decreases. The imposition of literary rich language on the tribal hinterland is gradually increasing and in some cases it is noticed that this is the last generation to have knowledge of tribal dialect. This urbanization has brought about a lot of changes. This new generation shows maximum interest in Hindi film songs rather then their own folk songs.

People in Rania block wish to listen programmes in Hindi, Sadri and Mundari. Here maximum. respondents know their tribal dialect *i.e.* Mundari. In Ambatoli village of Mandar, the tribals show their interest for programmes in Hindi, Sadri and Kudukh (Oraon Speaking). The place is less remote and the tribals also have scope to send their children to English medium schools. Hatma, located in Ranchi city consists of mixed tribal population of Oraon and Munda community. Here. in Ranchi city maximum school going children don't have knowledge of their own tribal dialect. Here the respondents show interest in Hindi and Sadri. Thus migration of tribals to urban places has affected the tribal dialects.

In remote tribal area of Rania, use of Hindi is minimum, Mundari and Sadri are the common language for interpersonal interactions. In these days, when nuclear families are growing up, village contact is gradually decreasing and as a result, the younger generation is not keen to learn it's tribal language. This is very much visible in Hatma.

(E&F) The point to be noted is that maximum respondents (55%) of our sample size belong to the category of Below Poverty Line (income less than Rs. 11,840 per annum). Out of the three field areas it is again maximum in Rania where out of 100 respondents, 84 are from below poverty line. Similarly the figure of Middle Income Group (MIG) is highest in Hatma *i.e.* 37 out of 100 where it is lowest in Rania *i.e.* only 3 out of 100.

Almost all the respondents in Rania belong to very poor economic strata. The tribals belonging to low and middle income groups settled in the heart of Ranchi city are found comparatively to be better in physique and in nutrition intake. The case of Rania is worst in respect of standard of living and as a result, they are prone to hazardous diseases and they suffer from physical deformity, malnutrition and ill health. Since standard of living is judged by a host of factors which include livelihood of the family, land and material possessions, nutrition level and energy consumption etc. attempts have been made to include all these queries in the interview schedule. Because of low standard of living, very few households possess radio sets in Rania.

Households enumeration study was taken up in Rania and Mandar only for the sole purpose of confirming our hypothesis that in the country side radio is the only largely accessible electronic media. In case of Rania out of 229 tribal households, only 34 households possess radio sets, only 3 households possess TV sets. The people were only able to visualize the TV programmes quite selectively after charging their battery sets from the nearest market place, Torpa which is about 20 kms away. No body is a subscriber to daily newspaper.

It is observed that the standard of living of the tribals professing Christianity is better off in all the field areas in comparison to their Hindu and Sarna brothers. Church has become an important centre of information for the tribals particularly for the Christians. Because of weekly congregations and religious teachings, their awareness level is comparatively high. It is also observed that the conversion is much more among Oraon tribes than that of Munda tribes who claim to have ruled Chotanagpur for a pretty long period.

Particularly among the category of Youth and Heads in Rania, the degree of listening is more. But the fact is that people here have not progressed accordingly. In Hatma, awareness from radio is minimum but the tribal people have got access to other modern mass media in comparison to a remote place like Rania where radio is the only easily accessible modern mass media.

Awareness is seen to be very high for Agriculture Schemes, Family Welfare Programmes, Employment Schemes and Panchayati Raj, little less for Bank Loan, IRDP, Non-Formal Education, TRYSEM, JRY, Indira Awas Yojana, Mahila Sammriddhi and far less for ICDS, NREP, DWACRA, PDS, RLEGP, Nutrition Support or Education, National Social Assistance Package, Watershed Development Projects, and Information about Small Scale and Cottage Industries.

The Youth seem to be best informed and most enthusiastic among the five categories of respondents. The adult population of respondents follow them. There is also good listening among people who are old. Women and children are least informed respondents.

In fact, this particular electronic media has a wide range of impact. It is more useful for a tribal village, which is far away from the city where people usually don't have access to modern mass media. Radio has become a popular medium for dissemination of information and diffusion of agricultural and allied innovations for progressive farmers.

When we compare listeners feedback with the background information, *i.e.* age group, education, religion, occupation and standard of living, we can find a close nexus in between respondent's status and listening behaviour, programme awareness and reactions on different function areas. The most important variable is standard of living, which determines accessibility to different channels of communication. The well-off tribal people in Hatma have got access to almost all available media channels while the poorest among them are deprived ones.

In Hatma, radio is the most entertainment channel because here the people usually listen Commercial Broadcasting Service (CBS). It is purely an entertainment channel having some relay of national news bulletins. Irrespective of occupation and standard of living, here tribals have chosen CBS as the first option. Here life is not slow as other field areas. Therefore, the migrated population of two to three generations old are not having crisis days like that of their brothern in Rania. People have opportunities to find regular engagement and labour. The commercial channel programmes mostly include Hindi film songs which is quite popular among all age groups and in all areas. Particularly first and third transmissions are having maximum listenership because during the period, the people do not have any engagement or work commitment.

Education is not at all a criterion for radio listening. Most of our respondents are either illiterate or having education upto middle school.

As far as language is concerned, it is also no more a significant factor. Although Mundari is dominant dialect both in Rania and Hatma, the tribals are tuned to Hindi programmes. Remoteness is one of the most important criteria for listening language based programmes. Therefore, Farm and Home programme is very popular in Rania unlike other places.

LISTENING BEHAVIOUR

Listening of radio is determined by various factors; such as socio-economic conditions, physical and environmental situations etc. Ranchi occupies a more significant position in this regard because it vastly varies from the plains of India. Ranchi has a large concentration of the tribal population; it provides rich forest cover to the country and what is more important is that it has long reserves of a number of precious minerals for chain of industries, large and small, in both private and public sectors have sprung up. It has given rise to an industrial culture influencing the native cultural contents of the original people in the region. Here in Chotanagpur, geographical, ecological, social, economic and cultural elements of the region together shape up the life pattern of the inhabitants which in turn determine their listening behaviour also.

It is noticed that the extent of average day listening continue to be very high for Radio Srilanka, Nepal and BBC besides AIR, Ranchi (Not shown in the table). Listening of various foreign broadcasting centres are due to musical entertainments and news. Within the country, National Channel has become very popular for its exclusive entertainment character.

Vividh Bharti, the important entertainment channel has been the most popular channel amongst all age groups.

The respondents were having quite good impression about Vividh Bharti sponsored programmes. Sometimes it carries different informative and welfare programmes, which are also full of music and entertainment.

The selection of variables to examine roles of broadcasting for tribal development is guided by the fact that there are different sources of information, entertainment and education for the people at all level. The present study is exclusively on the broadcasting media and variables selected reflect informative, informative - educative and entertainment dimensions. The various dimensions and the variables selected for inviting response from the respondents have been discussed.

For convenience, frequencies have been divided into three different categories.

Casual Listener (CL) : Frequency once in a week or less than that. In case of weekly programmes, frequency is even less than once in a month.

Regular Listener (RL) : Frequency is at least 2-3 times a week for daily programmes. In case of weekly programmes, frequency is at least twice in a month.

Very Regular Listener (VRL) : Frequency is atleast four times a week for daily programmes. In case of weekly programmes, it is, at least, three times in a month.

Table 7.2 : Frequency of listening of radio plays

	Rania (Remote)			Mandar (Less Remote)			Hatma (Urban)		
	VRL	RL	CL	VRL	RL	CL	VRL	RL	CL
I. Informative Dimension									
Pradesik Smachar	44	41	15	20	32	48	22	28	50
Sansad Samikshya/ Vidhan Sabha Samikshya/ Question Hour in Parliament	28	30	42	10	30	60	13	25	62
Radio Newsreel	12	26	62	02	08	90	–	10	90
National Hindi Bulletins	40	23	37	28	26	46	32	24	46
Samachar Dhwanichitra	14	26	60	02	11	87	04	11	89
Weekly Language Bulletins	58	19	23	32	20	48	20	29	51
Average figure	33	27	40	16	21	63	15	20	65
II. Informative and Educative Dimension									
Healthcare and Family Welfare	09	32	59	05	19	76	04	19	77
Suno-Kahani	32	42	26	20	19	61	16	16	68
Sports programme	18	17	65	22	22	56	16	16	66
F&H programme	38	42	20	20	28	52	15	22	63
Shramik Log	40	36	24	22	28	50	20	18	62
Yuv Vani	40	36	24	22	28	50	20	18	62
Bal-sabha/Chawa Sabha	12	20	68	10	18	72	03	08	89
Grihlaxmi/Gharni Sabha	14	18	68	03	13	84	14	08	88
Quiz	16	25	59	12	20	68	10	08	82
Educational B'Cast	03	10	87	–	12	88	–	08	92

	Rania (Remote)			Mandar (Less Remote)			Hatma (Urban)		
University B'Cast	03	09	88	–	10	90	–	06	94
Hindi Literature	04	08	88	–	08	92	–	06	94
Average figure	19	25	56	11	19	70	09	13	78
III. Entertainment Dimension									
Radio play/Prahsan	28	27	45	16	17	67	12	14	74
Light-music	20	20	60	06	10	84	04	08	88
Classical-music	–	07	93	–	02	98	–	02	98
Hindi film songs	68	32	–	80	20	–	70	30	–
Devotional songs	16	20	64	12	12	76	10	12	78
Patriotic songs	22	20	58	16	16	68	10	10	80
Folk Music	42	30	28	30	30	40	15	25	60
Short Story & Poems	16	20	64	–	10	90	02	08	90
Ram Charit Manas Gaan	29	20	51	20	20	60	08	12	80
Average figure	27	22	51	21	15	64	15	13	72

I. The listening of Pradesik Samachar and National News Bulletins in Hindi is quite high in all field areas. The respondents in the VRL (Very Regular Listener) category is highest in Rania (44). In case of Mandar and Hatma the figures are 20 and 22 respectively which is no doubt a good score. Weekly Language Bulletin is another important popular programme. The respondents in the VRL category is again highest in Rania (58). In case of Mandar and Hatma the score is 32 and 20 respectively. About Sansad Samikshya, Radio News Reel, Smachar Dhwanichitra, and recorded item of Question Hour in Parliament, it is clear from Table 7.2 that the listening gradually decreases as one moves from Rania to Mandar and Mandar to Hatma. Higher frequency of listening is not the sole criterion for development. Information dissemination should be supported by more access to resources.

Weekly language news bulletins in five regional (tribal and non-tribal) languages have brought about a new era in language broadcasting in this part of Jharkhand which is also evident from the table. Introduced on 19.11.94, it is an important milestone in the history of broadcasting here in Ranchi. The language dialects include Nagpuri, Kurukh, Ho, Mundari and Santhali.

The average percentage score in the VRL category is highest in Rania (33%) and lowst in Hatma (15%) in the informative dimension. The average percentage score in the CL category is highest in Hatma (65%) and lowest in Rania (40%). In Mandar, it is 63 per cent. In the RL category, the score is available in the descending order from Rania to Hatma. In Rania it is 27 per cent, in Mandar it is 21 per cent and in Hatma it is 20 per cent.

Pardesik Samachar, *National Hindi Bulletins*, *Weekly Language Bulletins* are having good scores in all field areas (in the VRL category). In Rania, the frequency is 44,40 and 58. In case of Mandar, it is 20, 28 and 32 and in the case of Hatma, it is 22, 32 and 20. In the urban places, the migrated tribals with the process of sanskritization are getting less language or dialect conscious. On the other hand, they are able to get information from various sources in the advanced literary languages (Hindi and English).

II. In the category of Informative and Educative Programme, it is noticed that the Special Audience Programmes *i.e.* Youth programme, Shramik log and Farm and Home programme register high listening in all field areas. It is again highest in Rania. These are all programmes of evening transmission. During evening hours *i.e.* 5 p.m. to 8 p.m., the listenership is highest in Rania. Being a remote place people prefer to go to bed early in the evening. The story of Mandar and Hatma is somewhat different. The people here wake up till 10 p.m. and don't sleep so early as that of Rania and therefore, they have scope to tune their radio sets till 10 p.m. or onwards. As the CBS programmes reach these places, usually people change their meters for Vivid Bharti programmes after listening Pradeshik Samachar (7.30 p.m.).

Running Commentary particularly cricket seems to be very popular programme in all field areas. The response is highest in Mandar, a place considered to be less remote. Bal Sabha and Chawa Sabha are weekly programme which have got comparatively low frequency of listening Educational and University Broadcast and Hindi literature register the lowest frequency in all field areas. 'Suno-Kahani' the newly introduced folk tale programme (3.4.95) which is being broadcast during morning transmission in all days has gained popularity particularly in the remote area of Rania. A fortnightly programme 'Quiz' is comparatively a popular programme particularly among youth.

Health and Family Welfare Programmes which are broadcast at different times are not very popular programmes as shown in the table. The listening is highest in Rania and it gradually decreases as one moves from Rania to Mandar and Mandar to Hatma.

As far as Informative and Educative Programme is concerned, the average percentage score in the VRL category is highest in Rania (19%) and lowest in Hatma (9%). It is 11 per cent in Mandar. The percentage score in the CL category is highest in Hatma (78%) and lowest in Rania (56%). It is 70 per cent in Mandar. In the category of Informative and Educative dimension, the score is again available in the descending order from Rania to Hatma as far as RL frequency is concerned. In Rania, it is 25 per cent, in Mandar, is 19 per cent, and in Hatma it is 13 per cent. The establishment of F&H units to provide relevant, timely and local area specific information has proved to be very useful. The medium can derive great satisfaction at having gradually own the confidence of traditionally conservative farmers and helping them through the use of new and improved techniques, to diversify crops and to achieve higher production with obvious economic advantage to themselves.

III. The frequency of listening Hindi film songs is highest in all field areas. It is interesting to note that in a remote place like Rania where the inhabitants usually like their folk songs are equally attracted towards Hindi Film songs. It can be noted that the position of Folk music listening comes next to film songs in all field areas. It is highest in Rania and lowest in Hatma. Hatma being a place of mixed population and situated in the heart of Ranchi, the tribals here are more inclined for other electronic media *i.e.* video films and other satellite channels. Devotional and patriotic songs, Hindi Short-story and Light music programmes register moderate response in all field area while classical music is having the lowest response. The frequency of listening of radio plays is comparatively higher in all field area (Table 7.2).

In the entertainment dimension, the average percentage score in the VRL category is highest in Rania (27%) and lowest in Hatma (15%). It is 21 per cent in Mandar. The percentage score in the CL category is highest in Hatma (72%) RL. In Mandar, it is 64 per cent. In the RL category, the average percentage score is available in the descending manner from Rania to Hatma (22%, 15%, and 13%).

Hindi film songs being the most important source of entertainment in Mandar (score is 80), the number of radio-sets was observed to be quite high in comparision to other places.

The film songs have got maximum listenership in all field areas and among all age groups and the people are found to have developed opinion about particular film only after hearing it's music from radio. The programme 'Chitralok' broadcast from Commercial Broadcasting Service contains latest film song; which is well received at Mandar and Hatma. The Commercial Channel is popular in both the places. It is also observed that the direct influence of broadcasting is greater among those sections of the population who are more exposed to other media. However, even those with little exposure are affected by broadcasting in indirect ways. Information, ideas and values originating in the media acquire currency by a process of diffusion. The respondents both in Hatma and Mandar are found to be regular listener of CBS (Commercial Broadcasting Service). Because of it's low power transmitter, the people of Rania can't monitor Ranchi CBS. But they can monitor Commercial channels of other high frequencies including National channel for listening film songs. There are some popular serials which have been introduced in radio recently, had mixed reactions. Ram Charit Manas Gaan is comparatively popular than Manav Ka Vikas and Dehlij which are now off in the AIR.

As the tribals are having more exposure to outside society and mass communication, their inclination to their own mother tongue is gradually decreasing. Tribals in Rania wish to listen more programmes in Sadri, Hindi an Mundari. While in Mandar, they aspire for more language based programmes in Sadri, Hindi and Kurukh programmes. Hatma and Mandar, almost all the respondents are of opinion that they can understand Hindi and Sadri. A number of people also understand Mundari language.

There are four tribal languages (Kurukh, Mundari Santhali and Ho) in Chotanagpur which are in dire need of patronage. It is, therefore, very important to promote language of the major tribes through this powerful electronic media.

In Hatma, the respondent in the CL category are of opinion that poor programme quality and access to other media channels are important reasons for poor listening of radio programmes while in the case of Mandar, over-burden of work, more interest for other media, poor programme quality and inability to afford cells are some of the important reasons. In case of Rania, the people don't have choice to modern mass media except radio. Therefore, the respondents here are almost silent about programme quality. Since most of them are having very poor standard of living, it is difficult on their part to purchase cells regularly for their transistor sets. They attribute poor reception quality and over burden of work life as important reasons for their casual listening.

Since 1989, it has been regular feature in South Bihar now Jharkhand to experience frequent power cuts and load shedding.

In the countryside, most of the villages remain without electricity throughout the year. This has been an important reason of good listening to radio programmes even in Ranchi city and other urban places.

The extent of exposure to national and international news on the radio is relatively higher among those also have same influence in the village, *i.e.* school teachers, the frequent urban migrators and the employed class.

AWARENESS

Communication is a complex process of information and influence. As such, it is seen as an essential component of development strategy. Traditional research in this area identifies five stages of diffusion process : awareness, interest, evaluation, trial and adoption. People are generally aware of development activities through various media like radio, television, film shows, newspapers, journals, posters, wall paintings, extension staff, village officials, and non-officials, NGOs and the general public. Development information is seen to percolate through every possible medium but in different ways. It is true that overall development of an area is certainly related with its mass media exposure.

This section aims at assessing awareness of development activities among tribals belonging to the three field areas. Awareness of development is a requisite of the adoption process. Listening behaviour is not exactly awareness.

The data on developmental activities indicate that information does not always result in action. Difference is seen not only between awareness and practice, but even among levels of awareness on different subjects. People are generally aware of development activities through various media like radio, TV, Film shows, news papers, magazines, posters, wall paintings, extension, staff, village officials and non-officials and the general public. In this study, in Rania (Remote) and in Mandar (Less remote) most of the respondents are deprived of modern mass communication channels except radio. In Hatma, maximum respondents in the category of Youth and Heads are service holders and other respondents are almost equally divided in other occupation classifications. In Rania and Mandar, the respondents in the category of Youth and Heads mostly belong to the class of agriculture labour, cultivator and unemployed youth.

Since each sample unit chosen for our study ought to be a radio listener, accessibility to different sources of communication could only, be enquired from those households having contact with the broadcasting media. As one moves from remote tribal area like Rania to semi-urban and urban areas, an individual is more likely to interact with other development media. It can be noted that higher socio-economic status is closely related with the degree of exposure to modern mass media.

In Hatma, unlike Rania, the inhabitants are having more exposure to modern mass mèdia *i.e.* newspaper and television. Few people are also noticed to have connections to cable channels. A number of people also subscribe magazines/journals. It is also observed that the people who can't afford a newspaper keep in touch with the neighbourhood so that they should not miss it. Few are the rickshaw pullers here who are better informed people. In Rania, awareness is seen to be very high for agricultural development activities while in Hatma, it is for local events. (Table 7.2)

As one moves from Hatma to Rania, the number of frequencies increase which speaks that the listening of radio is more common in remote places. The question was put to each individual as to whether he or she had awareness of a particular information from the broadcasting media.

1. The respondents belonging to Rania in the category of Youth (45%) and Heads (36%) are having maximum awareness on nutrition support for education. In all field areas, women don't have awareness of this particular information. In case of Mandar and Hatma, awareness is again higher among Youth and Heads. Respectively, the score is 29 per cent and 28 per cent for Mandar while it is 15 per cent and 13 per cent for Hatma. It can be mentioned that the figures are based on the response which is strictly based on radio listening. The people in all field areas consider radio primarily an entertainment media.

Table 7.3 : Distribution of respondents by awareness of developmental activities from radio

S. No.	Name of the scheme	Rania	Mandar	Hatma
1.	Nutrition Support for Education	22	18	08
2.	National Social Assistance Package	23	16	12
3.	Rural Group Life Insurance Scheme	22	16	10
4.	Indira Awas Yojana	49	32	20
5.	Tool Kits Distribution for artisans	16	15	10
6.	Employment Assistance Scheme	53	37	32
7.	Jawahar Rojgar Yojana	58	54	56
8.	Water-shed Development Project	19	13	09
9.	Revamped Public Distribution System	21	15	11
10.	Prime Minister's Rojgar Yojana	45	40	39
11.	Information about Small Scale and Cottage Industries	22	18	07
12.	Mahila Samridhi	50	42	33
13.	DWCRA	30	19	09
14.	Bihar Education Project	30	18	12
15.	Voluntary Social Work	25	18	10
16.	ICDS	48	40	30
17.	IRDP	54	37	23
18.	TRYSEM	44	32	30
19.	Panchayati Raj	60	50	41
20.	Family Welfare Campaign	72	70	54
21.	Bank Loan facilities	32	20	17
22.	Preservation of Environment	42	30	12
23.	Agricultural Schemes	58	60	28
24.	Social Legislation	38	28	20
		N=100	N=100	N=100

2. No body from the section of Women and Children is found to have information about National Social Assistance Package from this particular electronic media. It was not enquired if the respondents had information about the scheme from any other source. Here the Youth are having high reception. It is 36 per cent in Rania, 25 per cent in Mandar and 26 per cent in Hatma. Amongst Heads, the score is 33 per cent in Rania, 24 per cent in Mandar and 13 per cent in Hatma. There are a number of Aged people (29%) in Rania who have also information about this particular scheme. In a remote place like Rania, not only listening frequency is high but also people do take interest in radio listening.

Table 7.4 : Distribution of respondents by extent of awareness of developmental activities among different categories of respondents

S. No.	Name of the scheme	Field Area	Category of respondents					
			Children	Youth	Women	Heads	Aged	Total
1.	Nutrition Support for Education	Rania	2 (18%)	10 (40%)	–	8 (27%)	2 (14%)	22
		Mandar	1 (10%)	8 (29%)	–	8 (28%)	1 (7%)	18
		Hatma	–	4 (15%)	–	4 (13%)	–	08
2.	National Social Assistance Package	Rania	–	9 (36%)	–	10 (33%)	4 (29%)	23
		Mandar	–	7 (25%)	–	7 (24%)	2 (14%)	16
		Hatma	–	7 (26%)	–	4 (13%)	1 (8%)	12
3.	Rural Group Life Insurance Scheme	Rania	2 (18%)	8 32%)	–	10 (33%)	2 (14%)	22
		Mandar	–	7 (25%)	–	8 (28%)	–	16
		Hatma	–	5 (19%)	–	5 (16%)	–	10
4.	Indira Awas Yojana	Rania	03 (27%)	18 (72%)	06 (30%)	18 (60%)	4 (29%)	49
		Mandar	02 (20%)	12 (43%)	05 (26%)	10 (34%)	3 (21%)	32
		Hatma	02 (20%)	7 (26%)	4 (20%)	4 (13%)	1 (8%)	20
5.	Toolkits Disribution for Artisans	Rania	–	6 (24%)	–	06 (20%)	4 (29%)	16
		Mandar	–	8 (29%)	1 (5%)	4 (14%)	2 (14%)	15
		Hatma	–	4 (15%)	–	6 (19%)	–	10
6.	Employment Assistance	Rania	5 (45%)	25 (100%)	3 (15%)	14 (47%)	6 (43%)	53
		Mandar	–	15 (54%)	4 (21%)	12 (41%)	6 (29%)	37
		Hatma	–	12 (44%)	6 (30%)	12 (39%)	2 (17%)	32
7.	Jawahar Rojgar Yojana	Rania	5 (45%)	25 (100%)	4 (20%)	15 (50%)	9 (64%)	58
		Mandar	3 (30%)	20 (71%)	5 (26%)	20 (69%)	6 (43%)	54
		Hatma	3 (30%)	20 (74%)	7 (35%)	22 (71%)	4 (33%)	56
8.	Water Shed Development Project	Rania	–	07 (28%)	1 (05%)	08 (27%)	3 (21%)	19
		Mandar	–	07 (35%)	–	05 (17%)	1 (07%)	13

S. No.	Name of the scheme	Field Area	Category of respondents					
		Hatma	–	04 (15%)	–	04 (13%)	1 (08%)	09
9.	Revamped Public Distribution System	Rania	–	09 (36%)	1 (05%)	07 (23%)	4 (29%)	21
		Mandar	–	5 (18%)	02 (11%)	5 (17%)	03 (21%)	15
		Hatma	–	03 (11%)	–	06 (19%)	2 (17%)	11
10.	PM's Rojgar Yojana	Rania	–	25 (100%)	–	12 (40%)	4 (29%)	45
		Mandar	–	20 (71%)	2 (11%)	14 (48%)	4 (29%)	40
		Hatma	–	20 (74%)	4 (20%)	12 (39%)	3 (25%)	39
11.	Information about Small Scale and Cottage Industries and diff. Interpreneur schemes.	Rania	–	06 (24%)	2 (10%)	10 (33%)	4 (29%)	22
		Mandar	–	04 (14%)	3 (16%)	08 (28%)	3 (21%)	18
		Hatma	–	03 (11%)	1 (05%)	03 (10%)	–	07
12.	Mahila Samridhi Yojana	Rania	–	19 (76%)	6 (30%)	20 (67%)	5 (36%)	50
		Mandar	–	20 (71%)	6 (32%)	14 (74%)	2 (14%)	42
		Hatma	–	17 (63%)	3 (15%)	13 (42%)	–	33
13.	DWCRA	Rania	–	17 (68%)	2 (10%)	10 (33%)	1 (07%)	30
		Mandar	–	10 (36%)	1 (05%)	07 (24%)	1 (07%)	19
		Hatma	–	05 (19%)	2 (10%)	02 (06%)	–	09
14.	Bihar Education Project	Rania	2 (18%)	09 (36%)	3 (15%)	14 (47%)	2 (14%)	30
		Mandar	–	06 (21%)	–	09 (31%)	3 (21%)	18
		Hatma	01 (10%)	05 (19%)	1 (05%)	05 (16%)	–	12
15.	Voluntary Social Work and Social Action	Rania	–	10 (40%)	–	10 (33%)	5 (36%)	25
		Mandar	–	06 (21%)	–	09 (31%)	3 (21%)	18
		Hatma	–	04 (15%)	1 (5%)	05 (16%)	–	10
16.	ICDS	Rania	3 (27%)	20 (80%)	3 (15%)	20 (67%)	2 (14%)	48
		Mandar	03 (30%)	18 (64%)	4 (21%)	14 (48%)	1 (07%)	40
		Hatma	02 (20%)	16 (59%)	2 (10%)	10 (32%)	–	30

S. No.	Name of the scheme	Field Area	Category of respondents					
17.	IRDP	Rania	01 (9%)	22 (88%)	3 (15%)	26 (87%)	2 (14%)	54
		Mandar	01 (10%)	15 (60%)	1 (05%)	15 (52%)	5 (36%)	37
		Hatma	–	12 (44%)	2 (10%)	08 (26%)	1 (08%)	23
18.	TRYSEM	Rania	01 (09%)	20 (80%)	2 (14%)	18 (60%)	3 (21%)	44
		Mandar	01 (10%)	12 (43%)	7 (37%)	10 (34%)	3 (21%)	32
		Hatma	–	12 (44%)	3 (15%)	10 (32%)	5 (42%)	30
19.	Panchyati Raj	Rania	02 (18%)	23 (92%)	5 (25%)	20 (67%)	10 (71%)	60
		Mandar	02 (20%)	18 (64%)	5 (26%)	20 (69%)	5 (36%)	50
		Hatma	–	15 (56%)	6 (30%)	16 (52%)	4 (33%)	41
20.	Family Welfare Programme	Rania	04 (36%)	22 (88%)	10 (50%)	30 (100%)	06 (43%)	72
		Mandar	05 (50%)	25 (89%)	10 (53%)	25 (86%)	5 (36%)	70
		Hatma	04 (40%)	20 (74%)	7 (35%)	18 (58%)	5 (42%)	54
21.	Bank Loan Facilities	Rania	–	12 (48%)	2 (10%)	16 (53%)	02 (14%)	32
		Mandar	–	08 (29%)	2 (11%)	08 (28%)	02 (14%)	20
		Hatma	–	10 (37%)	2 (10%)	05 (16%)	–	17
22.	Preservation of Environment	Rania	–	20 (80%)	2 (10%)	18 (60%)	02 (14%)	42
		Mandar	–	12 (43%)	–	15 (79%)	3 (21%)	30
		Hatma	–	06 (22%)	–	06 (19%)	–	12
23.	Agricultural Schemes	Rania	02 (18%)	20 (80%)	3 (15%)	28 (93%)	05 (36%)	58
		Mandar	02 (20%)	22 (79%)	–	28 (97%)	8 (57%)	60
		Hatma	03 (30%)	10 (37%)	–	12 (39%)	3 (25%)	28
24.	Knowledge of Social Legislations/Social Security Measures	Rania	–	14 (56%)	1 (05%)	19 (63%)	04 (29%)	38
		Mandar	–	12 (43%)	1 (05%)	12 (41%)	3 (21%)	28
		Hatma	–	08 (30%)	–	10 (32%)	2 (17%)	20

Note : Percentage has been calculated with reference to number of respondents in a particular category as mentioned in Table 7.1

3. As far as Rural Group Life Insurance Scheme is concerned, the response is not different from above. In Rania, there is more awareness about the scheme.
4. About Indira Awas Yojana, the people of Rania are having maximum awareness in comparision to other field areas. The Youth of Rania are maximum in number (72%) who have awareness about this particular information followed by Heads belonging to the same place.
5. When asked about tool kits distribution for artisans the available score is highest in Rania (16 out of 100) and lowest in Hatma (10 out of 100). The Youth of Mandar and the old people in Rania register quite good response. As far as awareness of this particular scheme is concerned, it is almost nil among Children and Women while it is comparatively high among Youth of Mandar (29%) and Aged people in Rania (29%).
6. As expected, awareness of Employment Assistance Scheme is highest among Youth in the remote place. Almost all the respondents belonging to the category of Youth in Rania (100%) area aware of some of the employment schemes from radio. There are a host of reasons for their failure in adoption or finding an engagement for their own. Less qualification, poor infrastructure, poor family conditions and on the whole, poor-will-power are some of the important reasons. They are also disappointed by apathetic attitude of banking officials.
7. Jawahar Rojgar Yojana registers highest awareness level among Youth of Rania followed by Mandar and Hatma. Wide publicity is given to this programme particularly in F & H (Farm and Home) programme.
8. Awareness from radio about watershed development projects is higher among Youth and Adults followed by Aged people in all field areas. It is again minimum in Hatma and maximum in Rania.
9. My interviewees also reacted favourably about listening of Public Distribution Schemes from radio but their number was very less. 21 in Rania, 15 in Mandar and 11

in Hatma have understood this particular system from AIR, Ranchi.

10. PM's Rozgar Yojana is having largest awareness among Youth in Rania (100%). It is 71 per cent in Mandar and 74 per cent in Hatma. The Children and Women are having least information about this particular scheme. The Adults and Aged people too have information in all places.
11. Similarly 22 respondents from Rania, 18 from Mandar and 7 from Hatma confirm the fact that they do have awareness about small scale and cottage industries from their radio sets. Except children all groups have frequencies which can be seen in Table 7.4.
12. 50 out of 100 respondents in Rania, 42 out of 100 respondents in Mandar, 33 out of 100 respondents in Hatma have been able to hear about Mahila Samridhi Yojana. Here Women also have participation in the sense that about 30 per cent respondents from Rania, 32 per cent from Mandar and 15 per cent from Hatma have information about this particular scheme although they are outnumbered by other categories of respondents which include Youth and Adults.
13. About DWCRA, there is good information amongst the respondents particularly amongst the Youth in Rania. In Rania, respondents favourably opine that they have listened this particular welfare measure. It's number is 19 in case of Mandar and only 9 in case of Hatma.
14. The information about BEP (Bihar Education Project) is just moderate. In F&H programme, 'injore' was broadcast which included programmes on National Literacy Mission, Adult education and informal education for school going children and drop-outs. The score is maximum among adults in Rania (47%). Here Children and Women are also represented.
15. A lot of welfare activities are taken up by NGO's (Non-Governmental Organizations) in this tribal belt. From time-to-time, programmes are being recorded from experienced NGO's in different formats. Here the awareness about voluntary social work and different

social problems is noticeable amongst Adults and Youth and aged people. It's just moderate. In Rania, it is 40 per cent among Youth, 33 per cent among Adult and 36 per cent among Aged people. Similarly in Mandar, the response is 21 per cent among Youth, 31 per cent among Adults and 21 per cent among old people. In. case of Hatma, it is 15 per cent among Youth, 5 per cent among Women and 16 per cent among Adults.

16. When asked about ICDS (Integrated Child Development Schemes), good response was available from Youth (about 80 per cent in Rania, 64 per cent in Mandar and 59 per cent in Hatma) and Adults about 67 per cent in Rania 48 per cent in Mandar and 32 per cent in Hatma.
17. About IRDP (Integrated Rural Development Programme); there is good information amongst the respondents particularly belonging to the category of youth and adults in all field areas. Usually in F & H programme, regular comparing based programmes consisting of this kind of welfare schemes are aired.
18. 44 from Rania, 32 from Mandar and 30 from Hatma are the scores in the case of TRYSEM. Besides Adults and Youth, here there is also representation of Children, Women and Aged.
19. The respondents belonging to Rania in the category of Youth (92%) and Heads (67%) are having maximum awareness about Panchayati Raj. When compared field-wise, it is again Rania where the number is highest (60) followed by Mandar (50) and Hatma (41).
20. Different health awareness schemes include tips regarding methods of contraception, government facilities for birth control, balanced diet, causes and prevention of various diseases. Family welfare programme registers highest score in comparision to all other development programmes. Here all groups are represented. The score is all time higher and it is 72 in Rania, 70 in Mandar and 54 in Hatma. The figure shows that the listeners in all field areas have an inclination towards this particular programme and moreover, this programme is broadcast in all sections. The score is 100 per cent in Rania among

Adult respondents. Even Children and Women in all field areas are having scores.

21. Although there are multiple sources of information in the remote villages, it is observed that the people mostly relay on interpersonal communication when they hear some development message from credible source like radio. It is observed that illiterate and ignorant people mostly rely on opinion leaders and government officials for credit and subsidy. But they get all supporting information from time-to-time in radio programmes. Here, Table 7.4 shows that except Children all age groups have information about Bank loan facilities.
22. Particularly, Women are more involved in cutting of trees and deforestation in remote villages. This is a grave problem in the whole of Chotanagpur. It is evident from the fact that sometimes passenger trains reaching Ranchi Railway station carry more wood than human beings. A number of tribal young girls and adult women are involved in the race. After all, who is going to convince them when the legal and official machinery are all involved in exploiting them rather than discouraging them to stop cutting of trees. They are all ignorant, and poor people who don't possess even a radio set. If government provide them free radio sets, it may prove useful for them. This is an area where all available sources of information and communication have not yielded any result.

    Table 7.4 shows that there is more awareness amongst Youth and Adult population about environment conservation.
23. Different agricultural schemes include knowledge of chemical fertilizer and improved seed, pesticides/insecticides, improved implements, animal husbandry and scientific cultivation methods. As expected, the schemes have yielded more listening among Adults, Youth and Aged. people. Women and Children are having less awareness from this developmental information. In fact, radio has become a popular media for dissemination of

information and diffusion of agricultural and allied innovation for progressive farmers.

Of course, there is a big gap between learning and practice and this is due to a number of reasons. There is infrastructural problem and also the problem of resource. Utilisation of developmental inputs occurs mainly through agricultural programme broadcast in radio. It is also learnt that this special audience programme (F & H) has been able to retain it's listeners through broadcast of qualitative programmes since it's inception. It has a different world altogether which gives special focus on rural development. It is also learnt that the special audience programme has been able to retain it's listeners through broadcast of qualitative programmes since it's inception.

The Youth seem to be best informed and most enthusiastic among the five categories of respondents followed by adult population. There is also good listening among people who are old and consider themselves to be outdated while Women and Children are least informed respondents. In fact, this particular electronic media has a wide range of impact. It is more useful in a tribal village which is far away from the city where people usually don't have access to modern mass media.

24. In an attempt to uplift the socio-economic conditions of the rural population, the government has been taking up a number of steps such as initiating and highlighting some socially progressive legislations. The respondents were enquired about different social legislations and social security measures while response was quite encouraging among Youth and Adults. It was minimum among Children, Women and Aged people in all the three fields areas.

REACTIONS ON DIFFERENT FUNCTION AREAS

The need of the hour is that the existing roles of radio can be further widened in view of the fast changing social scenario. Undiscovered potential areas can be brought into book so that there can be more involvement of the people at the grassroots level. Since radio is the fastest and cheapest medium of information, it is important to explore the areas for greater listenability, participation and feedback. The opinion of the people in the countryside still holds good that what radio speaks is nothing but truthful information.

Many villagers mostly illiterate tribals follow even the simplified form of technical language used in the broadcasts. Others who can follow the language are troubled by the analytic mode of presentation, the unaccustomed categories of discourse and the impersonal nature of the radio. It has been observed that discussion often takes place spontaneously among villagers after they have heard a broadcast. In some cases, a few of them challenge the validity of some of the suggestions made in the broadcast on the basis of experience. Sometimes, the criticism stems from an incorrect understanding of the broadcast.

For any kind of technological innovation, cultivators prefer to rely upon practical demonstrations because their results can be more easily verified and the risk of uncertainty avoided.

Another important social function of this powerful electronic media is in the economic sphere. The information regarding the market conditions is very important to develop the economy. Secondly, advertisements through radio brings the sellers and the buyers together. The advertisements stimulate mass consumption and thus stimulate, in their turn, mass production. But in a tribal society advertisements have got very limited influence on the mass.

Reactions on different function areas speak of the social relevance of the broadcasting service. In each area, we get different kinds of response. The opinion sought has been divided into three types of responses, *i.e.* it Agree, Disagree and can't say. Rania being a remote place and most of the respondents being illiterate, here maximum respondents failed to give any response. It is followed by Mandar (less remote) and Hatma.

It is observed that as one moves from the city to the remote place, more people avoid to respond to the queries about different functional areas. There is more disagreement to different functions amongst respondents who are more literate and educated and who hold higher occupation.

Table 7.5 : Reactions on different function areas of radio

	Rania			Mandar			Hatma		
	Agree	Disagree	Can't say	Agree	Disagree	Can't say	Agree	Disagree	Can't say
(1) Radio is control-led by the govt. and it suppresses informa-tion. It is less credible.	05	66	29	09	69	22	21	61	18
(2) The Medium is particularly impo-rtant at the time of crises	72	-	28	60	10	20	78	06	16
(3) Very Useful to mo-nitor time	68	12	20	45	35	20	42	43	15
(4) Promote culture	67	05	28	60	21	19	50	35	15
(5) Promote commu-nal harmony and national integra-tion	55	15	30	55	30	15	40	46	14
(6) Sensitize people about urgent issues of society	62	14	24	55	16	29	46	44	10
(7) Radio is the fas-test source of in-formation	75	05	20	65	10	25	55	28	17
(8) Radio is the best modern entertain-ment media.	95	05	-	80	20	-	72	28	-
(9) Radio educates	56	18	26	51	29	20	42	48	10
(10) Radio advertise-ments are more credible	70	05	25	59	20	21	43	46	11

In recent years, ecological cultivation and environment have become issues of great concern. Land, water and forest degradation are serious threat to the livelihood of millions of people in our country. Deforestation and less output from agriculture have also endangered the very survival of our tribal people. Such degradation has caused poverty and uncontrolled exploitation of our resources. There is a close connection between poverty and environmental degradation. The pattern of ecological change is predominant after the change from a pastoral economy to agriculture. The area is gradually turning into desert because the land surface is rugged and undulating ranging from flat lands to almost steep slopes. Most of the tribals in Jharkhand are peasants, marginal farmers and agricultural labourers. Most of the marginal farmers are giving up farming and turning into agricultural labour due to faulty method of cultivation. The need for education and awareness for preserving the ecology and environment for the well being of the tribals is keenly felt.

Low agricultural productivity, limited potential for further growth and fragile ecological balance etc. are visible in tribal areas. Increased use of chemical fertilizers and pesticides have produced harmful effects on the productivity of their land. The researcher is of the opinion that in broadcasting media, there are regular programming on sustainable farming. Simultaneously knowledge of scientific methods can be imparted for sustainable agriculture development. In this connection, it can be mentioned that from time to time a number of agriculture scientists and experts are booked for studio based programmes.

The health and medical problems of the tribal villages particularly in the countryside are basically malnutrition, malaria, TB, infectious diseases, various water borne diseases and drug addiction etc. These problems are aggravated by illiteracy, ignorance and poverty. Here radio can arrange wide publicity about different health education schemes and also about health camps, which are usually taken place from time to time in far off places. Most recently radio played quite an important role in pulse polio movement.

Some of the tribal people who happen to be regular radio listeners opine that most of the programmes are not produced in a professional manner. News bulletins can't be trusted and on many occasions people listen to BBC for news about India and it is a sad situation. But in recent times, Samachar Prabhat and Morning News broadcast at 8 a.m. and 8.15 a.m. respectively are certainly good innovations presented in new formats. The news are not solely mere government opinions in these days. The news is more qualitative and credible. Credibility is lost sometimes because the field situation is fraught with problems unanticipated by communication agencies. The field relevance of information is of crucial importance here. Relevance and credibility of information, and learning and application by people are all linked.

Crisis and disasters are unexpected and sudden situations about which no anticipation can be made. To convey decisions, steps to be taken, impending dangers and prior warning and post crisis relief measures a full proof communication system is of paramount importance. In this context, it is only the electronic media, which can play a very important part to accomplish the desired result. Radio communication has assumed immense significance during disasters, calamities like flood, cyclone and now communal violence. Radio is the first to carry the information.

A good number of respondents opine that they listen to radio much frequently in certain situations like national calamities, general elections, political developments and sports commentaries.

In radio, programmes are usually fed at right time and the people without having watch of their own can monitor their time just listening still music from a distance. Particularly in a remote place like Rania, the respondents reply quite affirmatively.

AIR has helped us to keep our culture intact. It celebrates all important occasions throughout the year without any communal bias. Besides, coverage of festivals of different communities, this media is very careful while celebration of important birthdays and anniversaries of famous personalities. While in Hatma, 35 respondents have reservations above this role of radio, in case of Rania, it is 5 per cent only. The radio has been quite effective in bringing about change in the village communities on institutional and cultural areas of interest.

Being a government medium, radio gives wide coverage to important rituals and festivals which are celebrated by people of all faiths. Patriotic songs are regularly broadcast by all AIR stations. Important occasions connected with myrter's days, freedom fighters, national heros, religious leaders and festivals of all communities are given due weightage. The score is highest in Rania and lowest in Hatma.

The medium sensitizes people about urgent issues of society which include weather reports, market rates, information on different transport services, information about the special schemes launched by the government and development support communication. 62 respondents in Rania, 55 in Mandar and 46 in Hatma respond quite positively about the function.

Radio is by far the fastest electronic medium for millions of the people in the countryside. This fact is acknowledged by 75 respondents in Rania, 65 in Mandar and 55 in Hatma. Information is probably most important function. The power of radio to inform is almost incredible. Perhaps the most important information of all is information about the government.

It can be concluded that radio is the best entertaining media and 95 per cent of respondents in Rania approve it. Group listening is still prevalent in Rania. In Ambatoli (Mandar) and Hatma, group listening is hardly seen.

One question was very receptive for the respondents in the sense that no body tried to avoid it's response . In all field areas, the response was spontaneous. Entertainment is by far the biggest service of All India Radio.

One of the significant features of Indian tribal society today is that the tribal people living both in the countryside and in the urban areas now realise the value of educating their children. Due to helplessness, most of the children become drop-outs at a very early age. Particularly in the countryside, poverty is the singular cause of this grave misfortune.

The study carried out by the researcher in Rania and Mandar reveals the fact that a girl child is much more vulnerable. In Rania, it was very difficult to nab a female listener. Tribal women do hard work in the field from early morning to sunset besides usual cooking assignments. The researcher either found them with the hordes of cattles/goats or with HANDIA (a liquid rice bear) forming a parallel line near weekly markets. Mostly, they are impoverished lot suffering from malnutrition, exploitation and ignorance. In such a situation, radio is certainly an useful media. It educates people against social evils and superstitions. The result depends on the receptivity and adoption level of a particular individual.

It can be mentioned that more than eighty per cent of advertisements, which are aired in radio are commercial in nature. Social advertisements and slogons are very less in number A person having knowledge of different brands of a soap or tooth paste or consumer durables, sometimes feels important of himself so also a small or petty businessman having his shop at rural roads cross point who rushes to town or sends message to acquire some collection of the latest brand.

It is observed that in remote area, radio advertisements seem to be more credible. Gradually it decreases as the message reaches in an urban place. Since radio advertisement has got very powerful influence, it is important to boost up social advertisements on radio in the place of commercial advertisements In remote tribal regions, people might fall prey to claims of the advertisers particularly when the message is clothed in attractive slogans. The ability of the uneducated, unexposed mind to discriminate in a similar situation can well be imagined.

Bar Diagram showing average score of different dimensions

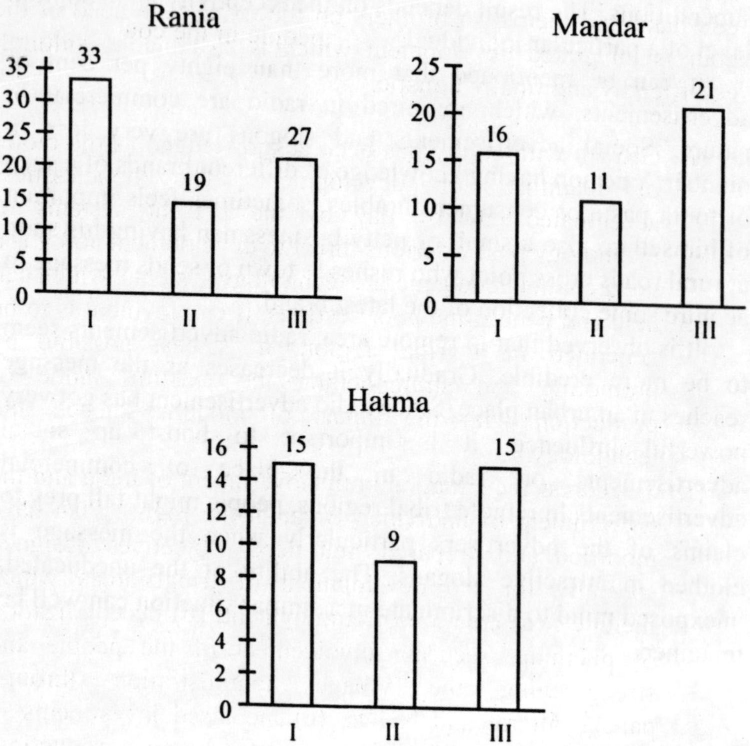

I. Information Programmes
II. Information and Educative Programmes
III. Entertainment Programmes

Figure 1 : VRL (Very Regular Listener) Category

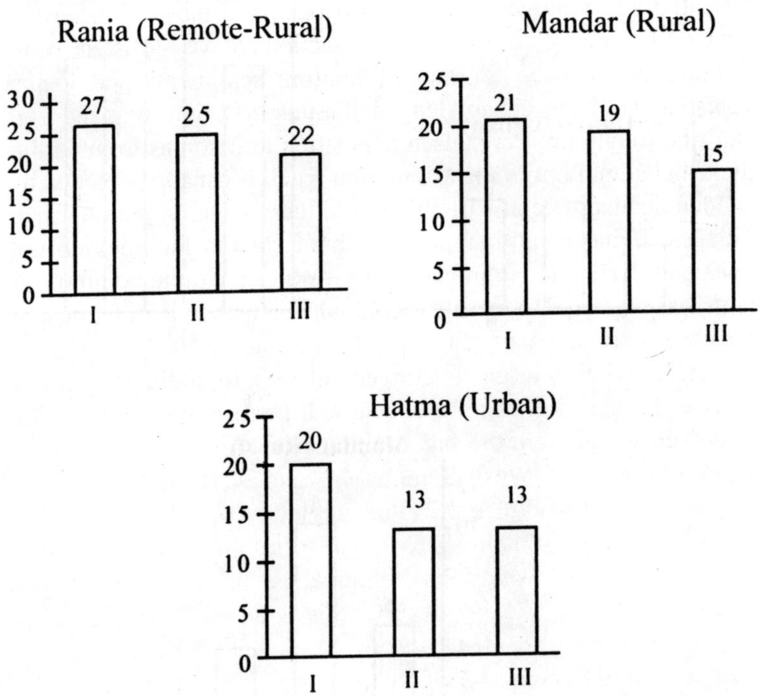

Figure 2 : RL (Regular Listener) Category

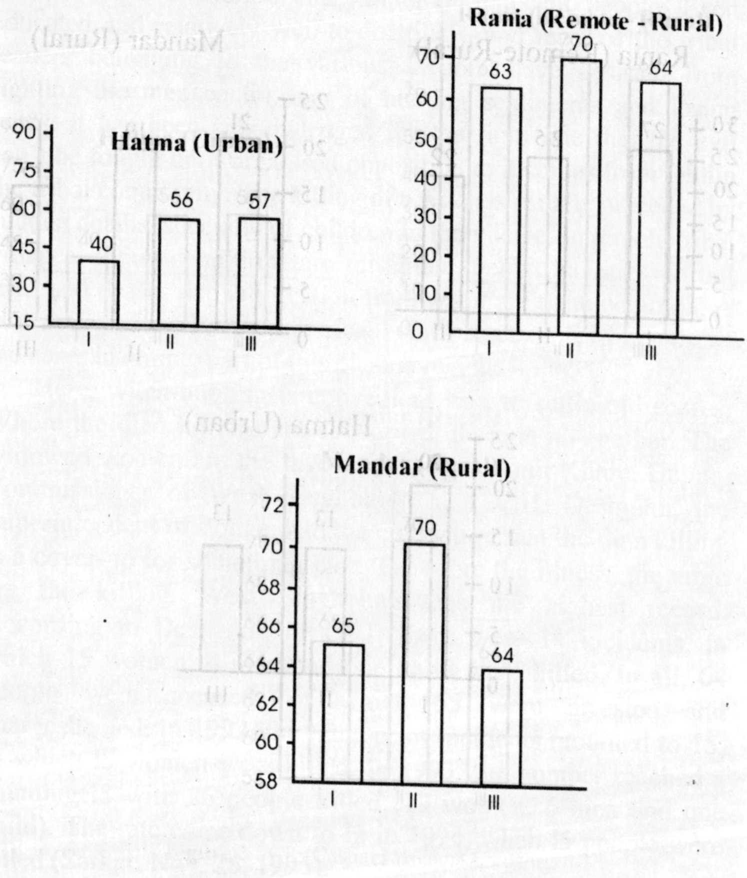

Figure 3 : CL (Casual Listener) Category

8

FINDINGS

There has to be an increase in the field based programmes so that broadcasting is not reduced to a one way traffic from the studio to the listener and the listeners should also have adequate opportunity to their views.

Success of the rural or tribal development schemes depends upon proper formulation of the communication policy.

An effective communication strategy for the tribal people may include the following :

(a) Conscientisation of audience and source;
(b) Democratisation of the communication process; and
(c) Setting up of local media councils.

This chapter takes note of the views of the respondents of the category of experts along with some general suggestions by the researcher.

The time has come to evolve a new communication strategy which takes into account the felt needs of the people, peculiar nature of land and people in different areas, constant monitoring and necessary follow up action. The strategy should lay stress on interaction between the government, voluntary agencies, the beneficiaries and the media.

Experts Report

Through my schedule, which was separately designed for media experts, I tried to collect opinion of some important people in and around Ranchi city having concern for tribal development. Attempt was also made to include some of the media people who are knowledgeable in their respective fields.

(i)	Members of Programme Advisory Boards (AIR)	06
(ii)	Tribal Social and Political Activists	05
(iii)	Anthropologists	03
(iv)	Few people from media which included editors of local press, Station Director and programme executive (Farm and Home) of AIR, Ranchi	05
(v)	Tribal friends who were able to speak on their problem areas	05
(vi)	Tribal artists and radio performers	06
	Total members	30

My schedule meant for the expert category consisted of mostly open ended questions on tribal life and tribal culture, tribal economy and standard of living, participation in broadcasting media, quality of programmes and language broadcast, different function areas of broadcasting and control of radio.

The media experts strongly endorse that cultural activity is an effective tool for including concepts of freedom, equality and justice. The cultural environment of India, particularly in the tribal pockets, lent itself excellently to these goals. The experts uniformly emphasise on inclusion of traditional contemporary cultural elements in broadcasting. There is need for preserving, documenting these aspects of rural and tribal cultural traditions which are in danger of extinction, particularly our heritage which has been sustained through oral communication. “Suno Kahani”, the recently introduced short story broadcast from AIR Ranchi every day during morning transmission is just wonderful. It is based on folk tales characterising environment, human values, truthfulness and morality. It is fine to listen all such entertaining programmes in the format of stories. AIR, Ranchi will preserve or document for the first time such an interesting endeavour. The stories are of several generations old and no body knows the original story teller.

Folk media are personal forms of entertainment and communication. This is important because behavioural changes are most easily brought about by personal interaction: These forms of arts are parts of the way of life of a community and provide acceptable means of bringing development issues into the community on it's own terms.

The present level of live performances in the shapes of invited audience programmes are not adequate, say the experts. They put too much importance on integrating electronic media with traditional and folk media for maximum efficiency. Instead of holding the invited audience programmes in city capitals or district headquarters, it is more desirable to organise them in panchayat level and in remote tribal pockets. The present practice is that maximum number of invited audience programmes are staged in urban auditoriums and maximum beneficiaries are non-tribals.

It's true that the tribal people continue to rely on human an oral communication. As far as modern mass media ar concerned, their effect on the bulk of the tribal population is ver insignificant. What's required for development is nc unregulated and so called free flow of information but optioni doses of communication, which might act as a support to an nourish the development process. The experts opine th considerable research and development work and action oriente studies need to be devised urgently to design optional, low cos human oriented communication system for this region.

Programme must be audience oriented. In order to produc an effective programme, a programme man needs to know wh the target audience/listeners are. For communicatio effectiveness, research from time to time; feedback abou response of the listeners and need identification of the targe listeners are very much desirable. The experts speak about th significance of research in the context of programme production.

The programme broadcast is able to stimulate improvemen in the present level of awareness, knowledge, attitudes, and favourable behaviour of the target audience. How to attract listenership to radio programmes is another major issue. The picture of Rania is different from Mandar. In the fast changing media scenario in the country, there is speculation about the survival and credibility of this great mother institution.

The experts strongly endorse radio as an informative and entertainment media for people living in the country side. They also opine that as a time monitor and particularly at the time of crisis situations, it's listening goes up.

The reactions of media experts for more qualitative programmes were clearly noticeable. Need identification of the people at the grassroots level through audience research cell of AIR from time to time invites overwhelming support by them. The listeners letters may be suggestive for conducting audience research among targeted listeners and on the basis of audience research report, there can be change in the fixed point chart. The provision is that the fixed point chart can be amended in every six month. The media experts strongly agree to the proposition of broadcast of important examination results, coverage of local sports, broadcast of competitive examination results, setting of radio clubs and radio forums in tribal pockets, introducing motivational schemes as in doordarshan, holding of useful competitions at school/college levels, and setting up of low power stations in tribal pockets.

This particular media should broadcast less about party politics and the corporate world and more about what ordinary Indian citizens are doing to better their lives. More time in transmission should be devoted to news of social developments of the people and the broadcast should be both continuous and in depth.

Community listening has failed in most part of the country. In Chotanagpur, there is no provision of community listening as found during field work. Farm Radio Forums also do not function here. Findings indicate that radio is behind other media in influencing farmers to adopt new techniques of farming. Demonstration and personal contact with village level workers and opinion leaders are far more important than listening to radio. To some extent, this is because the programmes are not always very lively eventhough some of them are very good. There is need of greater feedback and participation. Everywhere it is recognised that the centralised systems of mass communication is useless unless regional and local systems of communication are developed.

Communication potential among tribals of Chotanagpur is reasonably high. In Mandar, the Oraon speaking community are able to speak Sadri and Hindi; while the tribals of Hatma who are bit heterogeneous in nature, speak both Mundari, Sadri and Hindi. The Oraon Community here also know Mundari. In Hatma, most of the tribal inhabitants are migrants from remote parts of Chotanagpur. In Rania, only some people were found to be monolingual. Others could speak Sadri and Hindi. It was found that the tribals uniformly have got interest to listen programmes in their respective mother-tongues.

Radio can play a very important role to revive folk music, folk dance and folk drama in different regions of the country. It is true that the traditional means of communication through folk culture flourish at the grassroots level. Tribal music is dying out and we must keep it alive. Ethnic feelings of tribes should not be always taken as separatism.

What radio needs to do is to make a suitable balance between the credibility with responsibility and the credibility with objectivity. In a developing nation like India, particularly in the context of tribals, to appreciate and practice objective responsibility and thereby ensuring a greater degree of credibility should be the primal urge, whether it be a government controlled medium. Programmes based on creativity and professionalism should replace the present form of broadcasting.

Mass media can't win against traditional attitudes unless they are reinforced by personal influence. In this connection, it is important to popularise the stock characters in radio who usually claim popularity in the countryside. People know them by name who happen to be compel of rural special audience programmes.

The youth clubs existing in panchayat and village level can be encouraged to produce programmes at regular intervals, which are of local importance and may be cultural, entertaining and informative. An unemployed youth being a member of a club will enjoy the status of a casual production assistant. As the term comes, each club will be authorised to dispatch a production of it's own to the local radio station and as such instead of few urbanites, benefit will reach to grassroots level If such project becomes successful, Mahila Samities' functioning at village level can be taken up simultaneously.

The experts overwhelmingly support the concept of local radio–particularly in tribal pockets where there is greater scope of development communication.

Few important points were raised regarding the quality of programming as well as the decentralisation of the potential broadcasting media. Need identification of the people at the grassroots level through continuous audience research are stressed. The remote areas having less contact with urban places should be preferably covered. The requirements of people particularly those of the tribals in difficult area of South Bihar are quite different. Imagine the plateau area where there is poor transportation and communication network, no electricity, no access to modern mass media and the places still unknown to the outsiders. Rania is such kind of place, which has been covered by the researcher. It is well known a fact that Jharkhand houses about two lakhs population of tribals who have been declared as primitive by the government. Their exposure to modern mass media is very insignificant. Hence their awareness level is very low.

At present, the percentage of OB based programme is quite low. Special emphasis should be given on coverage of out side programmes particularly in rural areas as these kind of programmes not only increase the awareness level of listeners but also their involvement in programmes. OB based programmes do not exceed 5 percent of the total broadcasting hours in AIR Ranchi while in local radio stations (Hazaribag, Chaibasa and Daltanganj), it may be just above 5 percent. At a time when there is too much emphasis on human resource development, radio being an institution of learning can take up various training and development activities with the help of programme officers who can work as effective co-ordinators.

Provision of fixed chunck for grievance handling with public servants and inter-ministerial co-operation should be given more emphasis. Departments of Agriculture, Energy, Rural Development, Health and Family Welfare, Industry and HRD (Human Resource Development) should work with this potential media in close co-operation for appropriate and effective communication.

As opined by experts, in the language broadcast, Nagpuri should be given to priority as majority of the tribals use the medium as link language. More importantly, tribals as well as the sadans are emotionally involved with the dialect so much that they feel at ease to interact with others in Nagpuri and therefore, there is immense scope of broadcasting qualitative programmes in this particular dialect. While in the field work it was interesting to observe one remark from the tribal people when the researcher enquired about the programme having maximum listenership. The reply was, "We usually listen our own programmes, *i.e.* Hamari Dunia and Khetibari." Because of this dialect based programme the tribals identify this particular programme as their own.

Regional Language Media

When we talk about our regional language media, actually we talk about our huge masses. There is an urgent need for the regional language media to reshape itself in a proper manner for the well-being of the masses. The task is not different to our basic development programme. In the whole of Chotangpur, there is no circulation of any newspaper in regional or tribal languages.

Regional language media are suffering from many hindrances and contradictions. A poor tribal can't afford a newspaper. The cheapest medium is radio, which can promote language communication. Few experts opine that the present broadcast in five tribal languages should continue but in the place of broadcast of non-tribal languages, only Nagpuri (Sadri) should be the medium of broadcast. The four non-tribal languages are, Panchpargania, Khortha, Nagpuri and Kurmali and all languages are close to Hindi and Nagpuri.

About half of the scheduled tribes in India according to a survey have changed their traditional languages and registered non-tribal languages as their mother tongue. This is all due to increasing urbanisation and migration. Planning for these languages should include the mechanism through which the languages are dying out and the second is to evolve suitable measures to check their decline. A language without much literary tradition may not survive in the modern age, because contacts between those speaking folk languages and those speaking advanced languages are increasing. The new generations among tribal groups find that their languages are incapable of coping with the demands of modern knowledge. Such a situation invariably leads to a language shift. Had there been scripts of their language; and had the teaching in their own language been possible, such a situation would not have arisen. The identification of linguistic area for each tribal dialect is important for planning. Then it will be quite an easier task for a local radio station for programme planning and programme production. There are five major tribal languages in the belt and four non-tribal languages which require patronage. In this regard; more invited audience programmes in regional languages will be quite productive. Since its inception in the year 1957, AIR, Ranchi has recognised nine regional dialects for the purpose of programme broadcast which is certainly an important contribution.

Inventory of Folk Artists

A tribal's culture is so strong that it is very difficult to part with it even if there is more exposure to modern life.

The search for appropriate, relevant and honoured methods of evoking popular participation have to be considered at the earliest.

While interviewing it was observed that there are good number of people who claim to have, expertise in folk music and folk art. Due to lack of patronisation and the younger generation's diminishing interest, their interest may not survive more. There is no denying of the fact that Chotanagpur is culturally very rich endowed with an unique quality of simplicity and it's rich cultural heritage ought to be preserved at any cost. The folk-culture of indigenous tribes is dying out and has become diminishing art forms.

In order to revive them, local radio stations in tribal pockets can play a meaningful role. Through invited audience programmes, live audition and studio audition, the emerging artists can be encouraged. The present system of regional and capital AIR stations are incapable of eliciting skilled performance. Therefore, inventory of folk artists ought to be maintained at all levels of broadcasting. When there is requisition of artists from other AIR stations and different organisations, the process may help the station to recommend suitable groups or individual artists. The present system is not very scientific. Database of artists can be maintained by AIR.

Down to Earth Character

The weekly market is the most important mode of communication in tribal micro-region. It is not just a place for economic activity, but has a multipurpose role in the shaping of day-to-day life of tribal people. Besides the weekly markets, the festivals and folklores have got important bearing for the tribal people. The best course of effective communication in a tribal area like Rania is to make use of the traditional media in a more purposeful manner. Therefore, integrating of electronic media that is radio with that of traditional media can yield desired output. Conveying of message through tribal folk songs, taking up different development projects and disseminating information at a place very close to their place of living, monitoring and feedback are some of the measures that can be taken up by regional as well as local radio stations.

Thus the present system of centralised broadcasting can't satisfy the urges, aspirations and expectations of the people because of the multiplicity of the language and diversity of culture. The central and regional systems of broadcasting need to be supplied by local system of broadcasting in the dialects and idioms of the locals. Local Radio is a new concept in Indian broadcasting. Each of the station serving a small area will be basically utility service and reach right into the heart of the community which will use the microphone to reflect and enrich it's life and artistic expression. What distinguishes local radio from the regional network will be it's down to earth, intimate and inhibited approach and programmes will be area specific. They will be flexible and spontaneous to enable the station to function as the mouth-piece of the local community. It will demolish the division between the broadcaster and the audience.

It is learnt that at present, the functioning of local radio stations in different parts of the country has not been able to stick to its ideals set earlier. So far, it has only been able to attend a very partial success.

Radio through invited audience programmes can popularize for example tractors, electric pumps, small entrepreneurship and employment programmes with the co-operation of state government officials functioning at the grassroots levels in remote tribal pockets. It can utilise it's potential medium to inform the participants or beneficiaries much in advance. Radio succeeded in family planning campaign, AIDS awareness and more recently Pulse-Polio awareness programme. Needless to mention that it is blessed with unlimited potential to give boost to wide variety of human resources development activities.

Democratisation and Decentralisation

Radio's objective of bringing about social transformation and development in a pluralistic and traditional society has met only partial success. The Information and Broadcasting Ministry and other concerned have to wake up and make the electronic media truly viable and vibrant, which can cater to the diverse language groups and classes. Indeed it is a challenging task to meet the information needs of all strata in a tribal society, while there are fifteen major languages in India, hundreds of dialects are spoken in India. It's perhaps difficult to allot time for tribal languages broadcast in a radio station broadcasting primarily programmes in a major language. Say, in Chotanagpur tribal belt, when AIR Ranchi is having transmission in Mundari language, the Kuduk speaking people may switch off the set. There are nine regional languages, which are spoken by different tribals and Sadans (the original inhabitants of the tribal belt who are not tribals). Nagpuri is the only link language among them otherwise they don't have commonality as far as dialects are concerned. The question is how they are to be brought under the umbrella of information networks and who will produce programmes in their spoken language and in their idioms ?

Perhaps one of the answers to this lies in the principle of democratisation and decentralisation of infrastructure so as to include atleast one radio station in each district or block level in India particularly in tribal pockets. Only then the participation of all strata of people will be ensured and the fundamental right of people to be informed will become a reality. It will be quite appropriate to see that everything about programme, policy planning and production, be preferably worked out by the tribals for the tribals and of the tribals.

The programme planners, the programme producers, and the communicators can bring about an atmosphere of openness through sharing access to information with all targeted listeners. Only then the communications revolution can become relevant and meaningful.

Influential Factors

Radio listening is greatly influenced by a variety of factors. A sudden change in international, national and regional situations induces even an occasional listener of daily news to tune radio set regularly until the interest in the item is maintained. There might be some special programmes, which a person can tune in being inspired by frequent announcements done over radio. A lot depends on the mood of a listener. A sudden fall and rise in its listening curve may take place at any time. Language broadcast, news and musical programmes have got more attraction for the people.

Each individual is not having a set of his own. All members in a family can't be benefited equally from a single set. It is also found that people have not been able to establish contact with the media.

Making the Medium more Relevant

No doubt, TV programmes have effected very adversely radio listening among elite group, middle class and lower middle class. In countryside, the picture is altogether different. TV has not been able to attract substantial audience in tribal India because of their impoverished socio-economic status. It is also seen that people are gradually becoming selective to TV programmes. The question is how to re-establish the relevance of radio and explore it's potential in the direction of communication effectiveness particularly for it's targeted listeners majority of whom are tribals.

Every programme professional should address himself to the inherent strength of the radio in terms of formats which are distinctive to it. First and foremost, is the spoken word, which is another name of radio. It is also observed that a well produced radio talk is one of the most attractive formats of the radio. It is important to mention the directives of Govt. of India addressed to Station Directors of all AIR stations.

(i) Radio Talk should be qualitative and it's duration should be shortened and should not exceed 6-7 minutes.

(ii) Since Radio Drama is the art of imagination, it is a format that can involve the listeners in a very profound way. In an age which is becoming increasingly fast, there is need to tailor our programmes suitably. The duration of Radio play or Documentary should be identified.

(iii) The biggest weakness in radio is the straight, stiff, inflexible formal announcements which drive our listeners away. The basic point is that an announcement/compering ought to be very friendly, relaxed and where ever required hatty and informal style of presentation.

(iv) It is also necessary to take the radio mike out of the studios to the field to get on the spot, response from the common people. The radio mike should really travel out to the field more frequently than what it does now. 'Peoples Forum' programme to present the grievances of the people along with the response/reactions of the authorities must be encouraged. A weekly fifteen minutes program, Nagar Darpan recently introduced in AIR, Ranchi brought about lot of curiosity among public.

(v) In certain radio stations, the stock characters who use to present rural programmes have become so popular that they virtually turned into household figures. This tradition is on the decline, and the time has come for us to build up talented stock characters who can create instant rapport with the listeners. Stations have also been permitted to encourage casual composers for the purpose. A related question is one of building up media personalities to which adequate attention must be paid.

(vi) One way in which we can involve our listeners is to take up topics, which can generate a good deal of debate and divergent view points. We must try and get away from the confines of safe and academic topics and think in terms of issues, which can generate heat and light.

(vii) Radio being an instant medium, instant communication information with credibility is a must. According to the guidelines of the government issued in 1980, the dissemination of information must be done in fair, objective and balanced manner.

(viii) The Fixed Point Charts (FPCs) are revised twice in a year. This is the occasion for the stations to review critically the programme structure with reference to the needs and preferences of the audience. Programmes, which have outlived their utility have to be replaced. In making the change, the listeners letters, the audience research findings and the recommendations of the consultative committee should be taken into account.

Need for a New Information Order

All over the civilized world today, there is a debate on how to give the people access to the media of communication. With the rest of the world proceeding towards less and less rigid, centralised control over broadcasting in India can't continue with a system devised sixty years ago. In the absence of a communication policy, AIR has not been able to play its proper part in the progress of the country. What tribal people or people in the country side need is appropriate and relevant information which is both accessible and easily available to them. If people are provided with enough information, they would be able to think and decide on solutions for themselves to act and demand from governments the policies which will better their life. This will require a flow of information from the government down to the people, as well as from the people to upwards. This mass media should be better suited to this role, if it is able to flourish in an open and free manner unfettered by state control. Not only it will be more democratic but also it will be more pluralistic reflecting the diverse and challenging views of society.

We have to touch the heart and mind of the listeners so that the impulse to act and manipulate the environment for progress comes from within.

The establishment of local radio station with FM Transmitter had the sole objective to invite maximum participation through it's extensive OB coverage but ultimately failed to materialize. Even in places where, there are high power Transmitters, the duration of OB based programme does not exceed five percent of the total duration of daily programme broadcast. In the existing infrastructure, it is not possible to cover OB programmes extensively. If we study programmes of AIR, Ranchi, we can find that maximum OB programmes are covered within radius of twenty-five kilometers.

Tools for Media Planning

What matters most in the media is the total effect, words, sound and finally imagination which can be used through a medium that can communicate, rationalize anything from a spontaneous activity to a careful, considered programme. Viewed in the context, certain tools are suggested for media planning.

(i) It has to be determined in regard to the total duration of broadcast timing. It depends much on the credibility and quality of message and how do people receive it. The contents of a programme must convey a message that is purposive, value oriented and carry human emotions.

(ii) Communication is a way of reaching others with ideas, facts, thoughts, feelings and values. Authority influence is another significant tool of programme campaign and the message of popular figure and real opinion leaders carry quite weightage for influencing the mass. It promotes credibility in the media as well as formation of new beliefs and cognitions.

(iii) Hearing is with the ears but listening is with the mind. In order to boost up effective listening, a programme man/ broadcaster ought to establish contacts with the listeners and take care to see that feedback is maintained.

(iv) Semantics is the science of meaning. Many barriers exist for programmer with regard to language. Idea can be more emphasized than the words. The meaning that a listener grasps depends on his individual experience and attitudes, not the communicator's. Therefore, while programme planning, emphasis ought to be given on the beneficiaries. While addressing a rural or tribal listener living in the countryside, thus programmes have to be aired quite carefully.

(v) Message characteristics include how far the message is novel, valid, logical, persuasive, emotional, repetitive and capable of attitude formation.

(vi) There is always a difference between what the people learn/unlearn and what do they practise in real life. The programme producers are to minimize the gap between knowledge and practice by standardizing their programmes to be very receptive, understandable, educative, entertaining, ear-catching, value oriented and credible.

(vii) The combination of immediacy, intimacy, novelty and mass communication is what .gives the electronic media tremendous power, a power that is widely coveted, envied and trusted. Media research and media planning in the field of tribal welfare should be geared up. What distinguishes radio from other media is the primary emphasis it puts on the message.

Social Change and Responsibility

This particular media needs to be socially responsible in a number of ways. We need change in a number of areas for betterment of the people's life and mass media can play a very important part in this process. The change that we want to achieve is towards the positive realisation of plans, programmes and policies of the government and others. Social change and evolution are processes of differentiation and integration of various elements in the society.

Unlike the fast changing urban life style, in a tribal society, the pace of social change is very slow. Industrialisation and urbanisation have given rise to social problems like migration, child labour on the one hand and greater exposure to outside world on the other. The respondents cast doubts about radio's role in bringing about social change. However, it has got potentiality to spread the information inputs about different changes happening in society in a systematic and responsible manner. The tribal people ought to know the mixed influence of social change.

Fighting the Evil Forces

Ignorance, alcoholism and superstitions are three triangular evil forces in the path of progress in tribal India and radio has got to combat these negative forces. The story of Chotanagpur is almost the same as any part of the country where substantial population belong to tribal origin. There should be useful media campaign, which can promote good habits and work motivation among tribals. Say a child is disapproving the behaviour of his father who returns to home at late night with full stock of HANDIA. The whole theme of broadcast in local dialect will be quite impressive as there is no iota of doubt about it's efficacy in a society where almost eighty percent of adult male population are regular consumer of this alcoholic liquid. The picture of Hatma and Mandar is somewhat better but Rania tells the live story. That's a peculiar scene to look at when few women sit in a parallel line near a weekly market serving HANDIA to the passers by. Although less in number, women also consume the alcoholic liquid at regular intervals. A gentleman uttered when the researcher met him near a weekly market, "See, five per cent of people are earning bread spoiling ninety five percent of people, their home and family peace." Drug addiction, witch hunting and excessive intake of liquor are here some important evil forces.

Education for Tribes

A number of expert committees, task forces etc., which examined the issue of development of education among scheduled tribes have recommended adoption of a genuine tribal, cultural matrix in which educational contents are embedded. Another important hurdle in the spread of conventional education among tribes is the medium of instruction. Not withstanding claims to the contrary, it is known that physical inaccessibility to centres of learning constitutes a big obstacle to development. In the total perspective, the keystone of the arch is the teacher. The irony of the situation is that most such schools scattered in tribal pockets are single teacher schools and the teachers are very irregular in their attendance and they do not have adequate knowledge of the local languages too.

Viewed in the context, radio can play a role through frequent OB coverage of various literacy programmes. Recently there has been some experiments in AIR, Ranchi through serials for popularizing non-formal education but as per Audience Research Report, nothing substantial has been achieved. Perhaps methodologies have got to be changed.

The broadcast lesson must be placed on the time-table and must be part of curriculum. The teacher must prepare the student for the broadcast and must also clear doubts during the follow-up session.

It is unfortunate that educational authorities both at state and national levels have not so far appreciated the massive role radio can play in the better fulfillment of their plans and even a better utilization of their resources. Radio can reach isolated communities and regions which have no school buildings or trained teachers and minimum infra structural facilities.

There are a number of lacunae in the system right now. The schools scattered over different parts of tribal pockets can

multimedia campaign, there should be a message following each entertainment event.

The experiment of DBU (Development Broadcast Unit) in. Kota was quite successful. In tribal pockets of Jharkhand region, the experiment in a large scale is likely to pay much dividend. Here the producer is required to undertake baseline study and frequent field visits for search of programme ideas, content research, pretesting and feedback and make scrutiny of the same to avoid duplication in future. Not only can producer get many programme ideas but also clues about production methods, presentation and formats, music, language and other aspects of programming. The present practice is that the programme officers have got more table work than field-work.

It is time that a community oriented communication vision is formulated suited to the Indian milieu which is characterized by the supreme importance of local communication in the Indian social structure. The local radio will have a bright career, when the communication priorities are reformulated in respect to the community principle, which is so basic to Indian cultural heritage. A decentralized communication media under which planning becomes highly sensitive to the specific local milieu and local perceptions becomes inevitable. For promoting two-way communication between the community of farmers and producers at the bottom on the one hand, and technical experts, planners and administrators at the top on the other, the local radio has immense potentialities, which have not been adequately tapped so far.

A fuller and more intensive use of broadcasting should be made for dissemination of news and useful information.

With the passage of time, technology may change adopting to circumstance but radio is here to stay. For developing countries like India where poverty abounds and is not likely to vanish this prime mass medium.

Communication through radio should be viewed as a total process that includes understanding the tribal audience and their needs, dissemination of information, reception and feedback. What is needed is to exploit radio's potential fully and build up the listening habit through attractive programmes backed by vigorous and intelligent publicity. Radio is the only medium, which has the potential to reach so many people so efficiently and at a low cost.

The researcher from his own experience finds that cultural programmes in Nagpuri in small towns and even in block headquarters have become very successful (invited audience programmes). Both tribals and non-tribals (Sadans) rejoice for the whole night without a break. It is time to experiment similar programmes based on tribal language, say Mundari or Kudukh, in a remote tribal area may be in panchayat level. Invited audience programmes at frequent intervals particularly in tribal pockets need to be encouraged so that more and more artists will have recognition. It can be mentioned that as far as promotion of artists or talents is concerned, AIR is an important institution, which has been playing a key role.

Considering the main role of messages in communication, there is more scope for qualitative programmes both in literacy languages as well as in dialects. The message must be timely, meaningful and applicable to the situation. Quantitative and qualitative assessment of the audience is always a prerequisite to a good communication. The message and channels should be selected keeping in view the social and cultural life of the listeners within the broadcasting zone. Even if all the barriers have been removed, communication could still be a failure without good presentation. Good presentation requires complete understanding of the subject. Old stock characters in rural programmes are still remembered by the tribal people with lot of respect and pride.

India's diversity and the multiplicity of our languages, cultures, beliefs, histories and agricultural practices constitute a communication challenge of vast proportions. The present system of financing broadcasting should be so adjusted that a variety of opinions on public issues can be expressed. At the same time, every possible step should be taken to prevent political exploitation of the network and avoid consumerism and irrelevant programming. Social responsibility and public accountability should both be assured. Any type of autonomy that does not reject urban biased, undemocratic and commercial tendencies is likely to prove highly dangerous. If real autonomy is to be given to this particular electronic media, the government should also allow the setting up of private radio stations for healthy competition on regional basis.

Accountability signifies access. The unrestricted access of the powerful and wealthy Philistine to mass media should be controlled in ways guaranteeing honest, toiling, suffering Indians a right over finite programme time. Let not the well-nourished, well manicured and groomed experts in public policy monopolize prime-time. Let India's disadvantaged, dispossessed and depressed people speak. Let their suffering be newsworthy.

The immediate task is to improve the quality of the programmes and make them relevant for the common men. The programme must reflect the social awareness and concerns with regard to specific groups like tribals, women, linguistic and religious minorities. Credibility, social commitment and professional excellence have to be brought about in programming.

Mark Tully, a broadcaster of international fame opines that 'Radio, as a medium of mass communication, is friendly and has a far bigger reach. When you are listening to the radio, you are personally involved and your mind is working. This is because the mind is picturising the piece of information being communicated. The need of the hour is to explore it's potential for service of mankind in general and indigenous people in particular who live in difficult circumstances.'

Broadcasting in India is required to fulfil the objective of a public service system whether in terms of reach or content. The public service role of broadcasting, *i.e.* educational, extension, awareness building, facilitating participatory democracy and decision-making at the grassroots level of the district and below, etc. is, by and large, non-commercial. Far from earning profits, such service may need to be subsidized for quite sometime. According to Varghese (1991), privatisation of any description simply will not fill the requirement of the poor people. On the contrary, it will dismiss AIR/DDs feeble efforts as the privatised service might cater to urban, middle class elites mostly skimming the cream of advertising revenue. The middle class and urban elites have many alternative means of gaining access to information and entertainment through video, journals, magazines, films, travel, libraries, seminars, museums, etc. The deprived and the disadvantaged have little or nothing and it is they who need more access and participation through any second system, which must cater to their needs.

Thus, democratic decentralisation through setting up of more local radio stations at grassroots level, involving NGOs in broadcasting for local news and views, and finally mobilising local resources for participative broadcasting will yield dividend. This community oriented public broadcasting service will suffice, perhaps the urge of the rural and tribal people deprived of involvement from the city based radio station. This will definitely promote language broadcast and culture. Removal of government control means that the electronic media would have to show a greater sense of responsibility and accountability to the people.

The most popular medium of mass communication in tribal India where the majority of inhabitants are illiterate, is radio. India is a vast multilingual multiracial and multi-religious land. Yet a stray spark may ignite in and it's harmony may be disrupted. At this critical juncture, this particular media has a role to play.

The view electronic media have their own problem of elitism of access, infrastructure, skills and education. The radio should be better suited to the role of disseminating information to flourish in an open and free manner, unfettered by state control. It can help shape public attitudes and can challenge governments support and voice public demands. Politicians will certainly take notice of this vital electronic media, particularly when there is a free media willing and able to challenge the actions or inactions of their leaders.

What people around the world need is appropriate and relevant information, which is unbiased and is both accessible and easily available to them. If people are provided with enough information, they should be able to think and decide solutions for themselves to act and demand from governments the policies which will better their lives. This will require a flow of information from the government down to the people, as well as within the community and it's institutions, and from the people up to the government.

We live in an age of information revolution, and that this marks the start of a new era, as did the agricultural or industrial revolutions before. But the challenge we now face is how to harness the technological advances in communication to fulfill the visions and ambitions of our vast tribal population. How can they move towards a more sustainable pattern of development through this information revolution?

There is a lot of scope for NGOs (Non-Governmental-Organisations) to work with this broadcasting media : creating news briefings, radio materials and providing human interest stories from their own field areas.

Radio stations must assume greater responsibility of awakening people, of inculating moral, social and political values in them, of encouraging national and patriotic trends and of stimulating public opinion to usher in a political order that can meet the challenge of the time. They have to strive to become credible, responsible, objective, self-restrained, decent and development oriented as they are the watch dogs of democracy and freedom.

The Indian society at the grassroots level is a complex system of socio-economic, cultural, religious, and ideological pluralism. Besides traditional media, the only hope of bringing awareness to rural and tribal folk about national development programmes, seems to lie on the audio media, *i.e.* radio. The traditional media along with radio have continued to play a meaningful role in rural areas in educating the rural people about the consequences of social evils like alcoholism, illiteracy, untouchability, superstitions, communalism, population explosion, malnutrition, insanitation, dowry and many social prejudices. Unlike radio, doordarshan is not accessible for people at the grassroots level for a variety of reasons. It can be noted that the very modernity which has been considered as one of the causes for the decline of the use of traditional media or the traditional performing arts, is in some cases, partly or wholly, responsible for reviewing, revitalising, preserving and disseminating the traditional media.

Change is an on-going process in human communication environment, societal setup and communication technologies. Such change in these areas create new prospects. We decide about what to broadcast, when to broadcast without bothering much about the public or the listeners. And since the listeners have no way of communicating with the media, barring the occasional letters, we live in a world of make-believe thinking that whatever we broadcast is right for them and they will accept it. This is the view of D.C.Bhaumik, Ex-Director General, News Services Division, All India Radio, which the researcher shares wholeheartedly. Genuine participatory approach, not mere tokenism, at all levels from planning to production of media can facilitate the participatory development process to the satisfaction of all concerned. Communication has to be considered as an integral part of the participatory development approaches, without which participation and thereby development can't be expected to take place.

Community access sluts should be introduced for the purpose of sharing information and dialogue between rural communities and development agencies for bottom-up, top-down and horizontal communication flows. The interface should be dialogical so that tribal communities and development agencies share information, debate development problems and options and arrive at collective decisions on a suitable plan of action.

Instead of a daily hourly schedule of Farm and Home, which contains different dialectical programmes, there can be provision for four dominant dialects such as Mundari, Kudukh, Santhali and Nagpuri (Sadri) separately which will boost listenership. In view of the large tribal population, the duration for such dialect based programmes should be one hour each when there is no special channel for promoting dialect based programmes. Tribals knowing their own dialects should be recruited or kept in casual panel to give a fillip to programme compering and accessibility.

Programmes like Radio-Krishi-Pathsala should be a continuous process. In AIR, Ranchi, this is an occasional feature. Extensive coverage should be given to all development projects in its broadcasting zone.

One of the promising avenues is that local radio station ideally fits into the decentralized development initiatives. It also fits into the erstwhile idea of making districts as information centres and gateways for the local people. Because of poor infrastructure and inadequate funds, the project has not been able to yield results. It is worth mentioning that the tribal dominated districts such as Lohardaga and Gumla are still without a local radio station. In the existing setup, Local radio station (LRS) has not attended success due to a number of reasons.

Environmentally rich plateau areas, the home land of tribals are also called indigenous population. Because of poverty and unemployment, the poor tribals particularly women are involved in cutting of trees ceaselessly. According to a recent study, India is losing atleast 10 per cent of its national income due to environmental degradation. The environment has to be treated as a productive system where the annual accounting of natural resource capital should be linked with economic indicators. Viewed, in the context, there should be massive campaign against deforestation in this electronic media. Once upon a time, the tribals used to manage their livelihood for about a period of six months from the forest products. But this is not the situation now. The forest resources have been over exploited by not only the tribals but also the mafia groups, contractors and government.

From the survey of Rania, it is found that only 15 percent of the households are having radio sets. If this is the situation in the countryside, maximum people can't be benefitted by this potential media. Each household should possess atleast one radio set so that there can be maximum utilisation. Although community listening still exists in rural areas like Rania, government should take adequate measures to make some suitable arrangement so that each household should remain in a position to listen radio programmes. It is observed that there is large-scale migration to different far off places especially to take up work on bricks when the agriculture work is over. While returning from Bhatta (brick work) the young ones prefer to purchase radio sets, cycles and in some cases tape recorders also.

The message must reach the people who are to translate it into action and it must have immediate relevance for them. When one unemployed person approaches a bank official for a particular loan as a follow up action of radio listening and does not succeed in his effort, he doubts the credibility of the governmental medium.

The culture and day-to-day life of tribals in remote places are quite peculiar in the sense that they are deprived of all minimum health services. They have also a distinct culture of their own. While programmes should be made to bring these tribals to the mainstream, nothing should be done to destroy their customs. Their culture is their most valuable asset. The tribal artists should be given all possible motivation in the media, which is not possible right now because of the budgetary constraints. While analyzing tribal folk songs, it can be stated that the stanzas speak of worshiping of mother earth, environment, water and herbs. They all contain moral and spiritual values, which are not even visible in modern literary languages. A cultural pollution in the wave of new film songs is enforced on them, which is rather unethical. That's why the new generation is having more attraction for Hindi film songs rather than regional and folk songs. Therefore, the biggest threat to tribal culture springs from the dehumanization of all sorts overtly and covertly promoted by the media. So this tendency has to be arrested immediately.

Like other natural and human resources, information is also to be treated as a precious resource to promote and streamline the tribal development activities. It shall reflect the aspirations of the people and ensure their larger participation in the growth process.

Particularly in Rania, tribals are seen to rely most on traditional practices for health remedies. Many a patients are not in a position to get relief at right time and therefore, they remain sufferers. There is little infrastructure here and no qualified doctor is interested to serve these areas. Viewed in the context, radio can be an important medium for disseminating health information and removing prejudices. It is information, which can help to save the lives of many millions of children in remote areas. It is information which can drastically reduce malnutrition and help to protect the healthy growth of the next generation. It is information which almost all parents can put into practice, in some degree at very low cost. It is, therefore, information to which all families now have a right. Experience in all countries has shown that only frequent, varied repetition of new information from all sides and over many years can truly succeed in putting new health knowledge at the disposal of the majority.

Today's essential family information on maternal and child health care which include birth spacing, safe motherhood; breast feeding, weaning and child growth, immunization, diarrhoeal diseases, respiratory infections, domestic hygiene and malaria will provide tools to fight disinformation in remote places.

The mobilisation of the people and their integration into the process of information and dissemination can't be achieved if transparency of information and policy is lacking. The uneducated masses, the tribals with a poor environmental and economic base need to be strengthened through various programmes that include information about functional literacy, food for work, training in income generating skills, marketing, storage and credit facilities. Broadcast of examination results including that of competitive examinations will be very much beneficial for tribals living in remote places, which are not easily accessible and are not well-connected with transportation and communication infrastructure. Further the tribal people should not be deprived of the available employment opportunities. One thing is clear that although there is more radio listening in Rania (the remote place) amongst different age groups, the pace of progress is very slow due to poor infrastructure support on the one hand and minimum level of adoption by the beneficiaries on the other. Merely the quantum of listening programmes, can't be a measuring stick of development.

Programme presentation and are of improved formats by metro FM channels have brought about lot of attraction amongst general public and this is high time to replicate such experiences in various tribal pockets in different parts of the country.

BIBLIOGRAPHY

Aagnihotri, V. (1980), *Techniques of Social Research*, M. N. Publications, New Delhi.

Agrawal, B. C. (1978), *Television comes to Villages : An Evaluation of SITE,* Bangalore, ISRO.

Agree, Ault and Emery (1980), *Introduction of Mass Communications*, Oxford and IBH Publishing Company, New Delhi.

Akkara, (Jan 26, 1994), The Tribals are not Museum Pieces, *The Times of India,* Delhi edition.

Awasthy, G. C. (1965), *Broadcasting in India,* Allied Publications, New Delhi.

Bali, Y. (1989), An Agent of Change and Development, *Communicator,* (March-May) IIMC, New Delhi.

Banerjee, Mangobinda (1989), *An Historical out line of Pre-British Chhotanagpur*, Educational Publications, Ranchi.

Behari Sham (1994) Broadcasting for Development, *Communicator* (Oct-Dec.), IIMC, New Delhi.

Berelson, Bernard (1952), *Content Analysis in Communication Research*, Free Press, Illinois, USA.

Berlo. D. (1960), The Process of Communication, New York.

Berrigan, F.J. (1977), *A Manual on Mass Media in Population and Development*, UNESCO.

Bertrand, J.T. (1971), *Communication Presting, Community and Family Studies Centre*, University of Chicago.

Bhagya, Laxmi, J. (1981), *Communication and the Traditional Media*, IIMC, New Delhi.

Bhattacharya, V. R. (1976), *Communication in a Global Village*, Chetna Publication, New Delhi.

Bonnie, Remsberg and Doffin George (1975), Radio Television Spot Announcement for Family Planning, World Wide University of Chicago.

Carey, W. J., *The Communications Revolution and the Professional Communicator*, University of Illinois.

Carol, M. (1991), *Musicial and Cultural Interaciton in Tribal India*, University of Illinois, USA.

Chanda, A.K. (1966), Radio and Television Report of the

Committee on Broadcasting and Information Media, Government of India.

Chatterjee, P. C. (1987), *Broadcasting in India*, Saga Publications, New Delhi.

Chatterjee, R.K. (1978), *Mass Communication*, NBT, New Delhi.

Chawla, N. C. (1982, April & July issue), Social Challenges before AIR, *Communicator*, IIMC, New Delhi.

Colin (1965), *On Human Communication : A Review, a Survey, and a Criticism*, MIT Press.

Damle, Y.B. (1969), "Communication of Modern Ideas and Knowledge in Indian Village" in A.R. Desai's (Edn.) *Rural Sociology in India*, Asia Publishing House, Bombay.

Danielson, W.A. (1958), *Content Analysis in Communication Research – An Introduction to Mass Communication Research*, Ralfo Nafger & White D.W. (ed), Lovisiance State University Press.

Davision, W.P. (1966), Political Significance of Recognition *via* Mass Media – an illustration from the Berlin Blockade, *Public Opinion Quarterly*.

Dua and Gupta (1994) (ed) *Television and it's Impact on Rural Areas : A Doordarshan study*, Media and Developmetn, Har Anand Publications, New Delhi.

Dube, S. C. (1988), *Modernisation and Development : The Search for Alternative Paradigms*, The UN University, Tokyo.

Dubey and Burdhan A. (1981), Content Analysis of Messages and Programmes, Module on Research in Health and Population Communication, NIHFW, New Delhi.

Dubey, G.S. (1996), Paper Presented in a seminar organized by R.K. Mission, Ranchi (4-5-96).

Edwin, Philip and Ages (1975), *Introduction to Mass Communication*, D.M. Company, New York.

Gillin and Gillin (1950), *Cultural Sociology*, the MacMillan Co, New York.

Gulati, P. (1993), Language, Scripts, Folk-Arts : Their Development and Impact on Culture, paper presented in the workshop on Cultural Identity of Janjatis (conducted at Deen Dayal Research Institute from 21-5-93 to 23-5-93), New Delhi.

Gupta, V. S. (1996), Media strabgist is for Rural Dev, *Kurukshetra*, (Jan-Feb), Publication Din Ministry of I & B, ND.

Hartmann, Patil and Dighe (1989), *The Mass Media and Village Life*, Sage Publications, New Delhi.

Hollick, J. C. (1993), The Return of Radio. *The Illustrated Weekly of India*, Aug 26-Sep 3, Bombay.

Hotton, J. H. (1931), Ethnographic Notes by Various Hands, *Census of India 31*, Vol I, India, Part III B, Simla, Govt. of India Press.

Ishtiaq (1995), Saving the Languages of Tribals, *The Times of India*, February 3, New Delhi.

Jaiswal, Vittal, Jaiswal, and Ramchandra (1981), *Development Communication Process and Impact*, NIRD, Hyderabad.

Jamison and Mcanany (1978), Radio for Education and Development, Beverly Hills, Calif., Sage.

Janison and Mcanany, (1978) Kujur Alomane (1989), *The Oraon Habitate : A Study in Culture Geography*, The Doughters of St. Anne, Ranchi.

Johnson (1966), *Sociology : A Systematic Introduction.*

Joshi, P. C. (1989), Role of Local Radio (Article Published in *Communicator* (March issue), IIMC, New Delhi.

Joshi, P.C. (1986), Communication and Social Transformation *Communicator*, (August issue), IIMC, New Delhi.

Kakar, V.N. (1987), *Communication in Family Planning – India's Experience*, National Institute of Health and Family Welfare, New Delhi.

Khan, W.Y. (1993), *Fundamentals of Broadcasting*, Ideal Impressions (P) Ltd, New Delhi.

Kuppuswamy, B, (1976), *Communication and Social Development in India*, Sterling Publications Pvt Ltd, Delhi.

Lalithamva R, (1976), Study on Factors Responsible for the Gap between Awareness and Adoption in Contraceptive Practice, *Bulletin*, GIRH & FP II (C).

Laswel, H. D. (1960), The Structure and Function of Communication in Society in the Mass Communications ed. by W. Schramm, Chicago University of Illinois Press.

Laswell, H. D. (1959), Strategies of Inquiry : The Rational Use of Observation in Daniel Lerner ed. *The Human Meaning of Social Sciences*, New York.

Laxman Rao, T.V. (1967), *Communication and Development : A Study of Two Indian Villages*, University of Minnesota Press, Minneapolis.

Lazersfeld, Berelson & Gaudet (1948), *The Peoples Choice*, New York, Columbia University Press.

Leagans, J. P. (1961), *The Communication Process in Rural Development*, NY Correll Uni. Ithaca.

Learner, D. (1957), Communication Systems and Social Systems,

Behavioural Science, Oct. 57.

Lerner and Schramm (1969), *Communication and Change in the Developing Countries*, Honolulu, East-West Centre Press.

Lerner, D. (1967), *Communication and the Prospect of Innovation Development*, East West Press.

Luthra H. R. (1989, March issue), The Future lies in Villages, *Communicator*, IIMC, New Delhi.

Mac Iver and Page (1924), *Society*, Mac Millan Co, London.

Mahta, B. C. (1991), Voices form the Green Hills : Some Observations and Proposals for the Development of the Languages of Jharkhand, Seminar on Planning for Development and Social Justice in Jharkhand, Jamshedpur.

Mahto, P. P. (1991), Planning for Cultural Lingual and Educational Development for Jharkhand, Seminar on Planning for Development and Social Justice in Jharkhand, Jamshedpur.

Majhi (1995), Sustainable Growth of Chotanagpur : An Overview (Paper presented in the Seminar entitled "Rural and Urban Interface for Sustainable Development"), Ranchi.

Majumdar, D.N. (1958), *Caste and Communication in an Indian Village*, Asia Publishing House, Bombay.

Mani S. B. (1974), Culture and Communication, *Journal of Family Welfare*, Bombay.

Mathu, P. (1995), Towards Sustainable Agriculture : Dimensions and Components, *Employment News*, 18-24 November, Publication Division, New Delhi.

Mathur and Neurath (1959), *An Indian Experiment in Farm Radio Forums*, UNESCO Press.

Mazumdar, H. T. (1966), *A Grammer of Sociology*, Asia Publishing House, New Delhi.

Mehra, Mesani (1976), *Broadcasting and the People*, NBT, New Delhi.

Mehta, S. R. (1992), *Communication and Development*, Rawat Publications, Jaipur.

Mehto, D.S. (1992), *Mass Communication and Journalism in India*, Allied Publishers Ltd, New Delhi.

Menon (1993), Cultural Identity of ST, paper presented in the workshop on Cultural Identity of Janjatis (conducted at Deen Dayal Research Institute from 21-5-93 to 23-5-93), New Delhi.

Mishra, L. (1996), Three Facets of Communication in Rural Development, *Orissa Review*, (Jan.) I & PR Deptt. , Govt. of Orissa.

Modi, Bella (1991), *Designing Messages for Development Communication : An Audience Participation Based Approach*,

Saga Publications, New Delhi.

Mohanty, P. B. (1989), Radio for Education and Development, *Communicator*, (March-May) IIMC, New Delhi.

Mullick and Dubey (1974), *A Review of Studies in Family Planning Communication*, NIFP Monograph, Series No. 21.

Mullick, K. S. (1974), *Tangled Tapes, The Inside Story of Indian Broadcasting*, Sterling Publications, New Delhi.

Nacimento (1977), Using Communication to Support Development Guyanan, *Issues of Communications*, No.1, London, International Institute of Communications.

Narula, Uma (1994), Public Participation in Development Programmes – An Empirical Study, New Delhi, IIPA, Delhi Chapter.

Parmar, Shyam (1975), *Traditional Folk Media in India*, Geka Books, New Delhi.

Pasquali (1975), The Instrumental Use of Mass Media in America for the Purpose of Dependence, Caracas Univeridad Central deVeneivala.

Pati, Jagannath (1995), *Hopes Never Die in the Land of Virsha Bhawan*, Article Published in the Souvenir released on 9th August by JAAC, Ranchi.

Pey, Lucien W (ed.) (1963), *Communication and Political Development*, Princeton University, Press.

Prasad and Rao (1976), Village Communication Channels, *The Indian Journal of Survey Work 37*, Vol. 3.

Prasad, N. (1961), *Land and People of Tribal Bihar,* Tribal Research Institute, Ranchi.

Prasad, S. (1988, Nov 12), Communication and National Development, *Main Stream*, New Delhi.

Ramkrishnan, Uma (1993), Plant Plunder : 60,000 Species may vanish by 2030, *The Times of India*, Dec. 29, Delhi edition.

Ranganath, H. K. (1981), *Communication and the Traditional Media.*

Riggins, Herold Stephen (1991), *Ethnic Minority Media : In International Perspective.*

Risley, H. (1969), *The People of India* (Edited by W. Crooke, II Edition) Oriental Books, New Delhi.

Rogers (1976), *Communication and Development : Critical Perspectives*, Beverley Hills Sage.

Rogers and Shoemaker (1971), *Communications of Innovations – A Crossroad Approach*, Beverley Hills Sage.

Rogers and Singhal (1989), *India's Information Revolution*, Sage Publications, New Delhi.

Vatsyayan (1972-73), *Anthropology, Social and Cultural*, Kedar Nath Ram Nath, Meerut.

Verma, U. K. (1993), Education and Social Change, *Bulletin of Bihar, Tribal Welfare Research Institute*, Ranchi.

Vidyarthy L. P. (1970), Industrialisation in India : A Case Study of Tribal Bihar, Planning Commission, Govt. of India, Deptt. of Anthropology, Ranchi University.

Vidyarthy and Rai (1977), *The Tribal Culture of India*, Concept Publishing Company, New Delhi.

Vidyarthy, L. P. (1964), *Cultural Contours of Tribal Bihar*, Punthi Pustak, Calcultta.

Vittal (1980), Communication for Rural Development, *Kurushetra*, Vol. 28, Publication Div., New Delhi.

Watson, G. (1971), Resistance to Change in G. *Watsan* (ed.) Concepts for Social Change, Washington DC Coop. Project for Education Development Series.

Yadav, J. S. (1994), *Communication and Development – The Indian Expeience in Media and Development*, Har Anand Publications, New Delhi.

Yaspal (1986), A New Role for Mass Media, *Communicator*, (July-Oct.) IIMC, New Delhi.

REPORTS

A Chapter on Broadcast Journalism (1982), Parthasarathi Committee (Advisory Committee on Official Media headed by G. Parthasarathi).

Bank of India – District Credit Plan : 1993-94.

Bihar Tribal Sub-Plan – 1994.

Broadcasting in India (1993), (AIR), DAVP, Ministry of Information and Broadcasting, New Delhi.

Document of the World Bank (Bihar Plateau Development Project), Oct 28, 1992.

D.O. Letter of S. K. Kapoor, DG, AIR, dated. 5th Dec'94 (No.36/7/84 – P')

Literature of National Literacy Mission.

Monographic Work on Munda tribe by Soma Singh Munda (1993), Tribal Research Institute, Ranchi.

Monographic Work on Oraon Tribe by Prakash Oraon (1993), Tribal Research Institute, Ranchi.

National Census Report – 1991.

NIC, Ranchi (Block Profile).

Research and Reference Division (1973), Mass Media, Ministry of Information and Broadcasting.

Seminar on Rural Development and Communication Policies organized by IIMC, New Delhi and International Institute of Communication, 1979.

Sindhe on Future of Radio in Developing Countries, 1989.

UNESCO (1975), World Communications, The UNESCO Press.

UNESCO Report, The MacBride Commission, 1980.

INDEX